MADRID
— in your pocket —

MICHELIN®

MAIN CONTRIBUTOR: JACK ALTMAN

PHOTOGRAPH CREDITS
Photos supplied by The Travel Library: A Amsel 12,
18, 28-29, 36 (left, right), 44, 51, 64, 65, 68, 109, 115;
Stuart Black front cover, back cover, title page, 7, 9, 21,
23, 24, 27, 30, 31, 32, 34, 35, 37, 38, 41, 42, 45, 46, 47,
48 (top, bottom), 50, 52, 53, 59, 61, 62, 63, 66 (top,
bottom), 67, 69, 70, 75, 76, 78, 82, 83, 84, 87, 89, 91,
94, 96, 99, 100, 102, 104, 105, 106, 107, 111, 117, 120,
125; Philip Enticknap 5, 10, 11, 33, 39, 81, 88, 92;
R Richardson 85, 113, 123; Gino Russo 72.
Other photos: Prado, Madrid/The Bridgeman Art
Library 54, 55, 57; Giraudon/The Bridgeman Art
Library 60.

*Front cover: café scene, Plaza Mayor; back cover:
tapas bar; title page; statue of Philip III*

MANUFACTURE FRANÇAISE DES PNEUMATIQUES MICHELIN
Société en commandite par actions au capital de 2 000 000 000 de francs
Place des Carmes-Déchaux – 63 Clermont-Ferrand (France)
R.C.S. Clermont-Fd 855 200 507
© Michelin et Cie. Propriétaires-Éditeurs 1997
Dêpôt légal Mai 97 – ISBN 2-06-651201-X – ISSN en cours

Printed in Spain 4-97

CONTENTS

INTRODUCTION

In the last quarter of the 20C, Madrid has emerged as a capital whose dynamic cultural and social life bears honourable comparison with any of its older European rivals. More than the vision of its rulers, this has been the achievement of the town's artists, musicians, film-makers, fashion designers and, above all, the citizens themselves. As an improbable, even artificial, latecomer among European capitals, established only in 1561, what it may lack in spectacular architectural landmarks, the city makes up in its present-day ambience of boisterous modernity.

To achieve its new vibrancy, the city had to remove cold, hard layers of political calculation left by Philip II, who wanted a capital in the middle of the country without regional attachments, and by General Franco, who made it the chief focus of his dictatorship. Things have calmed down since the hottest days of the post-Franco *Movida* cultural movement, but the bars of the Chueca and Malasaña neighbourhoods still bounce all night. Gentler folk stick to the *tapas* bars *(tascas)* and cafés around the elegant Plaza Mayor and Santa Ana, but the scene is just as lively.

Not that higher cultural demands are neglected. Madrileños take pride in the golden triangle formed by the Prado with its Velázquez, El Greco and Goya treasures, the Thyssen-Bornemisza's awesome private collection and the Reina Sofía modern art centre displaying Picasso's *Guernica*. And the city's central location makes the architectural jewels of Toledo, Segovia and Philip II's Escorial Palace, or the royal gardens at Aranjuez, all easily accessible.

The monument to Alfonso XII is an imposing backdrop to the lake at Retiro Park.

GEOGRAPHY

Corresponding precisely to the needs of
Philip II when he chose it as his capital, the
city stands at the geographical centre of
Spain, equidistantly 300km (187.5 miles)
from the Mediterranean to the east and the
Atlantic to the north. Madrid's altitude of
646m (2 120ft) above sea level makes it the
highest capital in Europe. Sitting on the
peninsula's vast, open, arid Meseta plateau,
with the modest Manzanares river flowing to
the west of the city, it enjoys a dry
continental climate of extremes, with very
hot summers and very cold winters.

An oft-repeated proverb dating back to
the Renaissance says, with a little
exaggeration, *'Madrid, nueve meses de
invierno, tres meses de infierno'* (Madrid, nine
months of winter, three months of hell). In
August the temperature averages 30°C
(86°F), while in winter it can fall several
degrees below zero. The summers are, above
all, very dry, and dust brought in from the
surrounding Meseta has to be laid to rest
each night by municipal workers hosing
down the city's streets.

The city proper has a population of nearly
3 million, and covers an area of 531 sq km
(205 sq miles). The Communidad de
Madrid (the Madrid region) extends north
to the Sierra de Guadarrama and south to
Aranjuez on the Río Tajo (Tagus river). It
encompasses a total area of 7 995 sq km
(3 086 sq miles) and adds another 2 000 000
inhabitants. Population drift will continue to
favour this region over the metropolis as the

*The Sierra de Guadarrama marks the
northernmost extent of the Madrid region.*

more prosperous bourgeoisie moves to the suburbs north-west of the city around El Escorial, while the working classes migrate south and east.

Dotted with earth-hued villages, the plateau's endless horizons are covered with fields of wheat, olive groves and vineyards. The Guadarrama and Gredos ranges provide a mountain barrier to the north and west, rarely rising above 2 000m (6 562ft) but high enough for some serious skiing in winter, with the highest peak reaching 2 430m (7 972ft).

Inside the city, it is four man-made landmarks rather than geographical features that provide easy orientation: west of the city centre is the Royal Palace; on the east side is the Buen Retiro Park; to the north stands the AZCA district's Picasso Tower and Bilbao/Vizcaya Tower; and, at the very centre, is the clocktower of Puerta del Sol.

HISTORY

Much as its champions would like otherwise, Madrid is not an ancient city. The earliest evidence of human presence in the area is some bones found on the city's eastern outskirts dating to around 3000 BC. Later the Roman conquerors of the 2C BC encountered Celto-Iberian hunters and herdsmen on the Meseta plateau and founded towns at Toledo and Alcalá de Henares, but no evidence of a human settlement on the site of Madrid has been found.

Visigoths and Moors
When Spain's Visigoth rulers, not at all 'barbarian' but Romanized Christians, arrived from the Danube Valley in the 5C,

they established their capital at Toledo.

Even by the time of the Moorish (Arab and Berber) conquest of 711, Madrid was still little more than a hamlet and did not begin to grow until **Emir Mohammed I** built a fortress *(alcázar)* there in around 875. The walled town that grew up for the Muslim, Jewish and Christian population drew its modern name from the Arabs' fortress, Majrit, which was named after the small streams in the settlement.

In 1469, King Ferdinand II of Aragon married Isabel of Castilla, uniting the two great kingdoms of Spain.

Christian Reconquest

Over the next 200 years, the town was subject to constant raids by Christian kings on their way to Toledo. **Alfonso VI** finally took Madrid in 1083, with 200 cavalry and 500 infantry.

The city's loyalty in the Reconquista campaign was rewarded with the control of the mountains, pastures and hamlets between Madrid and Segovia. By 1346, the first real Town Hall *(ayuntamiento)* was established in the San Salvador cloister that is now Plaza de la Villa, and the bustling area around Calle Mayor, site of the Arabs' bazaar, became the focus for shops, brothels and gambling dens.

In 1390, **Henry III** launched Madrid's first campaign against the Jews. Their houses were

FERNANDO EL CATOLICO

plundered, and they were forced to wear distinctive signs of their religion.

From 1480, the Spanish Inquisition's tribunal in Toledo decided on the trial and execution of many of Madrid's Jews, Muslims and other 'heretics'. Jews were expelled from Spain in 1492, in the campaign to achieve *limpieza de sangre* (Christian blood-purity).

Becoming the Nation's Capital

Madrid's civic prestige rose as it was regularly chosen for meetings of the Cortes (parliament) and for the formal proclamation of King Charles I of Spain, in 1516. The future Habsburg emperor, **Charles V**, rebuilt the Alcázar and his son, **Philip II**, transferred the royal capital from Toledo to Madrid in June 1561.

At this time, Madrid's population was little more than 15 000, while wealthy, tradition-laden Toledo numbered over 70 000, but in a land of fiercely rival regions Madrid had the appeal of neutrality; it was also geographically central. More important, political power would now be separate from the church authority of Toledo. Philip emphasized the desire to keep his own counsel by building a retreat at El Escorial palace and monastery.

While these aptly austere edifices were being completed outside of the town, the monastery of San Jerónimo east of the city centre served as the pious king's retreat, the *buen retiro* that gave its name to Madrid's best-loved park.

Philip II (1527–1598) moved the capital of Spain from Toledo to Madrid.

Madrid of the Habsburgs

In striking contrast to the splendour of the Spanish Empire, Madrid remained architecturally unimpressive, with few of the Renaissance and baroque monuments that graced Europe's other capitals. With Philip's energies focussed on creating El Escorial, the city itself had no cathedral, university and few grandiose buildings. An exception is the arcaded Plaza Mayor, laid out in 1619 for royal processions, bullfights – and the Inquisition's trials and executions.

The Habsburg rulers made up for the lack of architectural grandeur with the splendour of their art collections – Flemish, Italian and native Spanish. **Philip IV** (1621–1665) was particularly active in encouraging Spain's

Pietro Tacca's equestrian statue of Philip IV adorns the Plaza de Oriente.

finest artists and writers. **Velázquez** and **Zurbarán** were both court painters; poet and playwright **Lope de Vega** was born in Madrid; and **Miguel de Cervantes** published the first part of *Don Quixote* in 1605 (completed ten years later) in the capital.

Under the French Bourbons

After a series of economic, diplomatic and military disasters, the 17C ended with the extinction of Madrid's Habsburg dynasty. The heirless Charles II chose as his successor Louis XIV's Bourbon grandson, **Philip V** (1700–46). Arch-conservative Carlists, supporting the rival claim of Austrian archduke Charles of Habsburg, subjected Madrid to a series of military occupations until a treaty secured Philip V's position in 1713.

Disappointed at not getting the French

Affectionately known as the 'mayor-king', Charles III left his mark on Madrid with the improvements he instigated.

throne, Philip V never took to Madrid, preferring the miniature Versailles he built at La Granja de San Ildefonso, between Madrid and Segovia. Replacing the alcázar destroyed by fire in 1734, Madrid's new Royal Palace put a neo-classical stamp on the city's architecture. Silks, laces and brocade, powdered wigs and other French frivolities replaced the stiff formality of Habsburg court dress.

Honouring him with the triumphal arch of Puerta de Alcalá (1778) and an equestrian statue on the Puerta del Sol (1994), Madrid regards King **Charles III** (1759–88) as the best mayor it ever had. The son of Philip V (by his second marriage), Charles paved the streets, improved the sanitation, put in street-lighting, extended the popular *paseo* promenades and planted more trees. In 1785 the Prado was opened, initially for the natural sciences but converted to a museum for the royal art collections 30 years later.

The 19C

Facing dangerous libertarian ideas filtering across the Pyrenees from the French Revolution, Madrid's rulers imposed censorship and gave renewed support to the Inquisition. The French invasion of 1808 did not improve matters, even after Napoleon replaced the heavy-handed **Joachim Murat** with his brother **Joseph Bonaparte**. On 2 May, riots against the French occupying force broke out in Madrid. The armed insurrection was crushed by a French force of 30 000 troops. In his paintings *Dos de Mayo* and *Tres de Mayo*, **Goya** immortalized the street battles and executions which left 450 dead. In an attempt at enlightened government, Joseph Bonaparte banished the Inquisition, encouraged literary cafés and demolished several churches and monasteries to make way for new city squares.

After the British drove out the French in 1814, the Spanish regime of **Ferdinand VII** proved more repressive than ever, abolishing the Constitution and dissolving the Cortes. Discord throughout the country continued, and not until the signing of the Constitution in 1876 was there peace in Madrid.

Civil War

In 1917, while the Bolshevik revolution was erupting on the other side of Europe, the army in Madrid repressed a general strike led by Spain's Socialist Worker's Party, formed some 40 years earlier. The city was ripe for the populist dictatorship of **General Primo de Rivera** (1923–30) and expanded under his large-scale industrialization programme. But in 1931, municipal elections brought left-wing government to Madrid, soon followed by a **Republican** victory at national level.

Amid church calls for a return to 'throne and altar', the city was caught up in a violent spiral of right-wing provocations by the fascist Falange party, leftist anti-clerical action and political assassinations on both sides. After a left-wing Popular Front coalition came to power in 1936, the murder in Madrid of a Socialist army officer and the reprisal killing of right-wing politician Calvo Sotelo led to all-out civil war. Anti-Republican troops led by **General Francisco Franco** surrounded the capital. Faced with the Republican forces' strong resistance, Franco launched a prolonged siege and called in aerial bombardment by units of

Mussolini's Italian air force, shelling university buildings, libraries, theatres and cinemas.

The three-year resistance of Madrid citizens became a symbol of the national struggle for democracy, but Franco's army, backed by superior Italian and German firepower, finally marched into the city on 28 March 1939. On the Paseo de la Castellana, the devout Franco, calling himself *'caudillo por la gracia de Dios'* (leader by the grace of God), called on the people to observe order, religion and absolute submission to the principles of his *Movimiento*. Over the next decade, in constant fear of 'godless Communists and Free Masons' Franco had, by the account of his own historians, at least 30 000 regime opponents executed, many more according to other sources.

From Franco to Movida

Spain's ties with the German-Italian Axis disqualified it from Marshall Plan aid, delaying Madrid's economic recovery from the devastating civil war until the 1950s. Prevailing influence in Franco's government was the Catholic **Opus Dei** movement (founded in Madrid in 1935 and blessed by Pope Pius XI in 1947), preaching a morally rigid form of modern capitalism. Puritanical censorship of films, books and newspapers was accompanied by Madrid's first skyscrapers and a glut of new cars in the city centre. Despite fears of immoral foreign contagion, Franco bowed to his Opus Dei economic experts' advice in opening the floodgates to mass tourism (one million in 1951, 16 million by 1965 and 60 million today).

Foreign 'contagion' was a reality, if only slight. In 1968, when revolt swept through Paris, Berlin and Chicago, the university of Madrid staged a fundraising concert by protest-singer Raimon for striking workers in the city suburbs. Franco felt secure. The next year, he named Juan Carlos de Borbón to succeed him as head of state, certain he would acquiesce in the Franquist policies of his prime minister, Carrero Blanco. 'Everything is tied up,' said Franco, 'and nicely tied up' *(Todo está atado y bien atado)*.

In 1973, Carrero Blanco was killed by ETA Basque extremists, who then launched a murderous attack on police chiefs in a Puerta del Sol café. At a last mass meeting in Madrid in October, 1975, the gravely ill Franco condemned 'an internationally orchestrated leftist Masonic plot', and died a month later.

After a prudent period of transition, **King Juan Carlos** replaced Franco's prime minister, Arias Navarro, with the moderate conservative, Adolfo Suárez. A new democratic constitution was proclaimed and censorship halted, but the economy, overheated by years of forced growth, went into recession.

In its first municipal elections since 1931, Madrid chose in 1979 a Socialist-Communist coalition headed by **Enrique Tierno Galván**. This forward-looking philosopher, revered by the young as *el viejo profesor*, 'the old professor', became the Mayor of the *Movida*, a slang word for the new mobile spirit of creativity in post-Franco Spain, spearheaded by Madrid. Tierno Galván reintroduced the carnival and neighbourhood festivities banned under the prudish old regime. The lifelong Marxist encouraged churches to ring their bells as never before, opened new libraries and cultural centres, and brought ducks and carp to swim in the newly cleaned Manzanares river.

In 1981, die-hard Franquists made a last farcical effort to turn the clock back when Colonel Antonio Tejero tried to hold up parliament, firing shots into the ceiling of the Cortes and shouting *'Nadie se mueva!'* – 'Nobody moves!' The putsch failed and a million Madrileños demonstrated in the streets, shouting: 'Everybody moves!' Many say that the *Movida* has ended, others that it has now evolved into the city's way of life, with the slogan: 'Everybody moves!'

THE PEOPLE AND CULTURE

For centuries, the Madrileños had a reputation for being austere. It reflected the heavy influence of the town's authoritarian rulers – 400 years apart – Philip II and Franco. In today's more liberal atmosphere, the people give vent to feelings that seem to mirror the extremes of their climate. Young or old, they can be astonishingly exuberant, partying till all hours of the night, but can descend to the depths of bluest melancholy – at the same party.

Madrileños do not like half measures. The same awesome fervour that the city's devout Catholics bring to Sunday mass, albeit in dwindling numbers, is there among pagan revellers at the *discobares*, the neo-flamenco clubs and the bullfights at Las Ventas.

There is also a new vehemence to the political and philosophical arguments conducted in literary cafés and *tapas* bars (*tascas*) in the post-Franco era. Equally extravagant are the street-fashions favoured

17

Traditional dancing in the Plaza Mayor.

by the young – and the not-so-young making up for lost time – setting Madrid uninhibitedly apart from the more sophisticated, traditional styles of Paris or Rome.

But not all is excess: ambulant *tuna* musicians strike a gentler note in *mesones* taverns, paying for their university studies with their guitars. And nothing could be more serene and dignified than the Madrileño bourgeoisie taking their evening stroll on the Paseo del Prado or Castellana.

Architecture

The demolitions of the Christian Reconquista, fires, wars and – most devastating of all – urban redevelopment in the 19C and 20C, have left little architectural trace of the city's Moorish beginnings. A piece of wall from the Moorish Alcázar fortress destroyed by fire in 1734 is to be found south of the cathedral. Even the **Mudéjar** architecture, a Moorish-inspired style combining brick and *azulejos* (enamelled ceramic tiles), survives only in three towers: the churches of San Nicolás (12C) and San Piedro el Viejo (1354) and the Torre de los Lujanes (Lujan Tower), a 15C prison across from the Town Hall.

Juan de Herrera, greatest of Spain's **Renaissance** architects, built his most important monument just outside Madrid: Philip II's solemn El Escorial palace and monastery. With the destruction of Herrera's work on the capital's Alcázar, the only Renaissance buildings to survive are the elegant Casa de Cisneros, the convent of Descalzas Reales and Segovia Bridge.

The city's great **baroque** monument is the beautifully laid out Plaza Mayor, an Italian-style piazza designed by **Juan Gómez de Mora** in keeping with the tastes of Spain's Neapolitan-educated monarchs. This Italian baroque influence is also evident in the oval-domed church of San Miguel. Madrid-born **José Benito Churriguera** gave his name to an extravagantly ornate baroque style (Churrigueresque) that has notably survived in the façade of the Municipal Museum.

The **neo-classical** style preferred by the French Bourbon and exemplified in the Royal Palace became the predominant style of museums, churches and government buildings. Otherwise, the 20C urban landscape is dominated by the highrise towers of the Franco era's building boom, most successfully the Torres Blancas (White Towers) of **Sáenz de Oiza**. Madrid's post-Franco era is characterized by its tallest building, the 45-storey Torre Picasso (Picasso Tower) by **Minoru Yamasaki** (1989), and the **post-modern** style of its new museums, its bars and its cafés.

The great Velázquez greets visitors to the Prado.

Arts and Letters

Paradoxically, Madrid's golden age in painting and literature accompanied the Spanish Empire's dramatic decline in the 17C. The transfer of the capital in the previous century from church-dominated Toledo to Madrid was paralleled by a similar transition in painting. The ecstatic religious works of Greek-born Domenikos Theotokopoulos, known as **El Greco**, gave way to the more worldly humanity of **Velázquez** (1599–1660). Born in Seville, Diego Rodríguez de Silva y Velázquez moved to Madrid in 1623 and quickly became court painter under the patronage of Count de Olivares. The painter's profound and subtle intelligence enabled him to serve his royal masters, Philip IV and Don Carlos, with portraits and battle scenes that somehow satisfied their self-esteem while uncompromisingly revealing their physical and psychological frailties. He brought the same insights to the more earthy subjects of drunkards and dwarfs, with his matchless technique, drawing on observation of Flemish and Italian masters.

The prince of Spanish painters undoubtedly influenced his fellow Sevillan **Zurbarán** (1598–1664). The latter's visits to

Madrid imbued his religious subjects, particularly portraits of Franciscan monks, with a striking simplicity and realism remote from the emotional religiosity of El Greco. The Neapolitan painter, **Luca Giordano** (1634–1705), worked for ten years at the court of Charles II, both in Madrid and at El Escorial, leaving his mark on Spanish painting with virtuoso frescoes of biblical and mythological subjects and monumental battle scenes.

Among Madrid's many brilliant playwrights in this golden era were **Tirso de Molina**, famous for creating the greatest of all lovers, Don Juan, and **Calderón de la Barca**, who wrote both cloak-and-dagger and philosophical plays. But the undisputed founding father of Spanish theatre was **Lope de Vega** (1562–1635), poet, wit, notorious womanizer and soldier in the Spanish Armada. Born in Madrid of peasant stock, he delighted Madrid audiences with his common touch, breaking down the barriers of comedy and tragedy. His plays are estimated to number between 1 500 and 1 800, of which 470 have survived.

Giant among novelists, **Miguel de Cervantes** (1547–1616) was the son of an impoverished aristocrat in Alcalá de Henares. Before making his home in Madrid, the author of *Don Quixote* learned the bitter truths of life in a Jesuit college, at the Battle of Lepanto where the Turks shattered his left arm, in Algerian captivity and in Spanish debtors' jails. The first part of *El ingenioso hidalgo don Quijote de la Mancha* was published in 1605 and proved an immediate success. In 1615, a plagiarized sequel forced Cervantes to complete the second part of his magnificent treatment of

Cervantes' hero Don Quixote and his companion Sancho Panza set forth in front of the monument to their creator.

idealistic dreams and cruel reality. Though his autobiographical short stories are almost equally masterful, Cervantes' poetry was unsuccessful and his numerous plays could never break through Lope de Vega's supremacy in the theatre.

Emblematic painter of Spain's often painful transition to a modern state, **Francisco de Goya** (1746–1828) began his Madrid career doing preparatory drawings for royal tapestries. He quickly graduated to

court portraits but, like Velázquez whose work he studied at the palace, painted his princes warts and all – even his beloved *Maja desnuda* has her faults. Made deaf, it is believed, by lead-poisoning, Goya became increasingly bitter in his treatment of aristocratic arrogance and social injustice. This culminated in his depicting the brutal violence of Madrid's struggle against the French in 1808 in the famous battle and execution scenes of *Dos de Mayo* and *Tres de Mayo*. He died in voluntary exile in Bordeaux.

Movida

Whether it has gone forever or is here to stay, the post-Franco creativity in Madrid expressed itself in the ephemeral culture of flashy, breathtaking advertising, photography, uninhibited comic strips, outlandish fashions and interior design.

In **music**, Madrid has been the most lively city on the national rock scene with singers such as **Luz Casal**, **Rosario** and the **Mecano** group. In jazz, **Pedro Iturralde** and **Jorge Pardo** are active, the latter working in the post-modern form of flamenco that with *nuevo flamenco* brings Andalucía to Madrid.

In the **cinema**, the acknowledged master has been **Pedro Almodóvar**, who has achieved international fame with *Women on the Edge of a Nervous Breakdown* and *Tie Me Up, Tie Me Down*. His studies of sexual excess, drugs and violence have epitomized the nervous reaction to the decades of national psychological repression and inhibition. It is perhaps a sign of the times that his latest films have been romantic comedies, calmer but still emotionally intense.

Goya, who was appointed First Royal Court Painter in 1799.

EXPLORING MADRID

MUST SEE

A newcomer to Madrid may
need help in choosing what to
see in and around the city.
Here are ten sights to include
on any first visit, six in Madrid,
and four from the surrounding
region.

Museo del Prado★★★
(The Prado)
One of the world's leading
museums, housing the
splendid royal art collections of
Velázquez, Goya, Titian,
Hieronymus Bosch and Pieter
Bruegel the Elder.

Museo Thyssen-
Bornemisza★★★
(Thyssen-Bornemisza Museum)
One of Europe's great private
art collections, ranging from
Jan van Eyck through
Caravaggio to 20C German
Expressionists and Francis
Bacon.

Palacio Real★★
(Royal Palace)
The imposing palace, built by
the Bourbons, was the official
royal residence until 1931.
Explore the sumptuous
apartments, the Throne Room
and Banqueting Hall, and visit
the Royal Armoury, Royal
Carriage Museum and the
lovely gardens.

Monasterio de las Descalzas
Reales★★
(Descalzas Reales Convent)
This handsome, still–
functioning convent of the
barefoot *(descalzas)* nuns of St
Clare is one of Madrid's few
surviving Renaissance
monuments. Its remarkable
collection of religious art
includes works by Titian and
Rubens.

Plaza Mayor★★
A theatrical setting for the city's
historic ceremonies at the
heart of Habsburg Madrid, this
elegant square is also a
delightful place to take a
morning coffee or an early
evening drink.

Parque del Buen Retiro★★
(Retiro Park)
This large area of landscaped
gardens not only provides
refreshing respite from
sightseeing, but also offers a
range of recreational activities
and entertainments, from folk-
dancing and concerts to
boating on the lake.

Toledo Catedral★★★
(Toledo Cathedral)
This grand edifice, begun in
the 13C, has magnificent choir
stalls and fine stained glass, and
no fewer than 16 works by
El Greco in the sacristy.

El Escorial★★★
(El Escorial Monastery and Palace)
Philip II's formidable Renaissance palace and monastery north-west of Madrid, notable for its basilica, royal apartments and pantheon containing the remains of Spanish monarchs.

Ávila's City Walls★★
Two kilometres (1 mile) of beautifully preserved 11C city walls are protected by 90 towers and contain over 2 500 niches for the medieval archers.

Segovia's Roman Aqueduct★★★
Built under Emperor Trajan (1C), the majestic dry-stone granite structure at Segovia is over 700m (2 297ft) long and was, until recently, still in operation.

Toledo's imposing cathedral.

THE CITY

The town was divided into neighbourhoods for Muslims, Jews and Christians, after Emir Mohammed I built his palace in 875, and ever since its citizens have referred to it in the plural, *los Madriles*. It is still true today. Architecturally, the city can be divided into distinct areas: Madrid de los Austrias (Habsburg Madrid), between Plaza Mayor and Puerta del Sol; Bourbon Madrid, separated from Habsburg Madrid by Paseo del Prado; and the modern city, north of Gran Vía. For the visitor, the town divides most simply into **Old Madrid**, **Modern**

The Royal Palace affords far-reaching views across Madrid.

Madrid and the **museums area** (principally the Golden Triangle consisting of the Prado, Thyssen-Bornemisza and Reina Sofía).

As churches and many shops close for the afternoon siesta while the main museums stay open all day, it is a good idea to do your street sightseeing early morning and late afternoon, and reserve your museum visits for midday. Large street maps posted outside each Metro station make it easy to find your way around. Following a time-honoured tradition, the names of many of the historic streets are displayed on attractive hand-painted ceramic tiles.

OLD MADRID

War, fire and over-ambitious city planning, particularly by Joseph Bonaparte and the Bourbons, have removed practically all trace of the Moorish city and many of the finer monuments of the Habsburg era. Yet a sense of the old city remains in the cluster of narrow streets south of **Calle Mayor**, where the Moors had their bazaar and the Christians of the Reconquista built their own shops, workshops, gaming-houses and brothels. Today, it is somewhat calmer and more respectable.

Puerta del Sol, one of the liveliest squares in Madrid.

Puerta del Sol

Historic in associations but thoroughly modern in atmosphere, the vast plaza lies at the very centre of the city. Indeed, a stone slab in the pavement outside the clocktower building of Madrid's regional government marks **Kilometre Zero**, the geographical centre of the country, from which all distances are measured. Sol (as the square is popularly known) takes its name 'Gate of the Sun' from a castle that was destroyed here during the insurrection of 15 cities against the monarchy in 1520.

The Oso y Madroño statue, a favourite meeting place.

At the corner of Calle del Carmen is the bronze **Oso y Madroño statue**, emblem of the city and, together with the fountain, a favourite meeting place. The oso is the bear and the madroño is a strawberry tree, symbolising forestry rights acquired in the 15C.

The **Metro station** opened up the country's first subway line in 1919, running north to Quatro Caminos. Bustling all day and most hours of the night, the plaza attracts shoppers to the major department store El Corte Inglés, the city's myriad gamblers to the jackpot machines and lottery kiosks, and New Year's Eve revellers to hear the midnight chiming of its clock tower. Following an age-old tradition, Spaniards swallow 12 grapes in time with the chimes.

Plaza Mayor★★

West of Puerta del Sol and just south of Calle
Mayor, the 'Main Square' was planned by
Philip II as the focus for his new capital's
royal ceremonies. It was finally laid out by
Juan Gómez de Mora for his son Philip III in
1619 and it is the latter's **equestrian statue**
that stands in the middle, the work of Italian
artists Giovanni da Bologna and Pietro Tacca.

Approached on all four sides through a
series of arched stairways, like passages into
an arena, the cobbled square is conceived in

*Take time for a
coffee and watch
the world go by in
the elegant Plaza
Mayor.*

the manner of an Italian piazza, a theatre with a spectacle to be watched by nobles on the balconies and by the common people in the shade of graceful arcades. The royal family watched from the much restored but decorative **Casa de la Panadería**, built between two slender bell-towers on the north side of the square and named after a bakery formerly located here. Of old, the spectacle might be a royal pageant, a bullfight on horseback, a gala première by Lope de Vega or an *auto da fe* confession and execution staged by the Inquisition. Today, the show is simply the world passing by: Madrileños and tourists sit at outdoor cafés and restaurants to chat and people-watch. On Sunday mornings stamp- and coin-collectors gather here, in summer, plays and concerts are staged, and in December there is a colourful Christmas market.

Plaza de la Villa★

Continue west along Calle Mayor to the peaceful square that groups three of the city's main architectural styles around a statue of Álvaro de Bazán, victor over the Turks at the naval battle of Lepanto in 1571. The 15C **Torre de los Lujanes** (Lujan Tower) on the east side of the square is one of the rare surviving examples of Mudéjar design, by Moorish architects working after the Reconquista. It is said to have held France's King François I for at least part of his 1525 imprisonment in Madrid. At the south end of the square is the 16C **Casa de Cisneros**, built for the nephew of the Inquisitor, Cardinal Cisneros. Its distinctively Spanish Renaissance style is known as Plateresque, from the Spanish *platero* meaning silversmith, featuring intricate

Coin-collectors discuss an interesting find on the Sunday stalls.

The Ayuntamiento (Town Hall) has impressive state apartments and a fine collection of tapestries.

detail reminiscent of a silversmith's craft. An arch links the house to the 17C **Ayuntamiento** (Town Hall), a fine baroque edifice originally designed by Gómez de Mora, architect of the Plaza Mayor. Its slate spires and towers are characteristic features of Habsburg Madrid. Behind it is the main city tourist office.

Iglesia de San Francisco el Grande

In a late-starting capital not noted for its churches, this 18C edifice makes a formidable impact, with its vast neo-classical façade and a colossal dome whose inner diameter measures 33m (108ft). Inside to the left, the **Capilla de San Bernardino** (Chapel of St Bernardino) has an early painting by Goya (1781) over the altar. It shows the saint preaching to the King of Aragón and what is believed to be a self-portrait of the artist (dressed in yellow, second from the right). Note, too, the Plateresque **choir stalls★**, brought here from a monastery near Segovia.

Palacio Real★★ (Royal Palace)
Overlooking the Manzanares river, the imposing mass of the sprawling edifice closing off the west side of the city centre is a clear expression of Spain's authoritarian monarchy in the 18C. Today, the Spanish royal family uses it only for formal ceremonies, living in more modest

San Francisco el Grande contains works by Goya, Maella and Bayeu.

The main entrance to the Royal Palace, facing the Plaza de la Armería.

Horseguards outside the Royal Palace.

apartments on the other side of town.

After the fire of 1734 destroyed the Habsburgs' Alcázar, shown in contemporary prints to be a charming hybrid of Moorish and Gothic, the Bourbon monarchs called on Italian and Spanish architects to design this neo-classical palace in the tradition of Louis XIV's Versailles. Built in white limestone and granite from the Guadarrama mountains, the long **façade** runs 140m (460ft), with alternating Ionic columns and Doric pilasters beneath a balustrade – the huge statues of the Spanish kings and queens originally intended to crown the palace have been installed on Plaza de

The monumental main staircase is decorated with fine frescoes by Corrado Giaquinto.

Oriente east of the palace and over in the Retiro Park.

Visits of the interior (entrance on Plaza de la Armería) are by guided tour only; including just 30 of the palace's 2 000 rooms, the tour is still something of a marathon. The imposing staircase leads through to the **Salón de Columnas** (Column Room). Among the highlights of the tour are the **Salón Gasparini**, a riot of rococo ornament, Alphonse XII's **Comedor de Gala** (Banqueting Hall) seating 145 guests, and above all the **Salón del Trono★** (Throne Room), with its décor of red velvet walls and gilded lions beneath the magnificent ceiling fresco of Spain's glories, painted by the Venetian master Tiepolo in 1764. Music lovers will appreciate the royal collection of Stradivarius instruments.

In an adjacent building, the **Real Armería★★** (Royal Armoury) is generally regarded as one of the finest collections of weapons and armour in the world. It displays the sword of 11C soldier-hero El Cid and the suit of armour of Charles V, plus the tools for bolting the parts together. The **Real Biblioteca** (Royal Library) includes a first edition of Cervantes' *Don Quixote* and the **Real Farmacia** (Royal Pharmacy) presents a set of elegant medicine cabinets to satisfy the most fastidious hypochondriac.

At the rear, the **Campo del Moro★** winter

Fountain in the palace winter gardens.

gardens, site of the 12C Moorish siege of the city after the Reconquista, provides an excellent view of the royal residence and the Manzanares Valley. The **Museo de Carruajes Reales★** (Royal Carriage Museum) here exhibits sumptuous royal vehicles from the 17C to the modern day.

Catedral de Nuestra Señora de la Almudena
(Cathedral of Our Lady of Almudena)
The gigantic but uninspiring cathedral south of the palace stands roughly on the site of the Moors' Great Mosque that was transformed into a church after the Christians captured the town in 1083. It was not until 1885 that the church hierarchy of

Nuestra Señora de la Almudena was rebuilt in neo-classical style after sustaining bomb damage during the Civil War.

Toledo grudgingly agreed to the Vatican granting Madrid the status of a diocese, with the accompanying right to a cathedral. In the spirit of its 19C conception, the church was originally neo-Gothic. It was bombed out in the Civil War and reconstructed with a neo-classical exterior in harmony with the royal palace, fulfilling the Spanish traditionalists' attachment to 'throne and altar'. Inaugurated by Pope John Paul II in 1993, the church celebrates the city's founding legend of a statue of the Virgin Mary found in the city walls *(Almudena)* at the time of the Reconquista.

Plaza de Oriente

The square has had a hard time overcoming gloomy associations with the grim nationalistic speeches which Franco liked to give here, surrounded by oversize statues of the Christian Visigothic monarchs with whom he liked to identify. Neo-fascists still assemble here to observe the November anniversary of his death. But the place is brightened, especially on summer nights, by the terrace of the fashionable **Café de Oriente** and by the refurbished **Teatro Real** (Royal Theatre and Opera House), built in 1850. At the centre of the square is the heroic **equestrian statue of Philip IV**, a veritable *tour de force* by 17C baroque sculptor Pietro Tacca, a pupil of Giovanni da Bologna.

The plain exterior of the Descalzas Reales Convent belies the wealth of art treasures contained within.

Monasterio de las Descalzas Reales★★
(Descalzas Reales Convent)

At the corner of Plaza de San Martín, this retreat for aristocratic nuns is a true haven of tranquillity in a district of heavy traffic. The stricture of the royal ladies to go barefoot – *Descalzas Reales* – clearly does not entail any other vow of poverty. Founded in the 16C by Philip II's sister, Joanna of Austria, the convent of the sisters of St Clare is a rare and opulent Renaissance monument, richly endowed by noble patrons over the centuries and still functioning as a religious institution. The resident nuns working the vegetable gardens keep out of sight during visiting hours. Beyond the cloisters, an elaborately ornate staircase leads to the former **dormitories**, decorated by art treasures that include Zurbaran's fine portrait of St Francis and 17C Flemish tapestries designed by Rubens. The **Relicario** (Reliquary Chamber) assembles a quite astonishing collection of jewels and sacred relics, mostly bones of unidentified saints.

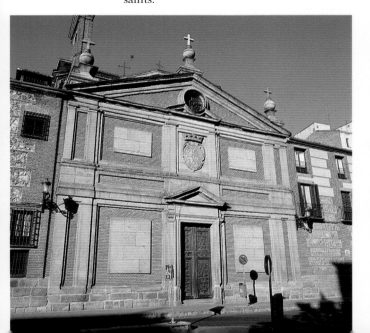

MODERN MADRID

Most of the modern city of interest to visitors
is situated on the periphery of Habsburg
Madrid, north of Gran Vía and east of Calle
Toledo to Retiro Park. Its main attractions
are the street life and *barrios* (neighbourhoods)
rather than churches and monuments. All
you need are good walking shoes and the
time to stroll or sit around and watch the
city's modern world go by.

Gran Vía

A dividing line between old and new Madrid, the city's main thoroughfare runs roughly west to east from Plaza de España, north of the Royal Palace, to join Calle de Alcalá at the great Plaza de la Cibeles. The non-stop traffic jam all day and much of the night is a spectacular display, with whistle-blowing police and car-honking drivers.

Gran Vía was opened up in 1910 – through the demolition of 327 buildings and the suppression of 14 smaller streets – and its monumental banks, cinemas, hotels, nightclubs, department stores and offices embody the city's 20C flavour.

The busy modern city of Madrid, near Plaza de España.

The architecture pays tribute, often in witty pastiches, to the Mudéjar, Gothic, Renaissance and baroque styles of the city's past. For admirers of commercial art, the cinemas' gigantic hand-painted **movie posters** are considered masterpieces of the genre. At the corner of Calle de Fuencarral, the stately **Telefónica Building** served as the Republicans' Civil War artillery position against the Nationalists occupying the Casa de Campo to the west.

Plaza de la Cibeles★

At the east end of Gran Vía, traffic swirls in perpetual paroxysm around the landmark 18C **fountain of Cybele**. The ancient fertility goddess, served by eunuch priests and extremely popular with Madrileños, is shown relaxing in a chariot drawn by a pair of watchful lions. But the plaza's most striking monument is the **Palacio de Comunicaciones**, the splendid yet stylistically indefinable post office, a secular cathedral completed in 1918 that visitor Leon Trotsky aptly nicknamed 'Our Lady of

Communications'. It is more fanciful than the reassuringly solid neo-classical **Banco de España** (Bank of Spain) across the plaza on the corner of **Calle de Alcalá**, Madrid's financial district.

The Paseos

Plaza de la Cibeles is also the junction of the broad, tree-lined boulevards, the Paseos, which provide the setting for that great Spanish institution, the *paseo* evening

The fountain of Cybele and Palacio de Comunicaciones are two of Madrid's great landmarks.

The busy junction of the Grand Vía and Calle de Alcalá at night.

promenade. Like the Italian *passeggiata*, it is the precious moment when the Madrid bourgeoisie and young couples take a stroll, to see and be seen, to talk of politics and bullfights, love and football. The Paseos have also witnessed the triumphal processions of Habsburg and Bourbon monarchs, of Franco's victorious army in 1939 and a million defiant Madrileños demonstrating for democracy in 1981. To the south, underlining the explicitly social function, the **Paseo del Prado★** was also known as the *Salón*. Its prestige is emphasized by two veritable monuments of luxury, the Ritz and Palace hotels facing each other across the grand **Neptune Fountain** on Plaza Cánovas del Castillo. To the north, **Paseo de Recoletos** extends into **Paseo de la Castellana**, with fashionable *terrazas* (terrace cafés and restaurants) along the grass strip in the middle.

Parque del Buen Retiro** (Retiro Park)

Within easy reach of the Prado and the other main museums, this delightful park offers a good opportunity to get away from the bustle of the traffic and the hard slog of sightseeing.

It originally provided a good retreat – hence its name – for Philip II while he was waiting for El Escorial to be completed. Its grounds belonged to the 15C monastery of San Jerónimo and to a later palace of Philip IV, both now destroyed.

There are numerous attractions scattered across its 130 hectares (321 acres) of French-style formal and English-style landscaped gardens: folk-dancing, concerts, a June book

The delightful Retiro Park offers a refreshing retreat from the noise of the city.

A captive audience for the puppet show in Retiro Park.

fair; art exhibitions in the **Palacio de Cristal** and **Palacio de Velázquez**; summer film shows at **La Chopera**; boats for hire on the oblong pond of **El Estanque**; and weekend **puppet shows** in the north-west corner, near the Puerta de Alcalá entrance.

Cortes

West of the Paseo del Prado, between Calle de Alcalá and Calle Huertas, is the largely 19C district around the **Cortes Españolas** (Spanish Parliament). Visitors are admitted on Saturday mornings to the rather undistinguished building of the lower house (Congress), and are shown the chamber with the bullet holes left by Colonel Antonio Tejero in his abortive coup of 1981 (*see* p.17).

Just to the north, on Calle de Alcalá, the

Círculo de Bellas Artes (Fine Arts Circle) is a highly agreeable cultural centre offering one-day membership access to its art galleries, concert hall, theatre, cinema and a bar in handsome, comfortable surroundings.

South of the Cortes, on Calle de Cervantes, the **Casa de Lope de Vega** (home of the playwright) includes an attractive reconstruction of the great writer's 17C Madrid. By ironic coincidence – for they hated each other – **Cervantes' burial place** is on Calle Lope de Vega, in the Trinitaria Convent, but this is rarely open to visitors.

A little further to the south is the lively **Calle Huertas** bar district. Here, the bars are more genteel than the *Movida*-style ones of the Malasaña district, and are highly recommended – as are the restaurants and

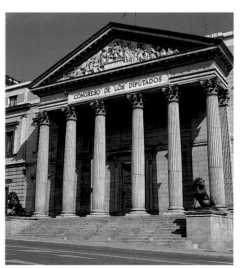

The neo-classical entrance to the Spanish Parliament is flanked by a pair of bronze lions cast from cannons captured in the Moroccan War (1860).

Lope de Vega's house has been preserved as a museum.

bars further west, on and around the delightful **Plaza de Santa Ana**.

Malasaña

Situated between the Gran Vía and Calle de Sagasta is the Malasaña district. This *barrio* (quarter) is beloved of Madrileños as the home of the Malasaña family, martyred on 2 May 1808 in the insurrection against Napoleonic troops that is commemorated annually on **Plaza del Dos de Mayo**.

The plaza's bouncy *terraza* cafés and music bars have prospered since the progressive spirit of the quarter was revived in the post-Franco era. When Malasaña became the major focus of the *Movida*, the poster advertising the *Dos de Mayo* celebrations showed Goya's hero with his arms raised before the firing squad – and an electronic guitar around his waist.

Chueca

Like Malasaña, the adjacent *barrio* of Chueca, west of the Paseo de Recoletos, remains one of the liveliest neighbourhoods of modern Madrid and is the hub of the city's gay scene. On and around **Calle Almirante** are several attractive art galleries, fashionable boutiques and restaurants. At night, the more cautious may prefer to avoid the area immediately around **Plaza de Chueca** itself, which is notorious for drug-dealers.

In the neighbourhood's north-west corner, a decorative note of respectability is added by the ornate Churrigueresque baroque façade of the **Museo Municipal** (Municipal Museum) on Calle Fuencarral. Maps and models of old Madrid trace the rapid growth of the city.

El Rastro

South of Plaza Mayor, Madrid's monumental **flea-market** sprawls along and around Ribera de Curtidores down to the Ronda de Toledo. It operates principally at the weekends, but antiques dealers and junk shops are open on week days – the best time to come if you want to browse and haggle in quiet. But the rollicking folklore, especially on Sunday mornings, is not to be missed. As with all big-city flea-markets, visitors need to be wary of fakes and pick-pockets.

Looking for a bargain at the El Rastro flea-market.

Puerta de Toledo

This triumphal arch was originally built to welcome Napoleon Bonaparte in the Peninsular War, but he never made it. It now provides an imposing backdrop to the **Mercado Puerta Toledo**, transformed from the municipal fish market into a high-class and attractive shopping centre for (genuine) designer clothes and antiques.

Puerta de Toledo, one of Madrid's two surviving city gates, was completed in 1817.

THE MUSEUMS

For many visitors the greatest treasures of
Madrid are its museums. Take them in
manageable doses. The so-called 'Golden
Triangle' along the Paseo del Prado,
between Plaza Cánovas del Castillo and
Atocha railway station, groups the Prado,
Thyssen-Bornemisza and the Reina Sofía.
The Prado needs at least a day to explore
comfortably, but the other two could be
visited in the same day.

To help you avoid the temptation of trying
to cram too much in, the modern
collections of the Reina Sofía are open on
Mondays when the other two are closed.
There are also a couple of other noteworthy
museums for those with the time and
inclination.

Museo del Prado★★★ (The Prado)
The royal collections assembled here are so
rich in quality and variety that to do them
justice needs some planning – and for

*The Prado Museum
houses the royal
family's collections
of art, providing an
outstanding
overview of Spanish
art.*

newcomers, some self-discipline in concentrating on the paintings they really want to see most.

Originally built in 1785 as a natural science museum, the Prado was established in 1819 by Ferdinand VII as the Royal Museum of Painting and Sculpture to house the huge collections of the Habsburg and Bourbon monarchs, much expanded since then by donations and acquisitions. Today, only one-tenth of the thousands of works are on display at any one time.

Ongoing renovation and reorganization of the collections may change some of the arrangement of the works exhibited. At present, since the main entrance on the Paseo del Prado, **Puerta de Velázquez**, is usually used by large groups, individuals are advised to use the side entrances, **Puerta de Goya** on Calle Felipe IV or **Puerta de Murillo** on Plaza de Murillo. The **main floor** (*planta principal*, above the street level) is devoted to the Spanish masters from the 16C to the 18C (El Greco, Velázquez,

One of the Prado's galleries.

Zurbarán, Murillo and Goya) and the Italians (Fra Angelico, Mantegna, Botticelli, Titian and Veronese). The street-level **lower floor** (*planta baja*) exhibits the northern European Flemish, Dutch and German schools (Bosch, Bruegel, Rubens, Dürer and Rembrandt) and Spanish art from the 12C to the 16C, plus Goya's so-called *Black*

El Greco's The Adoration of the Shepherds.

Paintings. The annex in the nearby 17C **Casón del Buen Retiro★**, a relic of the old palace of Philip IV, houses Spanish paintings of the 19C and 20C.

We propose here a selection of the museum's most important painters and their masterpieces.

Spanish★★★

El Greco (1541–1614) Signed Domenikos Theotokopoulos, *Nobleman with his Hand on his Chest* is an early work of realism from shortly after the Cretan-born painter arrived in Toledo, epitomizing the Spanish aristocrat in austere but elegant costume and serene yet unbendingly serious demeanour. Executed at the end of his life,

Velázquez's vast work The Surrender of Breda *records the defeated Dutch general Nassau before the Spanish commander Espínola.*

55

The Adoration of the Shepherds projects the artist's fervent spirituality, with dematerialized, almost surreal, human figures.

Diego Velázquez (1599–1660) The Prado's most celebrated picture, the endlessly hypnotic *Maids of Honour* (*Las Meninas*) presents the artist himself coolly appraising his royal masters, their servants – and us – with stunning command of space and colour. He tackles with equal facility and breathtaking technique a formal military scene such as *The Surrender of Breda*, a piercing psychological portraiture of *Philip IV*, and subjects of the common people, such as *The Drunkards*.

José Ribera (1591–1661) More Italian than Spanish after a long career in Naples, he uses in *Archimedes* a cheerful Neapolitan as a model for the august Greek scholar. The debt to Caravaggio's strongly contrasting light and shade is also evident in the dramatic *Martyrdom of St Philip*.

Francisco de Zurbarán (1598–1664) The graceful portrait of a defiant Spanish lady as *Santa Casilda* and the *Tavern* still-life of carafes and a goblet are outstanding examples of the naturalist style of this mystic who is best known for his scenes of monastic life.

Bartolomé Murillo (1618–1682) The sentimental but often highly personal charm of Murillo's religious pictures are exemplified in the portrayal of Jesus as a pretty little boy in *Good Shepherd* and a soulful Mary in the *The Escorial Immaculate Conception*.

Francisco de Goya (1746–1828) A revolutionary spirit is omnipresent. In *Wine Harvest*, aristocrats enjoy their grapes, oblivious of the hard-working labourers

Goya's celebrated portrayal of Charles IV and his family (1800).

behind them. The unflattering *The Family of Charles IV* shows the king's wife, Maria Luisa, very much in charge. The emblematic *Dos de Mayo* and *Tres de Mayo* depict the violence of Madrid's heroic fight against the French in 1808. Even the seductive *Clothed Maya* and *Naked Maya* express an impudence in the strangely superimposed heads.

Italian★★
Renaissance masters include **Fra Angelico** (an exquisite *Annunciation*); **Botticelli** (*Nastagio degli Onesti*, three panels illustrating a story from Boccaccio's *Decameron*); **Antonello da Messina** (a tragic *Dead Christ Supported by an Angel*); **Andrea**

Mantegna (*Death of the Virgin*); **Raphael** (a mysterious portrait, *The Cardinal*, and the superb *Christ Falling on the Way to Calvary*).

Venetian masters include **Titian** (an exemplary equestrian portrait of his patron, *Emperor Charles V*, and the bawdy *Bacchanal*); **Tintoretto** (the theatrical panorama of *Christ Washing the Disciples' Feet*); **Veronese** (an unusually playful *Venus and Adonis*); and the museum's one great **Caravaggio**, *David and Goliath*, which was so influential on Spanish painting of the Golden Age.

Flemish★★★ and Dutch
Rogier van der Weyden (the *Descent from the Cross* altarpiece, widely considered his finest picture); **Hans Memling** (a delicate *Birth of Christ* triptych); **Hieronymus Bosch** (three absolute masterpieces of surrealist eroticism and apocalypse, four centuries before the modern movement: *Garden of Delights*, *Table of the Seven Deadly Sins* and *The Hay Cart*); **Pieter Bruegel the Elder** (the profoundly humanistic and poignant *Triumph of Death*); **Rubens** (*Three Graces*, characteristically buxom, and an opulent *Adoration of the Magi*); and the museum's one authentic **Rembrandt**, *Queen Artemisia*, symbol of marital fidelity, painted at the time of the master's own marriage.

German
Albrecht Dürer (the penetrating *Self-Portrait* and a graceful duo, *Adam* and *Eve*); **Hans Baldung Grien** (*Ages of Man and Death*).

Museo Thyssen-Bornemisza★★★
(Thyssen-Bornemisza Museum)
At Paseo del Prado 8, the neo-classical Palacio de Villahermosa houses one of the

The magnificently restored Palacio de Villahermosa now houses the Thyssen-Bornemisza Museum.

world's greatest private art collections, inaugurated in 1993. Some 800 works, from the 14C to the present day, were donated by German-born industrialist Baron Hans Thyssen at the prompting of his Spanish wife, Tita Cervera. (The former 'Miss Spain' is portrayed in the foyer with the baron, King Juan Carlos and his queen.) The baron's father, Heinrich, assembled the bulk of the collection in the 1920s, advised by the greatest art historians of the day.

The works are organized chronologically on three floors, from the top down, with a bar and cafeteria in the basement.

Second Floor: European (14C–18C)

Italian primitives (Duccio di Buoninsegna); Early Flemish (Jan van Eyck, Rogier van der Weyden and Petrus Christus); Renaissance portraits (Ghirlandaio, Hans Memling, Hans Holbein, Carpaccio and Titian); German masters (Dürer, Lucas Cranach and Hans

Baldung Grien); Spanish (El Greco and
Zurbarán); Caravaggio, his disciple Ribera,
and a rare Bernini sculpture.

First Floor: European and American (17C–20C)

Dutch (Frans Hals); American (Whistler,
Winslow Homer); English (Gainsborough,
Constable); Impressionists and Post-
Impressionists (Monet, Manet, Degas,
Gauguin, Van Gogh, Toulouse-Lautrec,
Cézanne); Expressionists (Edvard Munch,
Egon Schiele, George Grosz, Ernst Ludwig
Kirchner and Max Beckmann).

Ground Floor: 20C

European (Picasso, Braque, Juan Gris,
Mondrian, Kandinsky, Magritte, Francis
Bacon, Lucien Freud); American (Edward
Hopper, Jackson Pollock, Mark Rothko,
Robert Rauschenberg).

Picasso's Guernica
*(1937) is the
centrepiece of
the Reina Sofía
collection.*

Museo Nacional Centro de Arte Reina Sofía★ (Queen Sofia Art Centre)

At the south end of Paseo del Prado facing Atocha station, the handsome modern transformation of a sprawling 18C hospital completes the city's Golden Triangle, with a fine collection of 20C Spanish art. Its centrepiece is Picasso's **Guernica★★★**. This monumental denunciation of the German bombing of the Basque city in the Spanish Civil War took a long time getting here. Picasso first hung it in the Spanish Republican pavilion at the Paris Exposition of 1937, and then sent it to New York's Museum of Modern Art, where it was to stay until, as he said, democracy returned to Spain. It was transferred to Madrid in 1981, at first in a much criticized display at the Casón del Buen Retiro before finally moving to the Reina Sofía in 1992. Here the stark work in black, grey and white is beautifully

Works by modern painters are exhibited on the second floor in the Reina Sofía.

exhibited, surrounded by preparatory studies and what the artist calls 'post-scripts' – moving detailed treatments of a mourning mother, a screaming horse and other symbolic elements of Guernica's suffering. Besides Picasso's earlier work, the museum also exhibits Salvador Dalí, Juan Gris, Joan Miró, Tàpies and Chillida.

Museo Arqueológico Nacional★★
(National Archaeological Museum)

Sharing the premises of the **Biblioteca Nacional** (National Library), Calle de Serrano 13, the collection traces Spain's origins, from the Stone Age through Roman times to medieval Christian and Islamic art. Among the more noteworthy pieces are two ornately carved **Celto-Iberian statues** (4C BC), the aristocratic **Lady of Elche★★★** and a goddess, **Lady of Baza★★**, plus a hoard of 8C **Visigothic jewels★★** recently unearthed in Toledo.

Museo Lázaro Galdiano★★

Housed in the neo-classical palace of the donor (Calle de Serrano 122), this personal collection is remarkable above all for its Spanish art, including El Greco, Murillo, Zurbarán, Ribera and some of

The National Library, built in 1892, has an ornate granite façade. It was one of the first constructions in Spain to be built with an iron framework.

Goya's more disturbing *Black Paintings*. There are also important Flemish works by Bosch and Quentin Matsys and an exquisite collection of jewels, ivories, precious **enamels★★** and antique clocks.

OTHER ATTRACTIONS

Casa de Campo★ behind the Royal Palace
An ideal spot for a day in the country without leaving town, where you can walk, picnic, swim (in pools), go boating or visit the amusement park and zoo. The parkland was reafforested by Philip II in 1559.

Cine Doré Santa Isabel 3 [Map:LZ]
The city's oldest cinema (1922), now home of the Filmoteca Nacional (National Cinematheque), with an Art Nouveau façade.

The Art Nouveau Cine Doré.

Real Monasterio de la Encarnación★
(Royal Convent of the Incarnation) square of the same name [Map:KX]
Augustine convent founded by Marguerite of Austria, wife of Philip III; 17C paintings, and an astonishing **Relicario★** (Relics Room).

Faro de la Moncloa (Moncloa Beacon) north of Parque del Oeste
An observation tower erected in 1992; it is 76m (250ft) high with a fine view from the **balcony★★** over the city and the Meseta plateau.

Jardín Botánico (Botanical Garden) south of the Prado [Map:NZ]
Cool shady gardens opened to the public in 1781 and renovated in the 1980s.

Jardines de las Vistillas (Gardens with Vistas) south of the cathedral [Map:KYZ]
Terrace cafés with **views★** across the Manzanares river to Sierra de Guadarrama.

63

La Corrala In colourful Lavapiés quarter, Calle Sombrerete [Map:LZ]
This balconied tenement building was declared a national monument for its cultural activities.

Museo Cerralbo★ Calle Ventura Rodríguez 17 [Map:KV]
Marqués de Cerralbo's grand mansion has been transformed into a museum of 19C aristocratic life, displaying paintings, furniture and porcelain, armour and weaponry.

Museo de América★ (Museum of the Americas) Ciudad Universitaria, Avenida Reyes Católicos 6
Artefacts from Latin America, including pre-Columbian art, the **Cortesano Manuscript★★★** (one of only four Mayan manuscripts) and the **Treasure of Los Quimbayas★**.

The delightful shaded Botanical Garden, where you can relax and unwind away from the bustle of the city.

The Plaza de España, where old and modern Madrid meet, is a popular promenade for Madrileños.

Museo Nacional de Artes Decorativas (Decorative Arts Museum) Calle de Montalbán, 12 [Map:NX]
Fine Spanish glass, ceramics, porcelain and jewellery.

Museo del Ejército★ (Army Museum)
Calle Méndez Núñez 1 [Map:NY]
Covers military history from ancient times to the Civil War; includes El Cid's sword and *Conquistadores* armour.

Museo Naval (Maritime Museum)
Paseo del Prado 5 [Map:NXY – M³]
A collection of **model ships★**, navigational instruments and charts, dating back to the first Spanish voyages to the Americas and including the **map★★** of Juan de la Cosa, the earliest known map of America.

Museo Romántico Calle de San Mateo 13 [Map:LV]
Costumes, jewellery and furniture, dating

from the crinolined age of rococo.

Palacio de Liria Calle de la Princesa 20 [Map:KV]
The splendid residence of the Duchess of
Alba; the private picture gallery is open only
by appointment.

Palacio de Santa Cruz Plaza Provincia 1, east
of Plaza Mayor [Map:LY]
Former court prison, whose inmates
included Lope de Vega. Now houses the
Ministry for Foreign Affairs.

Parque del Oeste★ (West Park) north of the
Royal Palace
This refreshing parkland includes the
ancient Egyptian Temple of Debod (4C BC),
salvaged from the Nile Valley, when the
Aswan Dam was built.

Plaza de Colón (Columbus Square) [Map:NV]
Christopher Columbus's statue stands above
a subterranean cultural centre, with films,
theatre and exhibitions.

Plaza de España [Map:KV]
Skyscrapers surround Cervantes' monument

*The statue of
Columbus, on the
Plaza de Colón.*

*San Fernando Royal
Fine Arts Academy.*

of Don Quixote on horseback, with Sancho Panza on his donkey.

Plaza de la Paja [Map:KZ]

The acacia trees and fountain make this one of the old city's most charming squares, a refuge of quiet shade in summer.

Plaza Monumental de las Ventas★ (Bullring) Calle Alcalá, east of Salamanca quarter

Considered by *aficionados* to be the high temple of bullfighting arenas, this is the biggest in Spain, seating 22 300 spectators.

Puerta de Alcalá★ (Alcalá Arch) Plaza de la Independencia [Map:NX]

A triumphal arch built in the 18C to welcome Charles III to Madrid.

This striking statue announces the great bullfighting arena of Madrid.

The church of San Isidro stands in the heart of the old town, close to the Plaza Mayor.

Real Academia de Bellas Artes de San Fernando* (San Fernando Royal Fine Arts Academy) Calle de Alcalá [Map:LX – M²]
Contains a fine collection of works, by Velázquez, Zurbarán, Goya and Rubens, among others.
Real Fábrica de Tapices (Royal Tapestry Factory) Calle de Fuenterrabía 8. Near Atocha station
The factory, founded in 1721 by Philip V, is still using Goya's designs for tapestries.
San Antonio de la Florida near Norte station
An 18C chapel with Goya **frescoes**** and the artist's tomb.
Iglesia de San Ginés Calle del Arenal 13 [Map:KY]

This church, dating back to Moorish rule, contains El Greco's painting, *Money Changers Chased from Temple*.

Iglesia de San Isidro Calle de Toledo 49 [Map:KZ]

The massive domed church of the city's patron saint, San Isidro, was the town's cathedral until Nuestra Señora de la Almudena was completed.

San Jerónimo el Real near Casón del Buen Retiro [Map:NY]

Juan Carlos was crowned in the abbey church of the long-gone monastery.

Pontificia de San Miguel Calle San Justo 4, south-west of Plaza Mayor [Map:KY]

An 18C Italian baroque basilica, with an attractively curving façade.

Iglesia de San Pedro south of Plaza de la Villa [Map:KY]

A 14C church, with a rare Mudéjar tower.

Santiago Bernabeu Stadium Del Padre Damián, off La Castellana

The city's most sacred secular shrine – the football stadium of Real Madrid and the Spanish national team.

El Pardo 9km (5 miles) north-west of Madrid

This town originated around a royal palace, Franco's former residence, and is now popular for its open-air *terraza* restaurants.

San Miguel church has an imposing curved granite façade.

EXCURSIONS FROM MADRID

All the excursions we propose here can be made comfortably in a day. However, some people may like to plan an overnight stay in Toledo for a more leisurely visit. Segovia or Ávila can be combined in a single round trip with an overnight stay in one of those towns.

TOLEDO★★★

All the strands of Spanish history and culture come together in this magnificent,

Majestic Toledo sits on a granite hill overlooking the Tagus river and the Meseta plains.

luminous hilltop town 70km (44 miles) south of Madrid. Dominating a loop in the Tagus river, the magical skyline of the Gothic cathedral flanked by the Alcázar fortress and San Juan monastery is a constant background in the paintings of El Greco, who made Toledo his home town. Its elevated position in the southern Meseta plain prompted the Romans to create the strategic garrison town of Toletum, which the Visigoths in turn made their capital in the 6C.

In the Middle Ages, Jews, Christians and Muslims enriched its cultural life, their sages working together to transmit the knowledge of Hebrew, Greek and Arabic scholarship. This enlightenment came to an end in the growing intolerance of the Reconquista, but Toledo retained its pre-eminence in the Spanish church even after the political capital was transferred to Madrid.

For a first truly awe-inspiring **view★★★** of the town, take the Puente de Alcántara (Alcántara Bridge) over the river to the numerous observation terraces on the Carretera de Circunvalación road running around the southern periphery. Once inside the town, lose yourself happily in the narrow winding streets that are the most obvious legacy of its cosmopolitan past and come across both its great monuments and other lesser, unsung beauties by serendipity – and an occasional signpost.

Catedral★★★ (Cathedral)
The silhouette of the great 13C church, more French Gothic than Spanish, can be appreciated only at a distance as its bulk is swallowed up in the maze of tiny streets around it. It took over 250 years to complete

and, like the imposing tower, the three portals of the main façade on Plaza del Ayuntamiento, most notably the profusely sculpted central **Puerta del Perdón** (Gate of Pardon), date from the 15C.

Enter left of this façade through the Puerta del Mollete past the cloister to the north side of the church. In the centre of the five-aisled interior, behind a fine Renaissance grill, is the **choir** with magnificently carved **stalls★★★**. The 16C wood panels recount in dramatic detail the conquest of Grenada, while the upper levels in alabaster portray scenes of the Old

The magnificent cathedral, one of Spain's finest Gothic buildings, provides splendid views from its north tower.

Testament. In the **Capilla Mayor** (Main Chapel) east of the Choir, the monumental **retable**★★ recounts the life of Jesus in five tiers of polychrome sculpture. In the ambulatory behind the chapel, the lavish 18C baroque **Transparente**, ornate screens in marble, jasper and bronze which are illuminated by an opening cut in the ceiling.

The **Sala Capitular** (Chapter House) has a handsome **Mudéjar ceiling**★. 'Mudéjar' refers to the highly decorative architectural style developed by Muslims converted after the Reconquista. Among the cardinals' portraits are two by Goya. The **Sacristy** contains 16 **paintings**★ by El Greco, works by Titian, Van Dyck and Goya, and ceiling frescoes by Luca Giordano.

Iglesia de Santo Tomé

With its fine medieval Mudéjar tower, this church is visited for the city's most famous wall painting, El Greco's **Burial of the Count of Orgaz** ★★★(1586). In masterful juxtaposition of the mystical and realistic, it recounts the miraculous participation of St Augustine and St Stephen in the 14C count's funeral. Among the celestial spectators is Philip II, still alive at the time of the painting.

Casa y Museo de El Greco★
(El Greco House and Museum)

Down the hill from the church, the house said to have been the painter's home is in what was the old Jewish quarter (Judería). The house was originally built by 14C financier Samuel Ha-Levi, financial adviser to Peter I of Castile (until the king lived up to his nickname of Peter the Cruel by killing him and confiscating his fortune). It has been restored in vague approximation of

El Greco's 16C studio. More interesting is the adjacent museum with some works of the master, including a view of the city.

Synagogues

Only two of the ten synagogues in the Jewish quarter still exist today. The **Sinagoga del Tránsito★★** (Synagogue of the Dormition) was built in 1355 by Samuel Ha-Levi. It was transformed into a church after the expulsion of the Jews, hence the name and the vestiges of Christian tombs. In the simple rectangular interior, with an upper gallery for women worshippers, Muslim artists crafted the stucco work in fine Mudéjar style, with intricate filigree decoration and inscriptions in Hebrew and Arabic praising God, the king and Ha-Levi. The adjacent **Museo Sefardí** (Sephardic Museum) traces the history of Toledo's Jewish community from Roman times until its expulsion in 1492.

Originally the most important Jewish house of worship in Toledo, the Muslim-built **Sinagoga de Santa María la Blanca★** (St Mary the White) became a church after the Expulsion. With its horseshoe arches on 24 octagonal pillars, it still resembles a mosque.

Alcázar

There have been fortresses on this site since the days of the Roman *castrum*, but they have been repeatedly destroyed in war, most recently in the Spanish Civil War in 1936. With the rest of the city in Republican hands, the Alcázar was occupied by pro-Franco forces and their families during a devastating 72-day siege. In a famous response to a telephone call warning him his

son would be executed if the Nationalists did not surrender, their commander, Colonel José Moscardó, told his boy: 'Pray to God, shout "Viva España" and die like a hero.' (A month later, the son was shot, but in reprisal for an air raid.) Franco finally sent in more Nationalist troops to relieve the beleaguered forces – and restored the Alcázar as a monument of fascist heroism. Roughly as originally designed for Emperor Charles V, it is still in part occupied by the army.

Near by, the triangular **Plaza de Zocodover** stands on the site of the Moorish

The 16C Alcázar stands at Toledo's highest point, on the site of a Roman fort.

market. The Inquisition staged its executions here. It is now a popular meeting place for Toledans on their evening *paseo*.

Museo de Santa Cruz★★
(Santa Cruz Museum)

With its elegant arcaded patio, the attractive 16C Renaissance building, built as a hospital, has been transformed into a museum. In addition to works by Ribera and Goya, there are 18 **paintings★** by El Greco, including the **Altarpiece of the Assumption★**, a late work of remarkable intensity.

Details from the façade of Santa Cruz Museum.

Other Attractions
Cristo de la Luz (Christ of the Light)
An early 11C nine-domed mosque, transformed into a church but still used for worship by visiting Muslims.

Hospital de Tavera★ (Tavera Hospital)
This 16C hospital, built outside the city walls, has important works by Tintoretto, Ribera and El Greco, including the latter's last work, **Baptism of Christ★★**.

Puerta del Sol
The 14C 'Gate of the Sun' is a fine example of Mudéjar design, featuring two horseshoe arches.

Monasterio de San Juan de los Reyes★
(St John of the Kings Monastery)
A 15C monastery built by Ferdinand and Isabella in a mixture of Gothic, Renaissance and Mudéjar styles.

Iglesia de San Román
Mudéjar church with 13C frescoes of the Councils of Toledo and now a museum devoted to Visigothic culture.

EL ESCORIAL★★★
(El Escorial Monastery and Palace)
Some 45km (28 miles) north-west of Madrid, Philip II's palace and adjoining San Lorenzo monastery express perfectly the essence of the sombre, single-minded creator of Spain's modern capital. In a resolutely Spanish interpretation of Italian Renaissance design, architect Juan de Herrera completed in 1584 a massive monument to his master's piety and authoritarian monarchy.

The rectangle of grey granite, 206m (676ft) long and 161m (528ft) wide, encloses royal apartments, a church, a mausoleum, a monastery and a museum. It is gigantic, with 86 stairways, 1 200 doors

and 2 600 windows. The king had it all laid
out in a grid-plan to symbolize the
martyrdom of San Lorenzo, the Spanish-
born saint roasted alive on a grill in Rome in
AD 258 – the grill is the Escorial's
omnipresent emblem. (It was on the saint's
day, 10 August 1557, after defeating the
French in battle, that Philip II had decided
to build El Escorial.)

The austere yet majestic design of El Escorial Monastery was a reaction to the excessively ornate architectural styles of Charles V's reign.

For a fine overall **view★** of the walled compound, drivers can follow signs 7km (4 miles) west from the town of San Lorenzo de El Escorial to **Silla de Felipe II** (Seat of Philip II), a group of boulders on a rise overlooking the site, where the king is said to have come to survey construction progress.

Palacios★★ (Royal Apartments)

On the second floor, built deliberately around the apse of the church, the **Habitaciones de Felipe II** (Philip II's Apartments) are austere in the extreme. The rooms are small and, apart from the 16C Flemish tapestries in the **Salón del Trono** (Throne Room), the furnishings are modest. A door in the king's bedroom opens to the church so that, when he lay dying in 1598 at the age of 71, he could participate in Mass from his bed. Still there is the chair on which he rested his gouty leg and, in another room, the sedan in which he had to be carried about. Away from the church in the north-east corner, the third-floor **Palacio de los Borbones** (Bourbon Apartments), renovated in the 18C, are more spacious, with ornate inlaid panelling and lively **tapestries★** based on designs by Rubens and, most notably, Goya's scenes of popular festivities.

In the handsome **Biblioteca★★** (Library), Herrera designed the shelves for Philip II's great collection of Arabic manuscripts and rare books, including St Theresa of Ávila's diary of her ecstatic dreams. Two new **museums★★** house Spanish, Flemish and Italian masters (**Museo de Pintura**, Picture Museum) and an architectural display devoted to the Escorial's original construction (**Museo de Arquitectura**, Architectural Museum).

Basilica★★ and Monastery

The church's interior follows the Greek-cross plan of St Peter's, Rome, its huge cupola soaring 92m (302ft) above the transept crossing, supported by four giant pillars. The 17C **ceiling frescoes** are the work of Luca Giordano. Herrera's monumental high altar, with columns of red marble, onyx and jasper, has bronze statues by Leoni and Pompeo Leoni. Father and son, they also carved the statuary for the **mausoleums** of Charles V and Philip II on either side of the choir. In a chapel to the left is a superb white marble Crucifixion by **Benvenuto Cellini** (1562).

Much of the royal art collection here has been progressively moved to the Prado, but the **Sacristía** (Sacristy) and **Salas Capitulares★** (Chapter Houses) have several fine paintings of Velázquez, El Greco, Ribera, Veronese, Tintoretto and Titian and two works by Hieronymus Bosch, including a second version of *The Haywain*.

The **Panteón de los Reyes★★★** (Royal Pantheon) is a 17C octagonal chapel beneath the church choir. Here, stacked in tiers of four, are the gilded marble tombs of all but three of Spain's monarchs since Charles V, kings to the left and child-bearing queens to the right. (Missing are the first two Bourbons: Philip V who is buried in the Palacio de la Granja, and Ferdinand VI who was laid to rest in Madrid.) In the 19C **Panteón de los Infantes★** (Children's Pantheon) are the tombs of some 30 royal infants – and the childless queens.

SEGOVIA★★★

This proud city enjoys a picturesque **setting**★★ perched on a triangular rock north of the Sierra de Guadarrama. In its 15C heyday, its favour with the kings and queens of Castilla meant that for a while it might have succeeded Toledo as capital of Spain rather than the less prestigious Madrid.

It is a handsome town in which some of the remaining fortifications serve as sustaining walls for dwellings, with many of the older quarters built in the region's attractive honey-coloured stone. It has also preserved several characteristic Castilian

The hilltop position of Segovia provides magnificent views across the Sierra de Guadarrama, especially from the towers of the Alcázar.

Romanesque churches with Mudéjar minaret-like towers, all much older than the cathedral.

Acueducto Romano★★★
(Roman Aqueduct)
Built in all likelihood under Emperor Trajan in the 1C, this masterpiece of elegant Roman engineering on the south side of town brought in water from the Acebeda river, well into the 20C. The two-tiered structure, built of local granite without mortar, is 728m (2 388ft) long and reaches 28m (92ft) in height where the ground is at its lowest, over the Plaza del Azoguejo.

Alcázar★
Soaring over the confluence of the Eresma and Clamores rivers are the pepperpot towers, dungeon and fanciful battlements of the royal castle. In fact the Alcázar itself is a pastiche: after being ravaged by fire in 1862, the fortress was reconstucted in a romantic

Perched on a cliff overlooking the valley, Segovia's Alcázar resembles a fairytale castle.

A testament to the engineering skills of the Romans, the aqueduct at Segovia was in use until recently, bringing water to the city from the Acebeda river.

pseudo-medieval style. The Alcázar served as the setting for the marriage of Philip II to Anne of Austria in 1570. In more recent times, the keep was used to incarcerate political prisoners. Visitors who climb the 152 stairs to the summit of the dungeon will be rewarded with a great **view** over the city and the Sierra de Guadarrama.

Catedral★★ (Cathedral)

The last of Spain's major Gothic churches was begun in 1525 under Charles V after the original was destroyed in the Comuneros' Revolt in 1511. In contrast to the Flamboyant Gothic exterior, the interior is surprisingly austere, almost completely devoid of sculpture and other decoration. The 15C **choir stalls** were salvaged from the old cathedral. Its **cloisters**, too, were transported here, piece by piece. Notice

The impressive Gothic cathedral dominates the Castilian city of Segovia.

the fine 17C Flemish tapestries in the chapter house.

Plaza de San Martín★

In the middle of a pleasant shopping area, this medieval plaza is in fact two squares on different levels, joined by stairs and bordered by several handsome **patrician houses** of the 15C. The venerable Romanesque **Iglesia de San Martín★** (Church of St Martín) is surrounded on three sides by a gallery, with finely **carved capitals** on its columns.

Capilla de la Vera Cruz
(Chapel of the True Cross)

Situated outside the city walls north of the Alcázar, this 13C polygonal church was designed by the Knights Templar to reproduce Jerusalem's church of the Holy

The Casa de los Lozoya, with its 16C tower symbolising the owner's status, adjoins the medieval Plaza de San Martín.

Sepulchre. Belonging today to the Maltese Order, it has a round nave for worshippers, encircling a chapel originally containing a piece of the True Cross – now in the nearby village church of Zamarramala.

Other Attractions
Synagogue (Corpus Christi)
east of the cathedral
Now a convent church in Segovia's old Jewish quarter.
Iglesia de San Esteban (St Stephen's Church)
Splendid 13C Romanesque church, with a five-storey **tower**★ and porticoes with finely sculpted capitals.
Riofrío★ 11km (6 miles) south of Segovia
The 18C palace of Isabella Farnese, wife of Philip V, stands in a lovely oak forest. A **Museo de Caza** (Hunting Museum) is devoted to the king's favourite sport.

PALACIO DE LA GRANJA DE SAN ILDEFONSO★
To compensate for not getting the French throne he so badly wanted, Philip V, grandson of Louis XIV, built this opulent baroque residence in the wooded hills south-east of Segovia, where he could escape from Madrid and the forbidding alternative of El Escorial. He is buried in a chapel here with his wife, Isabelle Farnese. The palace halls include a richly endowed **Museo de Tapices**★★ (Tapestry Museum).
   French landscape architects and sculptors have done fine work on the **Jardines**★★ (gardens), with formal gardens, topiary hedges, **fountains**★★ and statuary, yet the place derives its charm from the way the Sierra de Guadarrama forests have encroached to give the whole a most un-

French, more 'natural' touch of wilderness. Chestnut trees imported from France in the 18C have reached monumental proportions among the dense woods of local oak, elm, maple and poplar.

ÁVILA★★

An atmosphere of cheerful religious fervour reigns in the town. The home of St Teresa (1515–1582) attracts hundreds of pilgrims to her birthplace and the convents she founded, in particular busloads of Catholic schoolgirls whose teachers see in the great mystic a model for their faith. Against the growing trend in the Roman Catholic church towards a more relaxed attitude towards discipline in religious life, St Teresa reinforced the stricter observance of the Carmelite order.

Even the famous 11C **city walls★★**, still

Visitors can walk along the sentry path on top of Ávila's medieval city walls.

perfectly preserved in their embrace of the city, were initially an act of religious assertion. Alfonso VI had the granite ramparts, with their 90 towers, built by Muslim prisoners of war in 1093 after he had conquered the city for Christianity.

Catedral★★ (Cathedral)

Emphasizing the city's union of faith and force, the church's apse, with its crenellated outer wall, forms an integral part of the eastern fortifications. Begun in the 12C as a Romanesque church, Gothic and Renaissance features were added over the next 400 years. Inside, notice the fine **choir stalls**, two elegant wrought-iron **pulpits**, a monumental Renaissance **altar** in the apse by Pedro Berruguete and Giovanni da

Carvings over the entrance to the cathedral soften the rather austere exterior.

Bologna, and the elaborately carved **albaster tomb★★** of Bishop Alonso de Madrigal, nicknamed **El Tostado★★** (the Toasted One) for his swarthy complexion.

The Shrines of St Teresa

Built over the birthplace of Teresa de Cepeda y Ahumada on Plaza de la Santa, just inside the south city gate, is the **Convento de Santa Teresa (La Santa)**. Inside, you can visit the baroque church with a chapel marking the exact spot of the saint's birth, and paintings illustrating the miracles of her life. Next to the gift shop, a reliquary displays her rosary beads and one of her fingers. She was canonized in 1622 and declared a Doctor of the Church in 1970. Other pilgrimage shrines are outside the city walls:

The Convent of St Teresa was built over the site of the house where the saint was born.

north of the Parador Gate, **Convento de la Encarnación** (Incarnation Convent) in which she spent 30 years, first as a novice, then as prioress; east of the city centre, **Convento de San José (Las Madres)**, which she founded in 1562, the first of her 17 Carmelite convents; and on a rocky mound just west of town, **Cuatro Postes** (Four Posts) where the seven-year-old child was caught by her uncle after trying to run away with her brother, both seeking martyrdom at the hands of the Moors. This is a great spot from which to view the town, especially at sunset.

Other Attractions
Monasterio de Santo Tomás★
This Dominican monastery was expanded by the monarchs Isabella and Ferdinand in the late 15C as a summer residence. The tomb of Grand Inquisitor Torquemada lies in the sacristy.
Basílica de San Vicente★★
A huge Romanesque basilica with an ornate western porch. Inside is a 12C **tomb★★** of martyrs beneath a Gothic pagoda-shaped canopy.

ARANJUEZ★★
Like Spain's monarchs of old, many Madrileños head south in summer for the **Palacio Real★** (Royal Palace). After repeated fires, it has been renovated as a sparkling neo-classical summer residence. Among its showy splendours are the 18C rococo **Salón del Trono** (Throne Room) and the enchanting **Salón de Porcelana★★** (Porcelain Room), fashioned entirely in the porcelain factory of Madrid's Buen Retiro palace. The **Jardín del Príncipe★★** (the Prince's Garden) is a sprawling, shady, English-style

The Palacio Real, Aranjuez, seen from the lake.

landscaped park covering 150 hectares (370 acres) along the Tagus river. At the eastern end is the **Casa del Labrador★★** (the Labourer's Cottage), built in neo-classical style with sumptuous 18C decor.

CHINCHÓN★

This slice of Castilian village life is just 20km (13 miles) from Madrid. It is esteemed for its *anís* (aniseed liqueur) and, the people insist, the special qualities of its garlic. Centrepiece in every sense is the town's highly theatrical **Plaza Mayor★★** (Main Square). The two- and three-storey white stucco houses look down across wooden arcades at the oval plaza, alternating in summer as a stage for open-air plays and an arena for bullfights. Pride of the town's **church** is a Goya painting of *The Assumption*.

ENJOYING YOUR VISIT

WEATHER

Though that centuries-old adage about Madrid's 'nine months of winter and three months of hell' is grossly exaggerated, the continental climate in the middle of the peninsula does make for a very hot summer and bitterly cold winter. Ideally, April to June and September to October are the best times to go. If you must travel in July and August, follow the example of the Madrileños: wear light cottons and a good hat, and take frequent visits to the region's surrounding greenery. In the cold dry months from November to March, the dynamic spirit of *Movida* in the bars and theatres will keep you warm.

Enjoying a warm autumn day in Retiro Park.

CALENDAR OF EVENTS

In addition to national holidays (*see* p.122), there are a host of religious, sporting and cultural festivities in and around Madrid.

February
Carnaval (Carnival): Held the week before Shrove Tuesday, with costumed neighbourhood fiestas; Santa Águeda: (second weekend) in Segovia and the nearby village of Zamarramala, when women take over local government and medieval costumed processions take place.

March/April
Semana Santa (Holy Week): Festivities in Madrid and Segovia, with the most formal processions in Toledo; Passion Play in Chinchón.

2 May
Dos de Mayo: Week of celebrations of the 1808 insurrection, with concerts and dancing around Malasaña's Plaza Dos de Mayo.

15 May
Verbenas de San Isidro: Two weeks of festivals for Madrid's patron saint; bands, city parades, dancing in Jardines de las Vistillas.
Start of bullfight season at Las Ventas.

13 June
Fiesta de San Antonio de la Florida (St Anthony's Day): Festivities around the church.

24 June
Fiestas de San Juan: St John's summer solstice, saint's day for King Juan Carlos; bonfires and fireworks in Retiro Park; music and processions in Segovia.

July
Ávila Arts and Sports Festival.

9–16 July
Fiesta in Madrid's Chamberí neighbourhood (west of Castellana).

August
Virgen del Sagrario (Virgin of the Sanctuary): Fiesta in third week of the month in Toledo, culminating in spectacular fireworks.

15 August
Viergen de la Paloma (Virgin of the Dove): Festivities in Plaza de Paja in La Latina *barrio* and Las Vistillas gardens. Chinchón bull-runs through the streets.

September
Aranjuez concerts in palace gardens.

October
Festivales de Otoño: Autumn festival in Madrid, with theatre, opera, dance, concerts, circus, cinema and exhibitions. Feria de Santa Teresa: second week, Ávila festivities, market, concerts, bullfights, church organ recitals.

31 December
New Year's Eve: Big celebration on Puerta del Sol; good-luck grapes are eaten for each midnight chime.

Human statue in Plaza Mayor.

ACCOMMODATION

Accommodation in Madrid ranges from simple to luxurious, with prices to match. The *Michelin Red Guide España-Portugal* lists a selection of hotels. Prices do vary with demand, however, and while you can expect to pay more in high season, you will also be charged considerably more at times of popular feasts. Those travelling on their own also fare badly, as single rooms are in very short supply, and you may have to negotiate a reduced price for a double room.

Fondas (rooms) offer the most basic form of accommodation, and can be identified by a square blue sign with a white 'F' in it. They are often sited above a bar. Next come *casas de huéspedes* (CH on a similar background), *pensiones* (P, guesthouses), and *hospedajes*. More common than these four types of basic accommodation are *hostales* (marked Hs, hostels) and *hostal-residencias* (HsR, hostels with restaurant), both ranging from one to three stars and offering good en-suite or private facilities.

Hoteles (H) are graded from one to five stars, with a one-star hotel costing about the same as three-star *hostales*, but as you go up the scale the levels of luxury and pricing increase considerably.

State-run *paradores* are at the top of the scale, and these are often housed in beautiful restored historic castles, palaces and monasteries.

Details of youth hostels and other accommodation for students and young people are provided by TIVE, José Ortega y Gasset 71, 28006 Madrid; ☎ 347 7778. If you plan to take an extended trip out to the Guadarrama mountains, contact the Federación Española de Montañismo, Calle Alberto Aguilera 3, 28015 Madrid; ☎ 445 1382, who will provide you with information about *refugios*: basic dormitory huts offering cheap accommodation for hikers and climbers.

Recommended Accommodation

Madrid's better hotels are noted more for their modern facilities than for their romantic charm, but a few do stand out. Remember, when telephoning from abroad, dial 1 before the number. When calling from other parts of Spain dial 91 before the number.

Very Expensive (up to 49 000pts)
At the top end of the range are the Ritz and the Palace Hotel (*see* p.45), which will be beyond most people's budgets.

Expensive (20 000pts)
Gran Hotel Reina Victoria (*Plaza del Ángel 7*), with its colourful Bar Torero, is popular with bullfighters and *aficionados*.

Moderate (12 000-16 000pts)
Carlos V (*Maestro Vitoria 5* ☎ 531 4100)

The Palace Hotel offers luxury and old-fashioned elegance.

Comfortable hotel, pleasantly situated behind the Descalzas Reales Convent and within easy reach of Puerta del Sol.

NH Embajada (*Santa Engracia 5, Chamberí* ☎ 594 0213) Attractive building.

Moderno (*Arenal 2, Plaza Mayor/Puerta del Sol* ☎ 531 0900) Tourist hotel in the city centre.

Galiano Residencia (*Alcalá Galiano 6; near Plaza de Colón* ☎ 319 2000) Tastefully furnished stately mansion with comfortable spacious rooms; good value.

La Residencia de El Viso (*Nervión 8, Chamartín* ☎ 564 0370)

Inexpensive (6 000-11 000pts) − *234·8 ·*
Near the Plaza Santa Ana area's lively *tapas* bars and restaurants, the reasonably-priced Gran Vía is the place for bargain *Hostal* boarding houses.

California (*Gran Vía 38* ☎ 522 4703)

Centro Sol (*Carrera de San Jerónimo 5, Puerta del Sol* ☎ 522 1582)

FOOD AND DRINK

Madrileños nurture the habit of starting meals so late (lunch is rarely before 2pm, while dinner is usually 9 or 10pm) by whetting their appetites with delicious little *tapas* (snacks). Connoisseurs make the rounds of several *tapas* bars (*tascas*) to try, with a glass of wine or beer, the speciality of each place. Don't try to beat them, join them – unless you prefer to eat in an empty restaurant or one that caters only to early-dining tourists. The décor and lively atmosphere in the *tasca* and other bars and taverns serving *tapas* is often so much more attractive than the conventional *restaurante* or *cafetería* that many end up making a whole meal of the appetizers.

Tapas

Hot or cold, and eaten with fingers or a
toothpick, the snacks can be ordered either
as a *porción* (single-helping), a larger *ración*,
or *media-ración* (half-serving). Among the
classics, which you can point to at the
counter if you can't remember the Spanish
word, are: fresh anchovies (*boquerones*),
shrimp (*gambas*), squid (*calamares*), snails
(*caracoles*), garlic mushrooms (*champiñones*),
slice of potato omelette (*tortilla*), meatballs
(*albóndigas*), olives (*aceitunas*), eggplant and
pepper salad (*escalibada*), potato salad
(*patatas alioli*) and spicy sautéed potatoes
(*patatas bravas*).

A word about ham (*jamón*), a national
obsession: all over Madrid, literally
hundreds of dried hams can be seen
hanging in windows of restaurants known as
Palacios (palaces) or *Museos de jamón*
(museums) of ham. The most popular,
Serrano, is eaten in an open sandwich or by
the plateful. Gourmets compare its merits
with the prestigious *Jabugo* from Andalucía
and Granada, and the *Montánchez* of
Extremadura.

Main Dishes

Like many other capitals, Madrid offers in its
wide range of restaurants a chance to taste
regional cuisine from all over the country,
often proposing its own distinctive versions
of classic dishes.

Sopa de ajo (garlic soup) is a tangy peasant
dish, but Madrid's variation has made it a
delicacy – pieces of bread cooked in garlic,
olive oil and hot peppers, with an egg added
at the last minute to poach in the boiling hot
broth.

Gazpacho is a chilled soup from Andalucía,

a refreshing summer favourite of liquefied
tomatoes, chopped cucumber, green
peppers, bread croûtons, olive oil and garlic.

Paella, named after the two-handled black
frying pan in which the saffron rice is
sautéed and mixed with chicken, originated
in Valencia. It is now a national dish, found
Mediterranean-coast style with shrimp,
mussels and squid or, from Alicante, with
rabbit and snails. It is a dish, strictly cooked
to order, that Madrileños eat primarily for
lunch.

Cocido madrileño is a delicious version of
another national dish, presented in three
servings: first the broth in which everything
has been cooked, then the cabbage,
potatoes, young turnips and chickpeas, and
lastly the beef, marrow-bone, pork, *chorizo*
sausage and black pudding.

On your excursions, try the great Castillian

A typical meal of paella.

speciality, *cochinillo asado* or *Tostón* (roast suckling pig), at its tenderest best in Segovia, as is the *cordero asado* (roast lamb). Besides the humble, but succulent *carcamusa* (meat-stew), Toledo is reputed for game birds, particularly its red partridge, pheasant and quail.

Cheese and Desserts

Spain's most admired cheese is La Mancha's *queso manchego*, made from ewe's milk; it comes either dry and sharp or creamy and mild. Desserts (*postres*) include *arroz con leche* (rice pudding), *flan* (caramel custard) and Madrileño pastries known as *rosquillas tontas y listas* (ring-cakes with aniseed and sugar). Toledo produces delicious *mazapán* (almond marzipan), a Moorish legacy, and Ávila is famous for its *yemas de Santa Teresa* (candied egg-yolk).

Bar, with typical coloured tiled wall murals.

Wines

To most Madrileños, *vino* just means red
wine. To be more specific, they may say *tinto*
(full-bodied) or *clarete* (light red), more
rarely *blanco* (white), from Galicia or
Aragón. The most prestigious reds are *Rioja*,
from the Ebro Valley in northern Spain.
Madrid's table wine (*vino de la casa*) is more
likely to be La Mancha's *Valdepeñas*, which
are generally lighter and slightly acidic.

As an apéritif, sherry from Jerez de la
Frontera in Andalucía is served dry (*fino* or
seco) or medium (*amontillado*), and as a
dessert wine, dark and sweet (*oloroso*). The
cool summer drink, *sangría*, is a punch of
red wine, brandy, orange and lemon juice,
mineral water, ice and sliced fruit.

Recommendations: Tapas Bars

Since so many people find tapas a meal in
itself, we first propose a few of our favourite
tapas bars.

In the area of Plaza Mayor – Puerta del Sol

Historic **Casa Labra** (*Calle de Tetuán*), where
the Spanish Socialist Party was founded in
1879; delicious fried cod.

On and off Plaza de Santa Ana – Huertas

The old-fashioned beer-house and former
Hemingway hang-out, **Cervecería Alemana**
(right on the plaza), is expensive but
pleasant; the beautifully tiled bar of **Los
Gabrieles** (*Calle Echegaray*) serves modest
tapas but fine drinks; **Taberna de Dolores**
(*Plaza de Jesús 4*) is a charming early 20C bar,
whose façade is decorated with azulejos.

Around El Rastro

Try the bustling **Barranco** (*San Isidro
Labrador 14*) for its excellent shrimp
(*gambas*); **Los Caracoles** (*Plaza Cascorro 18*)
serves good snails and other tasty snacks.

Recommendations: Restaurants

With Madrid renewing its telephone system, some of these numbers may be changing; check with hotel reception before calling. Here are a few suggestions, but more complete listings are available in the *Michelin Red Guide España-Portugal*.

In the area of Plaza Mayor – Puerta del Sol

Casa Ciriaco (*Calle Mayor 84* ☎ 548 0620) Historic restaurant once frequented by artists and literati (moderate).

Café de Chinitas (*Calle Torija 7* ☎ 547 1502) offers authentic flamenco with traditional Madrid cooking (moderate to expensive).

Las Cuevas de Luis Candelas (*Cuchilleros 1*

Call in for a drink and to enjoy the elegant tiled bar at Los Gabrieles.

☎ 366 5428) Staff dressed in the costume of ancient highwaymen serve you in this traditionally decorated restaurant (expensive).

Botín (*Calle Chuchilleros 17* ☎ 366 4217) Historic tavern popular with tourists.

La Bola (*Bola 5* ☎ 547 6930) Popular taberna specializing in *cocido* (moderate).

El Asador de Aranda (at three locations: *Preciados 44, Puerta del Sol,* ☎ 547 2156; *Diego de León 9, Salamanca* ☎ 563 0246, *Plaza de Castilla 3, Chamartín* ☎ 733 8702) Castillan decor; roast lamb a speciality (moderate to expensive).

Around Plaza de Santa Ana – Huertas

Champagneria Gala (*Calle Moratín 22,* ☎ 429 2562) Pleasant decor with garden patio; speciality paella (inexpensive).

Domine Cabra (*Calle Huertas 54* ☎ 429 4365), where inventive efforts to update lusty traditional dishes for more refined tastes are made (moderate).

Plaza de España

La Rioja (*Las Negras 8* ☎ 548 0497) Medieval decor (moderate).

Salamanca

La Trainera (*Calle Lagasca 60* ☎ 576 0575) One of Madrid's most popular seafood restaurants, with an informal atmosphere (expensive).

La Giralda IV (*Claudio Coello 24* ☎ 576 4069) Andalusían decor and cuisine (expensive).

Parque del Oeste

Casa Mingo (*Paseo de la Florida 2* ☎ 547 7918) Traditional Asturian cuisine (roasted chicken and cider); a favourite haunt of students; outdoor dining (inexpensive).

Around Rastro

Malacatín (*Calle de la Ruda 3* ☎ 365 5241) Rustic tavern serving traditional hearty fare such as *cocido* (moderate).

SHOPPING

The *Movida* of the 1980s has breathed new life into Madrid's shops. Fashion for women and men is innovative, challenging the French and Italian 'establishment' with its freer spirit. In addition, a revival in traditional craftsmanship offers tourists a quality alternative to the tired old souvenir trade.

The city's main shopping area is along Gran Vía and around Puerta del Sol, where the **department store** El Corte Inglés has its flagship store. Besides the clothes of many of Spain's top fashion designers, these stores offer the shopper in a hurry a fair selection of handicraft goods. More offbeat and avant-garde shops can be found on Chueca's Calle Almirante and in the Malasaña neighbourhood.

Madrid has plenty to offer keen shoppers.

Clothes

Calle Serrano is one of Madrid's main fashion streets, with Loewe at nos 26 and 34, and the classic clothes of Adolfo Domínguez at no 96 (for men *Calle Ortega y Gasset, 4*). One of Spain's leading designers for women is Sybilla (*Calle Jorge Juan 12*), but prices are high. Her work is also sold at the avant-garde shop, Ekseption (*Calle Velázquez 28*). Two highly creative, more reasonably priced Chueca stores are Blackmarket (*Calle Colón 3*), for women's clothes, and Excrupulus Net (*Calle Almirante 7*) selling Spanish designer **shoes** for men and women. Alpargatería Lobo (*Calle Toledo 30*) specializes in **espadrilles** (*alpargatas*) in an amazing range of different colours.

For traditional **hats**, caps and berets, Madrid's oldest hatshop is Casa Yustas (*Plaza Mayor 30*).

These colourful Spanish fans make lovely gifts and souvenirs.

Crafts

The best all-round centre is El Arco de Los Cuchilleros (*Plaza Mayor 9*). Serving as an outlet for more than 20 modern and traditional workshops from all over the country, it sells embroidered goods, textiles, jewellery, leather, wooden games and ceramics. One of the city's leading **guitar** specialists, but expensive, is José Ramírez (*Calle Concepción Jerónima*). For **toys**, try Puck (*Calle Duque de Sesto 30*). The specialist in ladies' **fans** is Casa Jiménez (*Calle Preciados 42*).

ENTERTAINMENT AND NIGHTLIFE

There is more to Madrid's nightlife than **discos** (*discotecas* and *discobares*) but even if that *was* all, they alone could keep you up all night every night for a year – and you wouldn't need to go to the same place twice.

Start off the evening with a drink at one of the pavement cafés.

There are literally hundreds all over the city and suburbs, but most of them are on and around the city centre's Gran Vía, Puerta del Sol and Plaza de Santa Ana and in the neighbourhoods of Chueca and Malasaña.

Flamenco in Madrid has undergone the same modernizing influences as the rest of Spanish culture since the 1980s. To the insistent throb of the guitars, stamping heels, snapping fingers and heartfelt passionate song of the traditional form, perhaps of Arabic origin, has been added the new music of modern jazz and rock. The *nuevo flamenco* (new flamenco) can be heard

A visit to Madrid is not complete without experiencing the passion of traditional flamenco.

at the Revolver Club (*Calle Galileo 26*). The more traditional flamenco, alternating between the bouncy, cheerful songs known as *cante chico* and the sorrowful, heart-rending dirges of *cante jondo*, is performed at La Soleo (*Cava Baja 27*) and the historic Candela (*Calle del Olmo 2*).

Opera is more seriously back in business as the Teatro Real re-opens its doors, after lengthy renovation and **classical music** concerts are held at the Auditorio Nacional de Música, home of the Spanish National Orchestra *(Orquesta Nacional de España)*.

And every night-owl's last stop, whether rock fan or opera buff, seems to be the Chocolatería San Ginés, Pasadizo de San Ginés, near the Teatro Real. Since 1894, it has been serving hot chocolate and those sweet fried dough sticks known as *churros* before people head, at last, for bed.

SPORTS

There seem to be only two sports that really matter to Madrileños – **bullfighting** and **football**. Despite growing opposition inside Spain to the annual killing of 24 000 bulls nationwide, *aficionados* still make their way to Madrid's Plaza Monumental de Las Ventas, high temple of the national sport. The season is launched in May with two weeks of bullfights to celebrate the city's patron saint, San Isidro. Thereafter, the ritual of sun, blood and sudden death is played out every Sunday afternoon.

Football fans insist that this antique passion is overshadowed today by the joy and misery under the sun or floodlights of Real Madrid's Santiago Bernabeu Stadium, or at Atlético Madrid's Vicente Calderón. Here, defeat is as bitter as death, but less bloody.

The packed stadium at Las Ventas is testament to the popularity of bullfighting in Madrid.

THE BASICS

Before You Go

Visitors entering Spain should be in possession of a valid passport. No visa is required for members of EU countries or US, Canadian or New Zealand citizens, but visitors from Australia do require a visa, which can be obtained on arrival for a period of up to 30 days. No vaccinations are necessary.

Getting There

By Air: Most international airlines have flights to Barajas Airport, 16km (10 miles) east of Madrid.

There are numerous scheduled flights to Spain. Visitors coming from the US will probably fly direct to Madrid, though sometimes it is cheaper to fly to London or another European city first, then get a connecting flight to Spain. The superfast trains – the AVE and the Talgo – connect Madrid with Córdoba (2½ hours), Seville (3 hours) and Málaga (3-4 hours).

Scheduled flights leave all year round for Madrid from Dublin and Belfast.

Visitors from Australia and New Zealand cannot get a direct flight to Spain, and will have to make a stopover at another European city.

Low-cost flights from anywhere in the world can be arranged through flight agents or by booking a charter flight. These usually offer the best price deal, but return flights are fixed so that the maximum time you can spend in Spain is four weeks. Package holidays offer great value too, and sometimes the price is so reasonable that you can buy a holiday to a resort where you would not wish to stay, and still afford to stay in the place of your choice.

Apex or super-apex tickets may be bought directly from the airlines. The travel ads in the English Sunday papers or the various London listing magazines are the best places for travellers from the UK to look. Travel clubs and discount agents offer good savings from North America and Australasia.

By Coach: Coaches leave London for Madrid several times a week, and journey times are tediously long, so a stopover inside the Spanish border is recommended.

By Train: Le Shuttle takes cars under the English Channel from Folkestone in 35 minutes. A connection can be made at Paris with the Expresso Puerta del Sol, which leaves each night for Spain. Pedestrians can take the Eurostar from London through the Channel Tunnel, and must then change train stations in Paris (Gare du Nord to Austerlitz) to catch the Talgo Camas/ Couchette, which also leaves nightly.

There are various rail passes which offer substantial discounts on rail travel, particularly if you are planning to travel within Europe. Details are obtainable from Rail Europe in New York (☎ 800 438 7245), or Eurotrain in London (☎ 0171 730 3402), or British Rail European Information (☎ 0171 834 2345).

There are various options for those wanting to take their own car to Southern Spain.

By Ferry: Two ferries companies offer direct sailings to Bilbao and Santander from Britain: Brittany Ferries and P&O European Ferries. The advantage of this crossing is that the long – and expensive – drive through France is completely eliminated.

Several ferry companies carry cars and passengers across the Channel, with the quickest journeys being between Dover/Calais, and Folkestone/Boulogne. The hovercraft is even faster, crossing from Dover to Calais in just 35 minutes. Brittany Ferries offer crossings from Portsmouth, Plymouth and Poole directly to Brittany, arriving at St Malo and Roscoff.

Atocha train station, with its tropical gardens.

111

A-Z

Accidents and Breakdowns

If you are involved in an accident while driving in Spain you should exchange full details of insurance, addresses, etc. In an emergency, if you can find a telephone dial 091 *See also* **Driving**.

Accommodation see p.94

Airports see Getting There p.110

Babysitters see Children

Banks

Banks are open 8.30/9am-2pm, Monday to Friday. Main branches are also open on Saturday from 9am-12.30/1pm. Between June and September most banks are closed on Saturdays.

Most major credit cards are accepted by hotels and department stores. Girobank operates an international cash card system which allows cash withdrawals on personal UK bank accounts. For details of Delta Card contact Girobank at Bootle, Merseyside, GIR OAA; ☎ 01645 250 250.

Eurocheques backed up by a Eurocheque card can be used in banks, and to pay for goods in hotels, restaurants and shops. Most cheque cards, and Visa and Mastercard, can be used to withdraw cash from automatic cash machines.

Banks will usually change travellers' cheques, but charge high commission rates, and there are also specialist exchange bureaux. Exchange facilities at El Corte Inglés, a department store found throughout Spain, offer competitive rates.

Bicycles

Cycling is a cheap way of getting about in Spain, but the hair-raising traffic in Madrid makes it inadvisable here. A short cycling trip out to the surrounding countryside can make a pleasant outing, but the terraine is rather too monotonous for an extended cycle tour. There are several bike shops, and garages also sometimes carry bike spares.

Most airlines will take bicycles as ordinary baggage, although chartered flights may not have sufficient space. Bikes can travel in the guard's van on suburban trains only.

Breakdowns *see* **Accidents**

Buses *see* **Transport**

Camping

There are several good campsites situated just outside Madrid. For a free list of these sites, contact the Spanish National Tourist Office in your own country, or obtain one locally from any tourist office (*see* **Tourist Information Offices**).

Unauthorized camping is not recommended, and though you might just get moved on by the authorities, you may be unlucky.

For particular information on campsites or making a booking, contact the site directly, or Federación Española de Empresarios de Campings y CV General Oraa, 52-2°D 28006 Madrid; ☎ 562 9994.

Car Hire

Car hire companies are based in the city centre as well as at Barajas Airport. Airlines and tour operators offer fly/drive arrangements, which can be very good value. Make sure that collision damage waiver is included in the insurance. Automatics should be reserved in advance and are more expensive.

The lower age limit is 21, but few international companies hire to drivers under 23, or even 25. Drivers must have held their full licence for at least a year.

With the exception of Avis, there is an upper age limit of 60-65. Unless paying by credit card a substantial cash deposit is usually required. If you are driving a car that has obviously been hired, take extra precautions when parking it to deter thieves, and never leave anything of value inside.

See also **Accidents and Breakdowns** *and* **Tourist Information Offices**

Spanish guitarist.

Children

Children are welcomed in Spain, and hotel owners are usually happy to offer rooms with three or four beds to accommodate families. Babysitting services are generally available, or in smaller, family-run hotels the owners will often listen out for problems while you are out.

Baby food and disposable nappies can be bought from supermarkets and chemists, but you might want to bring your own powdered milk, as the Spanish type is heat-treated.

Children under three can travel free on trains, and those under seven are charged only half price.

Churches see Religion

Climate see p. 92

Clothing

The Madrileños are fairly liberal in their attitudes to dress, although they are very keen on looking smart and tidy at all times. In the evenings, in particular, they make a great effort; men often wear a suit for a night out clubbing. Beachwear is frowned upon, although mini-skirts and shorts are quite acceptable; places of worship and museums will often exclude those who are not dressed appropriately. Hats are a good idea at the height of summer, particularly in the early afternoon.
See also **Etiquette**

Complaints

Complaints about goods or services should ideally be made at the time. At a hotel or restaurant make your complaint in a calm manner to the manager.

All hotels, restaurants, camp sites and petrol stations are required by law to keep and produce complaint forms when requested by a customer. If this proves difficult, ask the local tourist information office to intervene on your behalf (*see* **Tourist Information Offices**).

Consulates see Embassies

Crime

Being the victim of petty crime – commonly pick-pocketing and bag-snatching – can ruin a holiday, so take every precaution to prevent this happening to you. The best advice is to be aware at all times, carry as little money, and as few credit cards as possible, and leave any valuables in the hotel safe.

Carry wallets and purses in secure pockets, wear body belts, or carry handbags across your body or firmly under your arm. Never leave your car unlocked, as this is an open invitation to thieves. Also make sure that you never leave any valuables or luggage in the car, even when it is parked in an apparently secure car park. If you have to leave things in the car, ensure they are well hidden. Hire cars in particular are targeted by thieves, and if possible you should remove any evidence that your car has been hired.

If you have anything stolen, report it immediately to the nearest police station or police office – Centro Atención Policial – where English-speaking officers can offer practical advice. Collect a report so that you can make an insurance claim.

If your passport is stolen, report it to your Embassy at once.

The Crystal Palace, Retiro Park.

Currency *see* **Money**

Customs and Entry Regulations

There is no limit on the importation into Spain of tax-paid goods bought in an EU country, provided they are for personal consumption, with the exception of alcohol and tobacco which have fixed limits governing them.

Disabled Visitors

Spain is not the most accessible country for disabled travellers, and public transport is particularly difficult for wheelchair users. The *Michelin Red Guide España-Portugal* indicates which hotels have facilities for the disabled.

In Britain, RADAR, at 12 City Forum, 250 City Road, London EC1V 8AF; ☎ 0171 250 3222, publish fact sheets, as well as an annual guide to facilities and accommodation overseas.

The Spanish National Tourist Office in your own country is a good source of advance information, and you are also advised to check with hotels and travel carriers to see that your individual needs can be met.

Driving

Drivers should carry a full national or preferably international driving licence, insurance documents including a green card (no longer compulsory for EU members but strongly recommended), registration papers for the car, and a nationality sticker for the car rear.

A bail bond or extra insurance cover for legal costs is also worth investing in. Without a bail bond the car could be impounded and the driver placed under arrest.

The minimum age for driving is 18, and cars drive on the right. Away from main roads cars give way to those approaching from the right. Front seat passengers must wear seatbelts outside of urban areas.

Speed traps are used, and if you are caught, the police are likely to impose a hefty fine.

Speed limits are as follows:
• Maximum on urban roads: 60kph/37mph
• Maximum on other roads: 90kph or 100kph/56 or 62mph
• Dual carriageways: 120kph/75mph.
Also note that Spanish motorways have tolls.

Dry Cleaning *see* **Laundry**

Electric Current

The voltage in Spain is usually 220 or 225V. Plugs and sockets are of the two-pin variety, and adaptors are generally required. North Americans will probably also need a transformer.

Embassies

American Embassy
Serrano 175,
28006 Madrid
☎ 557 40 00
Australian Embassy
Paseo de la Castellana 143,
28046 Madrid
☎ 579 04 28
British Embassy
Calle Fernando el Santo 16,
28010 Madrid
☎ 319 02 00
Canadian Embassy
Calle Núñez de Balboa 35,
28001 Madrid
☎ 431 43 00
Embassy of Ireland
Claudio Coello 73,
28001 Madrid
☎ 576 35 00

Emergencies

In an emergency, either go to the police or contact your embassy, who will offer very limited help. The universal emergency telephone number is ☎ 091.

Etiquette

As in most places in the world, it is considered polite and respectful to cover up decently in churches and museums. Be sensitive to conservative attitudes outside the city, and don't upset the locals by dressing provocatively or otherwise showing a lack of respect.

Excursions

For details of excursions and trips which can easily be made from Madrid, *see* pp.70-91. Information on excursions and attractions can be obtained from the local tourist information office or your travel agency.

Guidebooks *see* Maps

Health

UK nationals should carry a

Tiled street sign.

Form E111 which is produced by the Department of Health, and which entitles the holder to free urgent treatment for accident or illness in EU countries (forms are available from post offices). The treatment will have to be paid for in the first instance, but the money can be reclaimed later. All foreign nationals, including those from the UK, are advised to take out comprehensive insurance cover, and to keep any bills, receipts and invoices to support any claim.

Lists of doctors can be obtained from hotels, chemists and embassies, and first aid and medical advice is also available at the *farmacia*, from pharmacists who are highly trained and can dispense drugs which are available only on prescription in other countries.

The *farmacia* is generally open at 9.30/10am, close for lunch at 1.30/2pm and then reopen at 4.30/5pm till around 8pm. Some are open for longer; those which are open late or on Sundays display notices on their doors, and on the doors of other pharmacies.

You can get the address of an English-speaking doctor from your consulate, the police station, the *farmacia* or the tourist office.

Hours *see* **Opening Hours**

Information *see* **Tourist Information Offices**

Language

Most Madrileños speak some English, but are not generally pleased by tourists who make no effort to speak Spanish; even a few simple words and phrases will often be warmly received. In out of town areas very little English is spoken, and it is advisable, at the very least, to carry a phrase book.

Opposite are a few words and phrases that will help you make the most of your stay in Madrid.

Laundry

Self-service launderettes (*lavanderías*) exist, but are rare. More common are the service laundries where you are charged for someone else to do the work. For dry cleaning look for the sign *tintorería*.

Lost Property

Spanish airports and major railway stations have their own lost property offices. If something is missing in your hotel, check first with the front desk and hotel security. Report all lost or stolen items to the police, and always make sure to get a report to substantiate any

Yes/no / Sí/no
Please/thank you / Por favor/gracias
Do you speak English? / ¿Habla (usted) inglés?
How much is it? / ¿Cuánto es?
Excuse me / Perdone
I'd like a stamp / Quisiera un sello
How are you? / ¿Cómo está (usted)?
I don't understand / No entiendo
See you later / Hasta luego
Do you have a room? / ¿Tiene una habitación?
How do I get to …? / ¿Por dónde se va a …?

insurance claims, but do not expect the police to get too excited about minor thefts.

Should you lose any travel documents, contact the police, and in the event of a passport going missing, inform your Embassy or Consulate immediately (*see* **Embassies**).

Lost or stolen travellers' cheques and credit cards should be reported immediately to the issuing company with a list of numbers, and the police should also be informed.

Maps

There is a range of Michelin road atlases and sheet maps of Madrid and the surrounding area. The *Michelin Map 40 Madrid* covers the city, with a useful street index. The *Michelin Green Guide Spain* contains useful information on the sights and attractions in Madrid and also describes many of the towns and villages surrounding the city which you may be interested in visiting. The *Michelin Red Guide España/Portugal* lists accommodation and restaurants.

The spiral-bound *Michelin Road Atlas: Spain and Portugal* covers the whole of the Iberian peninsula, *Michelin Map 990* covers the whole of Spain, while *Maps 442-445* include Madrid and the surrounding areas and are useful for excursions around Madrid and for route-planning.

Hiking maps can be ordered from: Servicio de Publicaciones

del Instituto Geográfico Nacional, General Ibáñez de Ibero 3, 28003, Madrid. Bookshops, street kiosks and petrol stations offer a good selection of maps for sale.

Medical Care *see* **Health**

Money

The Spanish unit of currency is the peseta, with notes in denominations of 1 000, 2 000, 5 000 and 10 000 pesetas, and coins of 1, 5, 10, 25, 50, 100, 200 and 500 pesetas.

There is no restriction on bringing into or out of the country currency below the level of one million pesetas, but perhaps the safest way to carry large amounts of money is in travellers' cheques, which are widely accepted. Exchange counters are found at airports, terminals and larger railway stations, at the El Corte Inglés department stores and at banks (*see* **Banks**).

Lost or stolen travellers' cheques and credit cards should be reported immed-

Fruit shop.

iately to the issuing company with a list of numbers, and the police should also be informed.

Newspapers

There are several Spanish daily papers sold in Madrid, including *El País*, *El Mundo*, *ABC* and *Diario 16*. *El Mundo* and *El País* have useful entertainment listings supplements on Fridays, and *ABC* has one on Thursdays.

If you are looking for English language media, *Lookout* and *In Spain* are both monthly magazines, produced primarily for the English-speaking ex-pat community.

British and other foreign newspapers are widely available, and the *International Herald Tribune*, published in Paris, offers the latest stock market news from America as well as world news.

Opening Hours

Shops in Madrid normally open at 9.30-10am, close for lunch from 1.30/2pm, and then reopen at 4.30/5pm. They stay open till 8pm, or sometimes later in the summer.

Chemists *(farmacia)* are usually open the same hours as shops (see above), but some are open for longer and on Sundays, and some stay open late, or even 24 hours. These

are marked by a sign in the window, and other pharmacies also carry details. Call ☎ 098 for comprehensive information.
Monuments and museums tend to open between 10am-1pm and 4-7pm, with several variations, while many churches only open for the early morning or evening service each day.
See also **Banks** *and* **Post Offices**

Photography

Good-quality film and camera equipment are available in Madrid, and facilities for fast processing are plentiful, although this is often expensive.

Before taking photographs in museums and art galleries it is wise to check with staff as photography is usually restricted in these places.

Police

There are three types of police: the Guardia Civil, who wear green uniforms; the Policía Municipal, who wear blue and white uniforms with red trim and are generally sympathetic to tourists with genuine problems; and the Policía Nacional, who wear dark blue uniforms.

The national emergency telephone number is ☎ 091; the local emergency telephone number is ☎ 092.

Post Offices

Madrid's main post office
(*Correos*), in the Plaza de
Cibeles, is open from 9am-8pm.
It gets very busy at times, so if
you only want to buy stamps, it
is a good idea to buy them
from a tobacconist (*estanco*).

Poste restante mail should
be sent to the person
(surname underlined) at Lista
de Correos, followed by the
name of the town and
province. Take a passport
along as proof of identity when
collecting mail. British visitors
can withdraw cash on their UK
accounts with a National Girobank postcheque(*see* **Banks**).

Public Holidays

New Year's Day: 1 January
Epiphany: 6 January
Good Friday to Easter Monday
Labour Day: 1 May
Corpus Christi: 2nd Thursday
    after Whitsun
Assumption Day: 15 August
National Day: 12 October
All Saints' Day: 1 November
Constitution Day: 6 December
Immaculate Conception:
    8 December
Christmas Day: 25 December
    There are also other feasts
and public holidays which are
celebrated locally, when almost
everything shuts down:
Comunidad de Madrid: 2 May
San Isidro: 15 May

Public Transport
see **Transport**

Religion

Spain is a Catholic country,
and there are daily services in
the churches and cathedrals.
The location of churches and
the times of services are best
checked locally.
See **Tourist Information
Offices**

Smoking

Legislation protects the rights
of non-smokers over those of
smokers in Spain these days,
and smoking is banned in
many public places. Signs in
department stores, cinemas
and public transport indicating
that smoking is banned should
be strictly adhered to.

Stamps *see* **Post Offices**

Taxis *see* **Transport**

Telephones

International telephone calls
may be made from all Spanish
provincial capital towns and
most of the major holiday
resorts. Dial 07, wait for the
dialling tone, and then dial the
appropriate country code
(44 for the UK, 353 for Eire,
1 for USA and Canada, 61 for
Australia and 64 for New
Zealand).

Spanish telephones have instructions in English, and take 5, 25 or 100 peseta coins, or phonecards of 1 000 or 2 000 pesetas which can be bought at tobacconists (*estancos*). International calls may be made in either telephone booths, or at a Telefónica office where you pay after the call.

For calls within Spain, dial 9 followed by the area code. When telephoning Madrid from elsewhere in Spain, dial 91 before the number. Drop the 9 when dialing from abroad. The number for Directory Enquiries is 003, area codes 009, International Operator 008 for Europe and 005 for the rest of the world.

As in most countries, telephone calls made from hotels may be more straightforward and convenient, but they are more expensive.

Time difference

Spanish standard time is GMT plus one hour. Spanish summer time begins on the last Sunday in March at 2am when the clocks go forward an hour (the same day as British Summer Time), and it ends on the last Sunday in October at 3am when the clocks go back again.

Tipping

In Spain it is usual to tip between 5-10 per cent of the bill at bars, cafés and restau-

Shopping for souvenirs in Segovia.

rants, even though bills already include a service charge. The tip is related to customer satisfaction so the amount can vary each time. Porters, doormen, taxi drivers and cinema usherettes all expect a financial token of appreciation.

Toilets

There are many names for toilets in Spain, so look out for the following: *baños* (bathrooms), *aseos*, *servicios*, *sanitarios*, *damas* (ladies) or *caballeros* (gentlemen), *señoras* (women) or *señores* (men).

Tourist Information Offices

The Spanish National Tourist Office is an excellent first source of information for your holiday, on everything from where to stay to where and when the lesser known fiestas are held. Offices can be found at the following addresses:

UK
57-58 St James's Street,
London SW1A 1LD
☎ (0171) 499 0901
Canada
102 Bloor Street West,
14th Floor, Toronto,
Ontario M5S 1M8
☎ (416) 961 3131
Australia
203 Castlereagh Street,
Suite 21a, PO Box A685,

Sydney, NSW
☎ (02) 264 7966
USA
665 Fifth Avenue,
New York, NY10022
☎ (212) 759 8822, and
Water Tower Place,
Suite 915 East,
845 North Michigan Avenue,
Chicago, IL 60611
☎ (312) 642 1992

Tourist information centres, which can be found in most large towns throughout Spain, are well stocked with leaflets providing information on excursions, transport, entertainment, facilities for the disabled, and exhibitions, as well as accommodation and restaurants. Guide books and maps are also for sale.

Madrid's *Oficinas de Turismo*, usually known simply as *turismo*, can be found at:
Aeropuerto de Barajas
☎ 3 05 86 56
Duque de Medinaceli 2
☎ 4 29 59 51
Estación de Chamartín
☎ 3 15 99 76
Oficina Municipal de información, Plaza Mayor 3
☎ 366 5477
Torre de Madrid, Plaza de España
☎ 5 41 23 25

Tours see **Excursions**

Transport

Madrid has an excellent **Metro** service, although it is one of the oldest in Europe. It has 115 stations and operates between 6.30am-1.30am. The system is easy to follow and is generally efficient, although rush hours (between 8.30-9.30am, 1.30-2.30pm and 8-9pm) are extremely hectic, and the lack of air conditioning makes these times almost unbearable in the summer. Prices are reasonable, and there are various discounts available.

Madrid's **buses** run between 6am-12pm, and a special nightbus leaves every hour on the hour from Cibeles and the Puerta del Sol. A ticket costs 90 pesetas, regardless of the length of your journey. A 10-journey bus-pass known as a *Bonobus*, costing 410 pesetas, may be purchased from outlets all over Madrid, including bus information kiosks, newspaper stalls and tobacconists, and the Caja de Madrid bank.

An *Abono* costs 3 000 pesetas (2 000 for children and 1 000 for senior citizens) and covers you for a full month of unlimited journeys around Madrid. The main drawback is Madrid's terrible traffic.

Taxis are a fairly economical alternative form of transport. Although they also suffer

The impressive home stadium of Madrid's main football team, Real Madrid.

delays from the traffic, they are more able to dodge the trouble-spots, and are obviously more direct than buses. They are painted white with a diagonal red stripe along the side and bear the Madrid City emblem on the rear doors. When available they show a green *libre* sign, and a green light at night.

Fares vary depending on various factors. Drivers should have a list of approved charges for the different runs, and will quote on request before you set off. On top of the basic charge, there is a surcharge for night time, weekends and public holidays, and also for pick-ups and drop-offs at certain parts of the city. The driver is permitted to start charging double the amount shown on the meter as soon as he crosses the city boundaries into the suburbs, so trains are the best option for transport out of Madrid.

Trains from out of town areas may be caught from Chamartín, Nuevos Ministerios, Recoletos, Atocha and Príncipe Pío/Norte stations, all of which are connected to the metro system. For details of discounts on train fares

enquire at Spanish Railways RENFE, or a tourist office in your own country or in Madrid.
See **Tourist Information Offices** *and* **Driving**

TV and Radio
TVE 1 and TVE 2 are Spain's two nationwide television channels. Madrid also has Antena 3, Tele 5 and Telemadrid.

The choice is a mixture of good live sports coverage, game shows, dubbed foreign language films and series, and soap operas from the US, Australia, the UK and South America.

English radio programmes may be picked up on the BBC World Service on short-wave radio, as well as on the Torrejón American Airforce Base station at 100.2 FM.

Vaccinations
see **Before You Go p.110**

Water
Madrid's water is safe to drink, though most people prefer to drink the bottled variety.

Youth Hostels
see **Accommodation**

INDEX

He spoke h

She felt his hand t
smooth back the l
Rob was watching her all the while he touched her,
noting the loneliness mixed with apprehension in
her eyes. His gaze seemed to be questioning hers,
but Meg was still unable to lean forward the slight
little bit that would encourage him to cover her
lips with his own.

Help me. You take the initiative.

He did help her. Meg sighed in satisfaction when
he slipped his arms beneath hers to draw her
against him. She clasped him near the shoulders,
gripping those stringy hard muscles that had been
straining against the sleeves of his soft shirt all
evening. It was shockingly erotic to touch a man
after so long.

To my mother-in-law, Fay Shallenberger,
who has so generously shared her love with me

———————◆———————

SHARON McCAFFREE
is also the author
of these titles in
Love Affair

NOW AND FOREVER
MISPLACED DESTINY

and in
Temptation

ONE BRIGHT MORNING

Secret
Longings
SHARON McCAFFREE

A Love Affair from
HARLEQUIN
London · Toronto · New York · Sydney

First published in Great Britain in 1986 by Harlequin, 15–16 Brook's Mews, London W1A 1DR

© Sharon McCaffree 1985

ISBN 0 373 16110 7

18-0486

Printed and bound in Great Britain by Richard Clay (The Chaucer Press) Ltd, Bungay, Suffolk

Chapter One

"I need to reach Robbie Dowell immediately."

Despite the distortion of the telephone, the feminine voice sounded sexy and definitely eager. Absorbing the caller's urgency, Meghan Bronson set aside the Ultrasuede jacket she had discovered mismatched with a polished-cotton coatdress instead of being paired with the silk two-piece dress, and tried to think which male employee Robbie would be. Not the new teenager who would be coming into the store at four to help with shipment boxes; it was easy to remember that his name was Mike, like her son's. And she thought she knew all her other employees.

The caller, she decided, probably had the wrong number. Meg and the store's owner, Penelope Sands, only gave their office listing out to business associates, certainly not to breathless women who sounded one sultry pause away from bed.

"Would you repeat his last name?" Meg dutifully asked, trying to ignore the tangling of her long hair in the phone cord while she absently leafed through the sales slips on her spindle. They had had a good Monday so far, it appeared: two spring suits from the designer collection, seven pairs of Italian shoes, the usual half-dozen tennis dresses for Mrs. Marling and a number of separates. If that was the case by only noon on the first day of the week, the arrival of warm Louisiana weather had definitely been good for business. She was thinking how encouraging the spring season looked so far and only half concentrating on the words from the sensuous voice at the other end of the line while she reached in her drawer for the employee file.

"You say an emergency for Robbie Dowell?" Meg grinned to herself, doubting that the caller's problem could be explained to another woman.

How long has it been since I felt that way about a man? She thrust aside the cynicism and studied the alphabetized list, almost hoping there would be a Robbie there. Far be it from her to begrudge any lady a little happiness. She drew a blank, however.

"I'm sorry, but no employee here is named—"

"Is this Penelope's, at the Victorian Mall?"

The pain grabbing at Meg's scalp finally demanded immediate attention, and she paused to untangle her frosted blond hair from the phone cord. "Yes, but we don't have—"

"This is the home office of Allied Insurance in New Orleans. Our agent said he would be meeting with Penelope Sands this afternoon."

Her Robbie is Robert Clark Dowell? Astounded, Meg shifted the phone to her other hand and flipped her hair loose over her shoulder. Not the sedate Robert Clark Dowell! That confirmed bachelor kept such a low profile that she had certainly underrated him. Although, from what she'd observed during the year he'd been servicing the store's policies, she doubted that he wanted his women calling around to customers. Smiling in amusement, she glanced down at Penny's calendar.

"Ms. Sands has an appointment penciled in for Mr. Dowell later this afternoon. Do you want to leave a message for him?" Involuntarily her own voice became oily smooth, like finely toned leather. She almost laughed aloud. This was ludicrous. How could two women who had never met instinctively be at each other's throats over a man?

"Would you tell him to call his secretary in New Orleans," the caller responded aggressively. "It's important."

I'll just bet it is, Meg thought. *Robbie, dear, my husband is going to be gone this week, Hurry home.* Meg was aware that some of her acquaintances conducted such arrangements, but the situations had always seemed "no-win" to her.

"I'll tell him," she nevertheless promised smoothly.

After hanging up, Meg dutifully wrote down on the memo board: "Robbie, call your secretary."

She grinned knowingly at the note framed by the manicured nails of her slender fingers, then in better conscience pulled off that sheet and rewrote: "Penny—Mr. Dowell is to call his New Orleans office. Important—M."

Fighting a sudden, vague restlessness, Meg walked to the narrow floor-to-ceiling slot that served in some architect's mind as an appropriate window for a contemporary shopping complex. It was encouraging to see

that the parking lot was filling fast. Penelope's should
have a good share of those shoppers. She looked out
over parked cars to the surrounding neighborhood, reminded as always of how like heaven it had seemed
when Penny had opted to stick with the congestion
downtown and had sent Meg to establish a high-fashion
branch in one of Shreveport's loveliest residential
areas. Now, three years later, Meg was still charmed by
this mall. The small, nicely landscaped houses surrounding it had been converted into stylish boutiques;
beyond them, tall pines and water oaks heralded block
after block of elegant homes. She didn't particularly enjoy having to fight the many Cadillacs favored by the
mall's customers to secure a parking place for her little
Aries, but, otherwise, the store's lovely setting had
blended right in with the peace she was finally establishing in her life.

And the job had been just what she needed. Meg had
thrived under the responsibility of directing a business
catering to discriminating, trendy customers.

Thinking of her job, Meg turned resolutely toward
her desk, intending to review the stack of new winter
catalogs in preparation for her upcoming buying trip to
New York. But when she noticed that the first cover
featured a street-length mink coat, she paused pensively. The muted photograph was seductively erotic.
The model, draping the wrap loosely about her pale
body, was smiling mysteriously toward the vague outline of a male back. Obviously she wore nothing underneath that coat.

Meg's restlessness gnawed deeper and she wondered
what it must feel like to be naked beneath a fur coat. Of

course the wrap would be richly lined; but still, the effect must be caressingly stimulating to a woman's flesh, especially if the coat had been a gift from a lover.

That's the kind of coat Robbie would appreciate. The thought bothered her. Thrusting the fur catalog to the bottom of the stack, Meg cursed the call from that sultry-voiced woman for stirring her curiosity about the sedate Robert Clark Dowell. She simply didn't have time to waste speculating about someone else's love life.

"Look what I brought you, Mrs. Bronson."

Startled out of her reverie, Meg glanced up to see Susan Forsyth, the store's secretary-bookkeeper-gofer standing at the office door with a vase of crab-apple blossoms. The interrruption of her thoughts was welcome. And the gift was even more welcome. Meg loved flowers.

"These are gorgeous! When I drove in today along the south bayou, I noticed that those marvelous pinks and whites had finally burst out. Did you snitch some from there?"

Susan laughed and shook her head. "I don't want to get arrested—Shreveport treats the trees lining that bayou like the Washington cherry blossoms! I had lunch with a neighbor and she cut me an armload from her yard."

"Thanks for sharing." Meg set the vase on her desk and carefully readjusted one tilting branch back to its original position.

"Phyllis said you wanted me to do something with an Ultrasuede jacket."

"Oh, yes." She handed Susan the jacket. "Please put

this with that Gloria LaMotte two-piece—the toast-and-cream raw silk.''

"The size six?" Susan ruefully ran a hand over the hem of her bulging maternity blouse. Then realizing what she had done, she frowned self-consciously.

"Cheer up," Meg said sympathetically. "You'll be slim again before long. And it will be worth it."

"Keep telling me that!" Susan looked unconvinced as she took the jacket out with her.

Meg sighed knowingly to herself. The pregnancy was Susan's first, and it probably did seem a great burden. Unfortunately, there would almost certainly come a time when Susan would wish for a return of these days when the worst thing she had to worry about was regaining her girlish figure. Meg hoped that time did not come as soon for Susan as it had for her.

She bumped the desk slightly when she sat down, and a few of the delicate crab-apple blossoms broke loose. Lazily Meg watched one flutter down onto the stack of catalogs. How impossible it was to take work seriously when her senses were so titillated by the sight and scent of those beautiful, fragile flowers.

Meg realized now that she had been on edge even before that crazy call for Robbie Dowell came. The restlessness had started building subtly ever since she had discovered the unexpected burst of color when driving along the bayou that morning. Shreveport stayed relatively green throughout the damp winters, but each spring after the first extended spell of sunshine it underwent a breathtakingly beautiful metamorphosis. The sudden blossoming of the city always seemed to Meg a symbolic Easter gift, heralding a new beginning for everyone. Even for the swinging Robbies of this world.

She sighed again and touched a blossom. "I can't believe you," she chided herself aloud. Spring fever was definitely not a welcome development. What she needed was a quick chat with customers to get her mind back to business. She moved to the door, smoothing her mauve polyester skirt over her generous hips.

Too generous, she was grudgingly reminded as she caught a fleeting rear glimpse of herself in the full-length mirror at which she always checked her appearance before stepping out on the display floor. Those hips had kept her from a modeling career. Her slight weight and firm, small breasts, her long waistline, her slender ankles and five-foot-six-inch height had been fine for show modeling. But Meg took after her mother's side of the family, with the wide pelvis that was perfect for childbearing and lousy for high fashion.

She leaned toward the mirror and plucked a tiny, previously unnoticed glob of mascara from her long lashes. It was probably just as well, she thought. About the generous hips. Despite her classical blond complexion and high cheekbones, her face was a little too narrow to photograph perfectly, anyway. And only by knowledgeable application of makeup that played down the sensuous fullness of her mouth could her average blue-gray eyes appear to dominate her appearance.

I'm beginning to show my thirty-one years, Meg thought, without any particular regrets, as she noted the maturity evident in the planes of her face and in her carriage. Lately she had been frosting her blond hair to blend in the few strands of gray that were showing up with increasing regularity. But otherwise, the total natural look was what she strived for—elegant enough to give her customers confidence in her high-fashion taste, yet understated enough not to be competition. Meg didn't particularly care to be perennially youthful. In the ten years since she had graduated from LSU with a degree in fashion merchandising, there had been too many other things on her mind.

The final check indicated that her cotton designer sweater draped perfectly beneath the straw belt and that her hair was neat enough despite its bout with the phone cord. She glanced again at the note for Penny, sighed for some vague thing lost or maybe never attained and went out to mingle with her customers.

THINGS BECAME SO HECTIC in the early afternoon that Meg no longer had to fight the restlessness the spring weather and eager call for Robbie had created. Work took over. A couple of carloads of women came in from Alexandria for serious shopping, and a few of these customers insisted on consulting with Meg, even though she did not work directly in sales anymore. Penny Sands, who had recently appointed a manager downtown and now divided her time between the two stores, breezed in, waved and almost as immediately breezed out again. So she was no help. It was not until almost four, after the Alexandria customers had finally left, that Meg could settle back in the office and begin plowing through the New York catalogs.

"I'm glad I don't work on the floor every day," she told Penny when the store's owner eventually returned. "I've lost my stamina now that I'm out of practice."

"Managing and profit sharing are much better," Penny agreed, slumping into her own chair and meticulously picking a piece of lint from her navy spring suit. "Good day, I take it?"

"Looks as if it will be," Meg agreed, mildly concerned about the vibrant woman who had taken her under her wing five years earlier. They had been through lots of business crises together, but Meg had never noticed her mentor looking quite so tired.

No one knew Ms. Penelope Sand's age exactly, but people made guesses because her hair was the striking blue-white preferred by many Shreveport women who admitted to being over sixty. Of course she was more elegantly coiffed than most of her contemporaries; Penny religiously met a twice-weekly hair appointment in spite of floods, tornadoes or threatened bankruptcy. Meals, business meetings she would miss, but never her hair appointment.

Meg smiled affectionately. "Apparently your day didn't match ours," she said.

"Charlie's not resting as he should," Penny snapped angrily. "That damn man is going to have another heart attack if he doesn't do what the doctor says, but what did he insist on doing today? Cleaning out his damn caladium beds and—"

"You're getting into your cursing syndrome again," Meg warned.

"When he has two yardmen to do that kind of damn—that kind of work."

"When are you and Charlie going to get married

again?'' Meg asked, relaxing somewhat. Penny always seemed worn out when she took up nagging Charlie. "It's been seven years since your last divorce. Don't you think it's about time to—"

"I'm not marrying that man a third time! I've been Penelope Peabody twice, and that name alone is enough to cause separation. Besides, Charlie's the most damn stubborn..."

Meg's eyes drifted to the catalogs. There wasn't anything possibly new she could hear about that eccentric oilman, Charlie Peabody—she had heard it all. Why Penny kept a house of her own, yet consistently spent much of her time living with and ranting at her twice-ex-husband was an enigma Meg couldn't hope to figure out. Personally, Meg thought Charlie was a darling. She glanced over an ad on straw bags while she heard about Charlie's foul pipe tobacco, surreptitiously turned a page and looked at an Atlanta designer's new sports slacks while Penny ranted about Charlie's penchant for breakfast of chocolate bars and V-8 juice. The droning, irate voice had reached Charlie's irregular sleeping habits when Meg turned another page to see five women dressed in flimsy night wear and hanging over the shoulders of an eager-looking male. The restlessness promptly swamped her again, and she thought of Robert Clark Dowell.

"Oh! Did you get Mr. Dowell to call his office?" she interrupted Penny's harangue.

"No, I'd already canceled that appointment before I got back and saw your note."

"Great. His lady friend will be certain I sabotaged his message," Meg muttered.

"Lady friend—Rob?"

"Robbie, actually." Meg cocked an eyebrow suggestively. "And I describe the relationship with discretion, since he is too old for a girlfriend. The woman was most sultry and insistent."

"I guess I'm not surprised. That man's a hunk."

"Mr. Dowell a hunk?" Although Meg used the term, "hunk," favored by their teenaged customers, as naturally as Penny, she couldn't think of the man as other than Mr. Dowell. He was always so—so unobtrusively there. He came in at least once a month to take Meg and Penny out to a meal, during which he quickly settled their insurance concerns as if that were secondary to having an entertaining visit with them. His business methods were so pleasantly efficient that Meg always liked working with him. She even got a kick out of his inexhaustible supply of freebies—all those pencils, bookmarks and pocket calendars that stated his phone numbers and that incredibly formal "Robert Clark Dowell." She had often wondered if he thought people would forget him.

But on reflection she realized it was certainly possible that his customers needed to be reminded of his name. Meg, who saw him so regularly, couldn't even mentally reconstruct exactly what he looked like. He was relatively tall, she knew, for she remembered having to tilt her head slightly to catch his eyes. Fortyish plus, probably, judging from some of his nostalgia stories. Tanned. Meg could place no other recollections of his features. She guessed he was somewhat athletic, for he always told at least one golf tale, and his freebies included tees in a variety of colors. She thought he favored suits and leather shoes, although he might have been footless for all she remembered.

"Yes, a hunk," Penny was droning on. "It's no wonder you've never noticed. You treat him as you treat all eligible bachelors. Nonexistent."

"Please don't start on that you-should-remarry kick. You never take my advice, so I won't take yours."

"My situation with Charlie is different," Penny huffed out defensively. "You're not about to get involved with your ex-husband again, so after all these years you ought to be looking for someone new."

"Even if I didn't figure that anyone in his forties who is still a bachelor would be hopeless to live with, Robert Dowell is already taken," she said. "This sexy woman from his office says he *must* call her—an *emergency*. I suspect a let's-spend-this-week-together-type emergency. It's a shame you couldn't give him the message."

"You can give it to him tonight. I ran into him out in the mall at noon and shifted our appointment to dinner. But now I have to check on Charlie, so you can go instead."

"Me! Now, Penny..." Meg had never done business with the man alone, and the prospect was not particularly appealing.

"I don't ask you to fill in for me often. And you and I have gone over the employee benefits we want to incorporate in our next insurance policy. You can take care of it as well as I."

Meg sighed helplessly. Penny never ordered Meg to do anything. She merely reasoned and usually won. Mike was on a vacation fishing trip with Meg's parents and she had no plans for the evening, so there was absolutely no excuse for her not keeping a business appointment.

"Oh, all right." She gave in to the inevitable. "Where are you meeting him?"

"He was coming to the store at six-thirty. I'm leaving for Charlie's right now, but I'll have someone on duty send him to your house."

"I can wait around here for him," Meg offered hesitantly, not liking the idea of his picking her up at home, but on the other hand not all that fond of staying an extra hour and a half at work, either.

"You don't live that far. Besides, whenever we take separate cars directly from the store, he always follows me home after dinner to make certain I get in okay, so—"

"You're kidding!"

"He does. You'd think he was born a Southerner instead of in Kansas. Be ready by six-thirtyish. I told him I'd treat him to shrimp at the Old Shreve Inn, so put it on the store tab."

"I'm not sure I like this idea—"

"Just do it."

AND MEG TRIED TO DO IT. She went home on time, made reservations at the restaurant and arranged for the store to be billed, was freshened up by six-thirty and even solemnly shook hands with Robert Clark Dowell when he arrived. Then she blew the whole operation by asking if he wanted to use her phone to call the woman who had been so eager to talk to "Robbie."

"I'm not certain I like the way you roll that name off

your tongue." Robert Dowell's voice was steady and only his raised eyebrow indicated his grudging amusement. He was standing on her front porch, but even in the wavering twilight Meg could tell that his eyes were brown. She noticed other details for the first time—the freshly shaven smoothness of his broad, tanned jaw, the surprising light color of his eyebrows over the deep-set eyes. His was not a handsome face—the nose was too irregular and the mouth too stern. Especially right then.

"The lady who wanted Robbie said it was an emergency," Meg persisted.

"To my office maybe, not to me." His lips tilted wryly. "Quit worrying. My secretary reached me over at United Gas. The New Orleans staff got wind of a promotion offer they thought I'd be jumping at and couldn't believe I'd turned it down."

Quit worrying? Meg at first felt guilty that she had wormed the basis of that call out of him. Then she realized Robert Clark Dowell had never been free with personal information, so perhaps he was the one who manipulated *her*. She stood just inside her door, thinking that if he wanted to make her even more curious he had certainly succeeded. She could not help wondering what promotion he had been offered and why he had turned it down.

He wants to be in New Orleans with his secretary? He doesn't want to be in New Orleans with his secretary? His secretary wants him to accept the better job and take her with him? Cozy.

"Penny had suggested the Old Shreve Inn. Does that suit you?" His matter-of-fact question as he drew her out on the porch made her mental meanderings seem foolish. She reminded herself that she was supposed to be negotiating business with this associate.

"It's the place for us to go if you like shrimp," she agreed in her most polished and impersonal manner. "Their cook used to be over at Abe's Seafood place. Do you know the way?"

He did, which wasn't surprising to Meg. She supposed that for a man who flew regularly between appointments in Atlanta, Houston and New Orleans, finding his way around in a city of two hundred thousand was a snap.

The reminder of his competence heightened her peculiar sensitivity to the man and increased her compulsion to fill in the gaps her memory maintained about him. As she walked beside him to his car she realized that she was just shy of eye level with him in her highest heels. That made him almost six feet. Not unusually tall, but he seemed so because he was slender, moved athletically and had a thick shock of brown hair. Brown peppered with gray, she amended, when they paused under the streetlight for him to open the car door.

As she settled into the seat and watched him walk around to the driver's side she realized why she had never noticed him from the neck down before. His attire was tastefully chosen—her professional judgment told her that his tan suit was personally tailored, his tie a Pierre Cardin and the pale striped shirt an expensive version cut for athletes. But his garments hung so comfortably on his lanky frame that they seemed part of him. One noticed the whole person, not the packaging.

And that whole person seemed to fill the car with his charisma when he slid in beside her.

"Do you have to rent a car every time you come into town?" she asked, more to break the unexpected feeling of intimacy than from any real interest.

"Someone from Allied is here so frequently that we have a permanent contract for cars through the airport rental agency," he explained while he pulled away from the curb. "Our business in northern Louisiana and southern Arkansas is getting almost too good."

"You ought to open a branch here."

"I've been telling the board of directors that."

There was an unusual amount of traffic for a Monday night, so Meg agreeably lapsed into silence, grateful that driving required his concentration. She needed some time to come up with other impersonal subjects that could carry her through a whole evening of polite conversation.

Despite its name the Old Shreve Inn was a new place on a shaded drive bordering the levee of the Red River. When Robert Dowell eventually pulled into the parking lot, the bright security lights of the complex beamed through the windshield and reflected off his huge, tanned hands gripping the wheel. He seemed so lean and lanky otherwise that his broad palms and long fingers were an anomaly.

Like my hips, Meg thought in surprise.

"Is this all right? I can let you out at the door if you prefer."

His voice was amused, and she realized in embarrassment that she must have been staring at him.

"No, don't do that. Of course I can walk." She

jerked at the handle of the door and climbed out before
he could unfold himself from the car to help her. He
did, however, steady her at the elbow while they
crossed the parking lot.

Later, when they had ordered a final cup of coffee,
Meg decided that she must have covered the new tension she felt in Robert Dowell's presence well. The
meal went as pleasantly as all meals with him and
Penny had gone in the past, and they had managed to
finalize the new store insurance policy in between
good conversation. The coffee was served, and Meg
was listening to his question about a small antebellum
home they had passed earlier, when she was suddenly
swamped by a wave of relaxing inertia.

The long day was almost over! The job pressure, the
tension, her spring fever, all seemed to slip off her
shoulders as if she were a butterfly shedding a chrysa-
lis. She had never before felt anything quite like that,
and her welcoming sigh was enormously audible.

Robert Dowell looked startled. "You're tired, and
here I am, keeping you out longer," he apologized,
shoving aside his full coffee cup.

"No, it's not that." Instinctively Meg placed her
hand over his to keep him from rising. "It suddenly hit
me that I'm really off work. Do you know what I
mean?"

His questioning look indicated that he didn't.

"Don't you ever feel that your job puts you constantly on stage?" she asked. Surely selling insurance
was not that different from selling clothing. People still
had to be mollified. "I've been advising and soothing
customers for more than eight hours; my decisions at

Penelope's, as well as here, have affected the liveli-
hoods of seventeen employees, but now we're finished
and—''

"And now you can be yourself?"

"At least more myself," she admitted, so relaxed
that she couldn't even stir herself enough to remove
her hand.

"There are times when I get back to my motel room
at night and talk to the wall." He curled his fingers
loosely around hers. "I say all the careless things I can't
afford to let slip when I'm listening to clients. I brag
about my own golf score. I tell really boring stories just
because I like them."

Meg laughed. "I'm the opposite. I don't want to
speak or to hear the human voice. I must converse with
people so much at the store that sometimes when my
nine-year-old son starts chattering to me at home I
wish he had an 'off' switch. It's most unfair, and I try
to be a good listener, but . . ." She shrugged.

He smiled in sympathy with her problem and out-
lined her ringless fingers with his broad thumb. They
sat in a peculiarly comfortable silence, staring at their
linked hands. The marked contrast of his browned skin
against her fair complexion seemed fascinating to both
of them.

"Mrs. Meghan Bronson," he eventually stated quietly. "You're a puzzle, you know."

"I'm no puzzle." It occurred to her then that she was
not guarding her inner self as carefully as usual, and
she slipped her hand from his. But still there was a
slight hint of question at the end of her remark that
encouraged him to continue his lazy analysis.

"You always use 'Mrs.,' when most women now go to 'Ms.' Yet you don't wear a wedding ring. That's a puzzle."

Meg had never particularly thought about it, but he was right. Even married women used Ms. now. Meg had sent her diamond engagement ring back to Dane's family but kept the wedding ring. Although she couldn't bear to have the gold band on her finger again, it was still tucked away somewhere in the bottom of her jewelry box, just as "Mrs." was insistently attached to her name.

"I guess I want my son to be certain he has a legitimate father somewhere," she blurted honestly. Immediately regretting her candor, she settled her hands primly in her lap.

"You're divorced, I understand."

"You're a bachelor, I understand," she parroted rudely, feeling more and more uncomfortable with these revelations about her personal life.

"I'm a bachelor who's just been put in his place." He pinned his own impersonal facade back on as efficiently as she had, and Meg immediately regretted her thinly veiled reprimand. Robert Dowell undoubtedly needed his workday to be over as much as she did.

"I didn't mean that quite as it sounded, Mr. Dowell," she apologized.

"Couldn't we drop this 'Mr. Dowell' and 'Mrs. Bronson' bit?" he asked impatiently. "My name is Rob."

"Not Robbie?"

He looked pained. "Not Robbie. My two younger sisters grew up calling me that, and they flit into my New Orleans office often enough so that some of the

staff there have picked it up. I'm afraid I'll have to act
the heavy at work soon and put a stop to it."

Meg rather liked the seriousness of his expression. It
was touching that he hoped his employees would aban-
don the familiarity without his having to make a scene.
But Meg suspected that the sultry-voiced secretary
wouldn't easily give up on baiting Robbie, even if he
wasn't yet biting.

"Didn't you ever get stuck with a nickname?" he
asked defensively.

"I have an older sister and two older brothers who
still call me Pegghead." She cringed when he smirked.
"I've never told anyone that before. If you dare get
that started here..."

"You call me Rob, and I promise I'll only call
you...call you what?"

She couldn't help hesitating. "Call me Meg."

"Meg." The word escaped thoughtfully from his lips
as if he were hesitant to give it up. "I like that. Well, I
guess it's time to leave. Shall we, Meg?"

It was more than time, she thought, watching him
unwind his magnificent body from his chair. She was
losing control of this whole business situation.

THE AIR WAS A LITTLE COOLER outside. Meg lifted to her
shoulders the sweater that matched her dress, and Rob
Dowell helped her thrust her arms into its warmth. It
was a short walk to his car, but he drew her protectively
to his side as if shielding her from the changing elements with his body.

They said relatively little until they arrived at her
house.

"You've picked up very Southern traits, you know," Meg observed when they were walking toward her porch.

"A Kansan with Southern traits? None of your colleagues would agree. Everyone says I have a harsh Midwestern twang."

"Oh, your voice is still Yankee like mine, even though I've been in the South half my life." She laughed easily. "I mean the protectiveness to women—seeing Penny home in her car, not jumping down your secretaries' throats about 'Robbie' because you don't want to embarrass them or your sisters, insisting on walking me to the door."

"Do only Southern males care about their women?" he asked curiously as he watched her fit her key into the lock. She clicked it open, then turned back toward him.

"Well, it's a nice touch, whatever. Thanks for the evening." She thrust out her hand.

He engulfed it in his. "Penelope's paid for it, remember? Thank you for the evening."

"You're welcome."

That should have ended it. But it didn't. Her hand remained warmly in his while they stood close together on her darkened porch.

"Where did you spend the half of your life when you weren't a Southerner?" His eyes seemed to be roaming over her face, studying its shadows and highlights. Instinctively she lifted her chin to give him a better view.

"Born and raised in Indiana until my junior year in high school. Then we moved to Baton Rouge and I stayed on for LSU. Say! You haven't given me a new freebie this time."

"You think I don't have one?" He adjusted quickly to her change of subject, dropped her hand and dug into the pocket of his coat. "Here's a memo pad. In fact, here are two. Your son can doodle on one."

"He'll like that." She tried to see the logo in the dim light of the street lamp: "Allied Insurance. Robert Clark Dowell, Senior Analyst." She couldn't quite make out the series of phone numbers listed for numerous Southern cities. "You cover a huge territory." She glanced up at him, her lips suddenly tilting. "I can see why you get tired of being Mr. Dowell of Atlanta, Birmingham, Houston, Memphis—maybe you should quit talking to motel-room walls and change your image instead. Get a logo of a golf cart: 'Robbie Dowell, the—'"

"Uh, uh, uh," he cautioned, placing a mammoth finger over her teasing lips.

What am I doing, she suddenly thought in a panic, feeling her breath moisten his skin. She was actually flirting with this man. Here. On her own front porch, with her son gone for the night and the house dark. What stupid childish game was she up to, flirting with this stranger?

"I won't dignify that suggestion by calling you Pegghead," he said huskily, leaning toward her. "There are other ways to retaliate."

Her breathing caught, and she remained motionlessly unresisting as his mouth brushed tentatively across hers. He held her shoulders lightly while his lips skimmed along her jawline, hovered around her throat, then moved warmly back toward her mouth.

Once he began treating the other side of her face to

the same investigative caresses, her objection was wispy.

"Rob..."

"Sh, Meg. I'm only going to kiss you." His lips resettled on hers and his huge hands engulfed her waist to draw her body against his.

Meg was anything but soothed. *Only going to kiss me? Oh, Robbie!*

She hadn't kissed many men since Dane, and it showed. She stood against him stiffly, her purse dangled over her elbow and her hands, still clutching the memo pads, braced against his forearms. *Awkward! Awkward!*

If he tells me to loosen up, I'll— At the thought, Meg stiffened even more, having long ago learned that men liked to challenge divorcées. *Studs!* Her mouth tightened stubbornly under his. Only when his chest moved against hers did she realize that he was chuckling. Angrily she tipped back her head so she could see his face.

"Would you—"

His finger on her lips stopped her. He was smiling. "I have toothpasty breath, right?"

"What?"

"Or maybe it's my soap. Smells too much like a men's locker room?"

She couldn't help it. Definitely unnerved, she began to chuckle, too.

"Rob, I—"

"Sh, it's all right." He traced her mouth lightly. "I'm going to be here tomorrow, but I have no appointments after five. Spend the evening with me?"

Meg knew that she should have barked a polite excuse immediately. It was what she always did when men asked her out. But her son was on spring break with her parents, and her mind, usually so quick with polite excuses, went absolutely blank. Worse, the odd restlessness deep within her was churning again. Her hesitation lengthened.

"All right," she blurted, simply to fill the awkward gap of questioning silence.

His hand slid to her jaw, and he breathed the softest of kisses into her tightened throat before leaning away. "I'll pick you up here at five-thirty." He guided her inside and firmly closed the door between them.

Meg stared at the paneled wood, suddenly thinking that she should have told him she would have to work late. Immediately she slung the door open, but he was already loping out to his car like a kid. It was the hours of golf, she supposed—making a grown man lope gracefully like a virile teenager. Meg sighed and went back into the house.

Too late to change her mind.

A date? The reality was disquieting. She was thirty-one years old and she had just made a real, honest-to-God date. She couldn't imagine what had gotten into her.

I won't even remember how to act.

Chapter Two

Meghan Bronson's house sat fairly close to the street, leaving the bulk of its long, narrow lot for a spacious fenced yard to the rear. Rob Dowell hadn't noticed much about it when he had arrived at dusk the previous evening, but now, as he walked toward it, he thought the house was exactly what he would expect for her. Small, utilitarian, yet as tastefully cared for as if it were a mansion. A quality piece.

It was painted a pale yellow with a gray trim and looked almost like a storybook cottage, sitting as it did in an intensely green yard. He was glad to see that she had a carport to protect her as she came in and out during Shreveport's many rainy days. Although the backyard seemed heavily wooded at the far end, only one tree shaded the house in the front—a huge magnolia with waxy green leaves and dozens of small buds filling for a burst of white blossoms later in the spring. Geraniums and pansies were blooming in a tub on the front porch, but otherwise Meg had kept her plantings to a minimum, adapting, Rob supposed, to the reality that inexpensive yard help, like daily maids, went out with the sixties. The South was still noted for its beautiful lawns, but more and more Rob saw owners of all races and ages out taking care of the work themselves. Despite what some old-timers said, it undoubtedly was, he thought, a positive evolution.

Having a house of one's own must be rewarding, he mused as he leaned the fishing rod he had been carrying up against the porch railing. For years Rob had never been in a position seriously to consider buying a home, and as he got older it seemed less likely that he would ever do it. An apartment was so much more practical for a single traveling man.

Frowning at that thought, he punched the door bell. From the shuffling sounds, then silence inside, he judged that Meg was doing what most women he knew did after hurrying to a door—patting her hair, straightening her clothes and checking numerous unnecessary things about her appearance. Unnecessary, because Meghan Bronson always seemed absolutely perfect to him. Impatiently he waited for her to decide that she looked all right; it seemed months instead of only twenty-four hours since he had seen her.

When the door swung open, however, he couldn't hide his surprise. She was wearing an exquisite pink linen cocktail suit and the highest heels he had ever seen. Not exactly what he had expected. She took one look at his white knit golf shirt, khaki slacks and tennis shoes, noticed the rod angled against the railing behind him, then burst out laughing.

"I thought Susan was kidding when she gave me your message. You really meant that we'd go fishing at your friend's place on Cross Lake!"

"I'm afraid I did. It must have been a bad idea."

"Oh, no! I love to fish. In fact, my parents and son are reeling them in at Toledo Bend right now. But I've just never thought of Cross Lake as a place to fish."

"What do you do out there?"

"Play bridge and go to coffees. A lot of my customers have places on the lake, but they use them mostly for business entertaining."

He had a sinking feeling about this date. Fishing had seemed such a good idea when he'd run into Diego and Molly Preston, and his good friends had urged him to make more use of the place they'd long ago given him a key to. The Prestons weren't going to be out there that evening, and Rob had thought Meg might feel more comfortable with him in a casual setting. But now...

"Please, Rob, don't look so embarrassed. It's my fault."

"We can go someplace nice for dinner. I'll run back to the motel and—"

"But I'd love to go fishing! It will only take me a moment to change."

Rob opted to believe that she really meant it; there wasn't any percentage in embarrassing them both further by exchanging polite arguments on what to do.

"I hope that's an extra rod and reel you brought up," Meg added in apparent enthusiasm as she motioned him inside. "My mother borrowed mine."

"It sure is. I couldn't remember—are you left-handed?"

"What? Oh, no, I'm not."

He retrieved the rod before coming in the house.

"That's why I got it out of the car. This reel is set for a lefty, but it won't take me a minute to switch it over." He paused just inside the living room. The plush carpeting and deep velvet love seats flanking the little gas fireplace didn't seem an ideal place to work. "Mind if I use your kitchen? I don't want to mess up your nice room."

"Make yourself at home. I won't be long."

And she wasn't, either. He had barely finished reassembling the reel with the handle on the proper side by the time she came in wearing tennis shoes, khaki slacks and a short-sleeved white blouse.

She's dressed as if we were twins. He dismissed the intimate reflection on closer inspection. The clothes might seem to match, but that ruffled blouse of hers with the deep neckline did a heck of a lot more for her figure than his favorite old golf shirt did for him. He couldn't seem to tear his eyes away from the soft cleft that the lacy frills did so little to hide.

"I didn't realize I was duplicating your outfit," Meg said self-consciously, misinterpreting his interested look for one of distaste. "Maybe I'd better change?"

He took her arm and rushed her to the front door.

"If we don't quit being so polite to each other, we'll never get out of here," he warned.

She had to go back, of course, to grab her purse and a jacket. But before long they were driving along the curving, shaded road approaching the big lake that was Shreveport's source of drinking water.

"Do you expect to catch our meal tonight?" Meg was sitting primly enough at his side, but she kept hitching at the neckline of her blouse, as if it didn't sit quite comfortably on her shoulders. He wished she'd leave it alone, because he liked the way it kept sinking lower until a man could get a really pleasant glimpse of her nicely rounded little breasts.

"The box I brought along from the deli probably answers that question." He tore his fascinated glance away from her neckline and concentrated again on his driving. "Actually I usually do catch several catfish, but they don't start biting early enough to make a decent supper. I clean them and leave them in the freezer for the owners of the cabin."

"You fish at night?"

"I fish anytime I can. Early morning's best—about five o'clock, when it's still cool and the mist shrouds the water."

They didn't talk much once they had passed the congestion of new developments on South Lakeshore Drive and were headed toward the more remote homes on the far side of the lake. It was companionably pleasant to remain silent and watch the passing scenery along the lightly traveled road. Tall pines covering the high ground were sporadically joined by the willows and canebreaks that liked the lowland environment nearer the water. Although it was a little early to hear the night-talking of the lakeland creatures, occasionally a rabbit darting through the underbrush reminded them of the complexities of wildlife hidden all around them.

Rob slowed down as an elderly lady on a motor scooter approached them, then eventually wobbled past. He slowed even further when in the distance they could see jogging toward them an elderly man wearing a red sweatband around his shaggy gray hair.

"This road gets interesting traffic."

"That poor guy's wasting his energy," Meg observed sympathetically. "He looks as if he's on a slow pogo stick."

When they pulled far to the side to pass the jogger safely, Rob noted the man's florid face. He didn't appear to be in the best condition for running. "I wonder sometimes about doctors advising—"

Meg suddenly twisted completely around and stared behind them.

"Oh, my, oh—*Stop*!"

Rob slammed on the brakes in alarm. His first reaction was to check in the rearview mirror, expecting to see the man sprawled out on the ground. Instead he saw the fellow still bouncing doggedly away from them, but with Meg scrambling along behind.

"Charlie?" She was shrieking. "Charlie Peabody, you wait for me!"

Rob pulled shut the door Meg had so hastily left ajar and thrust the car into reverse.

"And Penny will have a fit."

Rolling down his window while he drew alongside them, Rob heard only part of Meg's warning to the runner.

"Hello," the huffing man named Charlie said pleasantly to Rob, as if being followed by a shrieking woman and a stranger driving in reverse was all in his day's routine. Rob nodded an acknowledging greeting and adjusted his reverse speed to about zero. The runner was covering as much area up and down as he was forward.

"Charlie, would you please walk," Meg insisted breathlessly. "This is killing me."

"You shouldn't try jogging if you're out of shape," Charlie objected, nevertheless adjusting to a normal stride. Rob was surprised to find that he then had to increase his reverse speed. The fellow was quite spry when he resorted to walking.

"Charlie, your face is bright red." Meg changed her gait to a racing-walk. "You shouldn't be jogging."

"I got sunburned on the dock this afternoon. Happens every spring. Who are you?" The question was directed to Rob.

"Robert Dowell. Allied Insurance, out of New Orleans." Rob grabbed the wheel with his left hand and awkwardly reached across to thrust his right out the window. Charlie shook it formally without missing a step.

"Oh, yeah. You have the insurance contracts at the mall." He released Rob's hand. "Charlie Peabody. Retired oil bum out of Texas and Louisiana."

"Penny wouldn't be having nervous fits over you if you behaved like a proper retired person." Meg seemed frustrated and worried as she scrambled to keep up with the old man and with Rob's car. "Every time you go down to the gulf to check out a new oil lease, Penny comes into my office and raves for hours. She's had us all tearing our hair over this heart murmur your doctor discovered."

"My father had the same murmur and he lived to be ninety-three," Charlie Peabody explained to Rob, apparently not feeling that it did any good to reason with Meg. "I've probably had it for years and the quacks never found it before, but Penny can't get it out of her head that I've had a heart attack."

"I take it you have something to do with Penny Sands." Rob spoke with his eyes on the rearview mirror. Driving backwards down a narrow, curving road, even at two miles an hour, required concentration.

"Married her twice. Our first divorce settlement paid for the Penelope's downtown, and the second one eventually got her the branch in the mall." Charlie seemed to be proud of the accomplishment. "Alimony keeps her with new carpets. But you know, her business has really grown enough so that she could expand again. I've been telling her that we should set the date soon. Our second marriage lasted half as many years as the first, so if we keep that same ratio, she would be ready to open another branch store with my money by—"

"Charlie, I hear a car coming. Would you please get in with us?"

Meg was right about the car. Twisting to look over his shoulder, Rob could see someone approaching from a far curve of the road. He turned on his hazard lights and maintained his speed. Much as he also hoped Charlie Peabody would get in with them and relieve Meg's mind, he was pleased that she did not try to tug him along forcefully. It annoyed Rob when younger people used their physical strength and mental quickness to manipulate the elderly. The car approaching them was honking, but Charlie doggedly continued his pace a few more steps until he heard Meg's muffled sniffing. "Oh for—you women!" He took Meg's arm and hustled her toward Rob's car as if she were a fragile darling and the actual cause of their current difficulty.

"Where to?" Once they were both in the back seat,

Rob flicked off the hazard lights and started forward again.

"Where were you going?" Charlie asked.

"My friends have a cabin halfway up this next lane that they let me use."

"You planning to fish?" One could almost feel him eagerly looking over the rods he had shoved aside to make room for Meg and himself.

"We are, later in the evening. We have plenty of food if you'd care to join us for supper first."

"Okay."

"Does anyone want to consult me in this?" Meg asked, apparently still worried about Charlie's heart.

"Not if you're going to lecture me on my health."

"Charlie, dear, it's my heart I'm protecting now." Meg patted his arm affectionately. "If you'll refrain from jogging again until I'm out of sight, I promise not to nag you about your health."

"Why do you jog, anyway?" Rob asked curiously. "You have one of the best race-walking strides I've seen."

"I was getting into training to shock Penny."

"You don't have to train to do that," Meg said with just a trace of sarcasm.

"Penny is on this kick about my heart. At bedtime she keeps bringing me hot skim milk and tells me to go to sleep. Treats me like some impotent invalid. I'd molest her if I didn't think she'd kill me afterward."

Rob burst out laughing. He glanced in the rear mirror and saw that Meg's face was red and that she was apparently speechless. His grin grew wider.

"I figured Penny would hear about my jogging

around Shreveport," Charlie continued, unembarrassed, "and start raving more about my heart. Then I'd tell her she has a choice. I'll either drop dead jogging in the street or have my heart attack in bed with a sexy old woman. She can take her pick."

Rob could hear Meg's reluctant chuckle. "If I know Penny," she said carefully, "she'll hand you a list of other options, all of which are unpleasant, and none of which threaten your long life."

"Dammit, I'm tired of all this celibacy."

"Why don't you tell her about your prostate gland?" Rob asked.

"Why should I? There's nothing wrong with it."

"Good. All the more reason to keep it that way. Don't you know that having sex is the best preventive medicine for prostate troubles?"

Rob's assertion brought both Meg and Charlie up to lean over the front seat.

"Where did you hear that?" Meg asked suspiciously.

"Between them, my two sisters have produced five babies, so they've had lots of time to read all the helpful literature in their gynecologist's waiting room. Of course I can't vouch for what they read, but they've been giving me lots of free advice lately about what I should do for my prostate gland."

"The publications in an obstetrician's office have certainly been upgraded since I had my son," Meg observed wryly, leaning back again. "All I ever read about was cradle cap."

"You know, that just might work." Charlie also relaxed against the seat and stared thoughtfully out the window. "Penny's father died after prostate surgery ..."

"Charlie!"

"It would beat this jogging," he reasoned. "Being out on the street is dangerous! Why just this evening, some gal on a motor scooter almost ran me down."

"YOU'D BE A PRETTY GOOD FISHERMAN if you'd use the right lure." Rob watched Meg efficiently take a blob of cheese off her weighted line, move the bobber up another ten inches, then attach a wriggling worm on her small hook.

When the three of them had gone out to the Prestons' dock just after the sunset faded completely, Rob had quickly cast several times with three different artificial lures before hauling in his first catch. After that test he had stuck with the successful lure and thus far had four pan-sized catfish to Meg's none on worm bait.

"I told you worms wouldn't work in this hot weather," Charlie told Meg unsympathetically, having caught two catfish on lures himself before he had let Meg have a turn with the rod Rob had converted for her.

"Using that plastic thing seems ... unfair. The fish might as well get a good snack in return for being caught."

"Don't tell me you're one of those women who won't cook or eat what they catch," Rob remarked.

"Wrong. I'll even clean it if I have to."

"I love the way she says 'have' to," Charlie told Rob. "Makes us feel so guilty we'll clean 'em ourselves."

Rob watched Meg swing her bobber away from the dock and let it settle on the water until the worm dangled below it. She was a natural at casting. He would like to see what she could do if she ever made up her mind to resort to artificial lures. Fly fishing—that's what she would really be good at. He could visualize her standing in a mountain stream in hip boots and a damp shirt, whipping out that delicate line to the hidden reaches of an overgrown stream. She'd probably want to tie her own flies—gorgeous things with vibrant colors that all the fish would flock to. Rob smiled contentedly.

They waited in silence for several minutes with nothing happening. The crickets and night creatures were talking by then, and occasionally you could hear the tail of a big fish breaking the water. But nothing was attracted to Meg's wriggling worm. Finally she sighed in defeat and reeled her rig in. Rob pulled his stringer full of fish out of the water and began to gather together their gear.

"If you two are going to be such wonderful gentlemen and clean those fish," Meg teased, "I'll make us a pot of coffee."

"I'll clean 'em," Charlie volunteered. "Rob can load the gear."

It took only a few minutes for Rob to get everything packed away in the trunk of his rented car. There wasn't any food left to take care of, Charlie having built up a good appetite with his jogging efforts. And Rob was an old hand at disassembling his rods. When he came into the kitchen, the rich smell of coffee was just beginning to touch the room, and Meg was opening cabinet doors, looking for cups.

"They're probably right in front of me," she apologized. "But I don't like to nose around too much in someone else's house."

"Wait a minute. I think Molly keeps mugs in the dining room. She and her husband aren't coffee drinkers."

"In a thousand years I wouldn't have matched up Charlie Peabody and Penelope Sands," he remarked idly when he returned with three mugs. Through the window over the sink he could see Charlie still out on the dimly lighted dock, happily rinsing off the cleaned fillets in a bucket of fresh water. "He's as genuine as my best friends among the Texas roughnecks. And Penny's one of the grandest old-style ladies I know. But as a couple?"

"They've been divorced twice, but are still together, so I've given up trying to figure them out. Thanks so much for including Charlie tonight. I think he needed the company." The silence between them was comfortable, and Meg filled two of the coffee cups before continuing easily. "My folks said that for the first year of their own marriage they didn't agree on anything, but after my oldest brother was born they suddenly got along beautifully. What about your parents?"

"They're both dead now. I remember that they seemed to love each other and never fought. But I think they both would have been better off if they'd never married."

"That's a sad thing to say." She seemed concerned about him and unconsciously rested a hand on his shoulder in a brief gesture of comfort before handing him his coffee. He felt some explanation was necessary.

"My mother was the youngest in a big family of girls who grew up like the Brontës, Kansas-style—highly intelligent and well-read in a time when rural girls were supposed to marry the neighboring farmer and raise little farmers. None of her sisters would have minded that part, I guess, but no males nearby were as interested in intellectual endeavors as they were. Eventually they gave up trying to communicate with others; their big house full of family and books became all the world they needed. Mother was the only one who married. We had our own home down the block, but her ties were always to the sisters."

"What about your father?"

"He was sensitive, intelligent and very impractical. He wanted to be an artist, but not quite badly enough to go for it."

"Did he give up painting for your mother?"

Rob hesitated. She had been right. It made him wrenchingly sad to think about these things. More so, because for the first time he could remember, someone had instinctively sensed his pain and cared that he hurt. "No, he didn't give it up," he finally managed to continue. "All his life he painted seriously in a shed behind our house."

"He didn't work elsewhere?"

"Never. Occasionally he earned money doing a commissioned portrait or hand-lettering christening documents. After he died, mother took her favorites of his work and moved us back to her sisters' home. I was in my last year of high school then, and I took the remainder of his finished things to Kansas City for art

dealers to look over. They said the work was amateur-
ish, but marketable as interior-decorating fluff.''

"Did you sell it?"

"No. I kept some and saved the rest for my own
sisters. All the dealers agreed that he might have been
quite good if he'd had adequate formal training and
equipment. In the early years of their marriage Dad
considered going to Paris to study, but Mother refused
to leave her sisters, and he didn't want the school-
ing badly enough to find a way to get there on his
own.''

"For you, the situation must have seemed such a
waste of both their talents," she said empathetically.
"Especially since you were helpless to change it. How
did they live?"

How indeed? That was the hardest part to talk about.
But when she watched him with such open caring, he
was tempted to try.

"My maternal grandparents had done fairly well on
their wheat farm. Mother and Dad managed to get
along on her share of the sisters' inheritance from
them until I was almost out of high school." Meg was
leaning toward him, listening intently. But he couldn't
go on. "Charlie must be finished by now. I'll help bag
up those fillets." Abruptly he stalked to the door, hoping Meg wasn't shocked by his sudden dismissal. But
additional useless speculation about the past simply
wasn't in his capacity.

Indeed, Meg wondered what she had done wrong.
He had seemed to need to talk, but now she regretted
her questions. Having secreted away parts of her own

life that she never discussed, Meg understood if people needed to guard their words.

Pensively she poured coffee for Charlie and carried the mug out to him, watching while the two finished cleaning up from their fishing efforts. Rob seemed to feel more relaxed by the time they had exchanged a few tall fish stories over a final cup of coffee. And once they were driving down the lake road toward the house where Charlie wanted to be let off, Meg began to wonder if she had merely imagined Rob's tension. She had the most pleasant feeling of family as she sat beside him, with Charlie leaning up from the back seat and absentmindedly patting her shoulder with his gnarled hand while he chatted enthusiastically about sports. Meg listened contentedly, grateful that they enjoyed each other so much. She adored Charlie and suspected that she could easily learn to adore Rob. The fact that he, unlike most of her acquaintances, appreciated Charlie's unvarnished personality was enough to make her admire him. The man had a wonderful sense of people.

All in all, Meg hoped that her first date in years wasn't going too badly. She had enjoyed Rob Dowell thoroughly and wanted to give him pleasure in return. Dating, she decided, was rather like riding a bicycle. Once you learned, you never forgot how. You might wobble and falter, but the determination to succeed was still there. Then, remembering one awkward aspect of dating, the embarrassing fumbling around in cavernous purses hunting for door keys while your date hovered nearby, Meg dug out her own key ring and tucked it into her hand. She wasn't going to embarrass

Rob Dowell by making him feel obligated to kiss her good night. Not after her miserable failure at it the night before.

Charlie was just finishing an outrageous story about a friend of his who had bet an oil well on his golf score— and lost—when they pulled into the driveway of a secluded home.

"Do you own this place?" Meg asked in surprise when she saw the initials "C.P." on the mailbox. It was a large contemporary home, one-level on the street side, with an entry garden full of blooming flowers and neatly trimmed rosebushes. To the rear of the fall-off lot the house was two levels of shaded glass, ringed with a deck. A large swimming pool was in a fenced garden off to one side, and two boats were anchored at the spacious dock below.

"Yes, I own it, but don't tell Penny you've seen it." Charlie grunted. "She doesn't want any of her friends to know she comes out here to rough it. She's afraid someone will drive by and see her without her makeup."

"You call this roughing it?" Meg laughed in disbelief.

"Penny calls it roughing it," Charlie corrected sourly. "I think it's too fancy. I wish I had my old fishing shack back. But you can come in and see it, if you want."

Meg glanced over at Rob. He was leaving it up to her, but she thought he looked tired. Protectively, she didn't want to lengthen his day. "I think it's beautiful, and I'd love to see it another time," she told Charlie sincerely. "But I must get home now. I have to be at the store around seven tomorrow."

"You two can come out anytime." Charlie grabbed Rob's hand for a final shake before ambling into the house.

"I thought the store didn't open until nine," Rob said when they were on the road again. "Did you beg off for my benefit, or do you always go in to work so early?"

"I only go in early when we have some special projects coming up that I can't get to during regular hours. Which I really do have to do tomorrow because I'm arranging a trunk showing and it's going to be a big one."

"What's a trunk showing?"

"Your sisters haven't advised you on that?" she teased, recalling his earlier story. "Wait till they're out of maternity clothes for good and start investing in wardrobes. You'll hear all about the high-fashion world and probably even receive a few hints for special birthday presents."

"That may be a while. Tell me now."

"Trunk showings are a way we can offer our customers originals without having to carry them in inventory. Representatives of the top New York designers come once a season with sample garments and we take orders."

"Do you select your own clothes that way?"

"I appreciate the compliment, but hardly. You haven't looked at me very carefully."

"Oh, yes, I have." His glace hovered on her deep neckline.

Worrying that he thought the blouse was too revealing, Meg self-consciously hitched it up at the shoulders and wondered why she had chosen to wear that thing, since it always tended to droop. She glanced nervously at her watch. "It is late."

He pulled to a stop in her driveway. "Is that a not-so-subtle way to tell me that you're not going to offer me a nightcap from that wet bar I saw in your dining room?"

"The wet bar came with the house, but I never keep alcohol at home. So, actually, I can't offer you a nightcap."

"That firm statement is intriguing. I know you're not a teetotaler, because we shared a split of wine at dinner last night."

"I drink occasionally at business functions."

"Well, I won't pretend that this has been business." Rob grinned, climbing out of the car. When he didn't ask to come in, anyway, she knew for certain that he was anxious to leave, and her self-confidence sagged. Worse, his close presence at her side while they walked up to her dark house brought on a sharp attack of sexual awareness.

"I forgot to turn my night timer on again," Meg babbled when they reached her porch. She regretted that kissing wasn't anything like riding a bicycle. You *did* forget how to do that. Confusing thoughts raced through her mind. *Would he, or wouldn't he?* A kiss from Rob Dowell would be nice, but how could she encourage it after her awkward fumbling the last time?

With a trembling she couldn't quite control, Meg fitted the key into the lock. However, getting the door open expeditiously did nothing to stop the heat and expectancy building between them. He wanted to hold her in his arms. She could sense it, even though he didn't violate the space she maintained between them.

When she reached inside to turn on a lamp controlled by the wall switch, he was still leaning lazily against the door frame, watching her.

"I know you feel a little rushed by all this," he surprised her by saying, "but I'm not in town frequently enough to give you time to get used to me. I'll be in Shreveport next weekend. Shall we spend Saturday together?"

Meg gulped. She had been wanting a good-night kiss. Another date seemed almost too much to handle. "I've already made plans with my son for the afternoon."

"Dinner, then? I could pick you up as late as eight."

He made no move at all, no macho action that might force her acquiescence. It was hard having the decision rest so simply with her. She wished he'd take her in his arms. Then she might know if she would still freeze up so much that she could never be an entertaining companion on another date. She felt so terribly inadequate. And still he waited.

"All right, all right!" Her vehemence jarred him from his passive stance. He immediately straightened up, an understanding smile on his face.

"Feeling pressured?"

"Do you want to withdraw your invitation?" she countered bleakly, her eyes on his lips.

"Never. So we'll go to dinner?"

"Yes!"

He grinned when she bit out the words, as if a mere whispered acceptance, perfectly audible in the stillness of the cool night, would never have managed to escape her. He had decided to kiss her. It was there in his expression, even though her own was probably unwelcoming. She wanted to show some encouragement but the look wouldn't come. For she knew she would disappoint him; already her body was threatening rigidity. When Rob reached for her hand, she retreated a step inside her house.

"Eight o'clock Saturday, then."

He nodded, looking very amused.

After he was gone, Meg sagged against the closed door, every nerve tingling with disappointment. She heard the closing of his car door and listened for the start of an engine, but the night sounds remained undisturbed. It was obvious that he had been waiting for some encouraging sign from her before taking a kiss, and why not? What man would want a repetition of her stiff reaction of the night before? She felt throbbingly aware and regretted that she had sent him away without the caresses that might have put such needed warmth back into her too-carefully constructed life.

When the sound of footsteps crunched on the sidewalk, she threw open the door joyfully with no attempt to hide that she had been leaning weakly against it all along, hoping he would come back.

"You forgot your purse."

"What?" Meg stared at the small, tan cloth bag in his hands. She absolutely never forgot her purse. It was almost a religious thing with her, holding on to that purse with its comb and credit cards and Mike's baby pictures—all the things she had to have to survive.

"Isn't this yours?" He placed the bag in her hands. Of course it was. She had carefully closed it and laid it in the divider between the bucket seats after she had dug out her key. But to forget it? Positively Freudian. She looked up at him in total confusion. The heat from both their bodies seemed to intensify and reach out to mingle into steamy longing.

"Meghan Bronson."

He spoke her name reverently. She felt his hand trace along her forehead, smooth back the long blond hair at her temple, cup along her jaw. He was watching her all the while he touched her, undoubtedly noting the loneliness in her eyes mixed with apprehension, the shortness of breath that had the lacy neckline of her blouse rising and falling in puffs over her breasts. His eyes seemed to be questioning hers, but she was still unable to lean forward that slightest little bit that would encourage him to cover her lips with his own.

Help me! You take the initiative.

He did help her out. She sighed in satisfaction when he slipped his arms beneath hers to draw her against him. The purse fell to the floor and she eagerly clasped him near the shoulders, gripping those stringy hard muscles that had been straining against the sleeves of his soft shirt all evening. It was shockingly erotic to touch a man after so long.

"Mm."

Her undisguised murmur of pleasure drifted into his mouth when he finally kissed her. She closed her eyes, slanting her head slightly to taste more of him.

"Mm." His own satisfied sigh mingled with hers and the tentative kiss became greedy for them both. "Ah, you taste good."

You taste even better, she thought. Remembering his

sadness when he talked of Kansas, she began to meet each short foray of his with matching enthusiasm. His lips felt so good and healing to her that she ardently wanted to share some of that healing in return.

He rubbed her lips warmly, forcing them open just enough for their inner softness to cling to his mouth. She was vaguely aware that they must be creating quite a scene for the neighbors, standing as they did in the concentrated light of her doorway, but it felt so good to be wrapped in his arms within that haven from dark loneliness that she didn't care. She kissed him again— once for his artistic father, once for the intellectual mother, for the sisters—over and over before breaking away, laughing aloud. *Was she trying to pleasure him, or herself?*

Then he, too, was laughing and hugging her up off the ground. Meg flung her arms around his neck and clung there.

"This is crazy!"

"This is wonderful," he countered, kissing her so thoroughly this time that she felt some part of him must have thrust to the very core of her caring. She started to slip down along his body, and he broke away to steady her, but the minute her toes touched the ground, his lips again hungrily coupled with hers. One broad hand remained threaded in her hair while the other roved down to mingle with the lacy ruffles and soft fabric covering her breasts.

She wanted to be touched more thoroughly. He must have felt that in the way she lifted against him, for he immediately slid his fingers into the neckline of her blouse and warmly felt for her body.

"Women are shaped so much nicer than men," he praised huskily as he fondled her briefly before trying to slide her bra and blouse far enough away from her flesh so that he could see what he was shaping so tenderly.

Involuntarily she stiffened. It was one thing to be touched, another to have him turn her to the light and want to admire. Even though one part of her sensuality wanted to open her clothing for him, the wary, jaded part of her was grasping his hand and pulling it out of her blouse. The lacy neckline fluttered back into place. His fingers remained warmly quiet within hers, going no farther than she was ready to encourage.

"I, uh..."

"There'll be other times for us." He clasped her hands more tightly, trying to calm their trembling.

"Rob, I'm sorry."

"Sh," he murmured against her lips. "I'll see you at eight, Saturday." He hesitated only briefly before letting himself out.

Again she leaned against the door, feeling even more shocked and deprived than before. But this time she knew he wouldn't be coming right back. She'd have to wait until Saturday to make it up to him.

Chapter Three

Meg's regret that she had driven Rob away so precipitously lasted only a few moments. Then euphoria took over. Smiling foolishly, she thought again of her whimsical conclusion that dating was like riding a bicycle. She felt much as she had that day years ago when she had stomped into her parents house in Indiana with bruises all over her gawkly little legs and proudly announced that she had ridden her two-wheeler by herself for the first time.

Hey, everybody, I'm falling in love! I haven't forgotten how after all.

She floated toward her bedroom—"walked" was too earthbound a word for her present state of mind—glancing only cursorily toward the lamp table where she had hastily piled the mail hours earlier. Saturday and the chance to see Rob again seemed the only important thing to consider at that moment and she passed on, having no premonition about the ominous envelope buried between a catalog and a solicitation from a charity.

Meg was in no mood for forebodings, anyway. All

she could think about was Rob Dowell and what a surprise he was to her. Being able to let a man into her life again was such a welcome gift.

I really needed this boost, Meg mused as she wandered into the master bathroom and scrubbed the makeup off her glowing face. *And Rob did, too.* It pleased her that he had seemed to benefit as much from their evening together as she. That was the way it should be between a man and a woman. Noticing her reflection, she disbelievingly checked the mirror again—she *was* glowing! There was a radiance coming from within that told of excitement and awe that were all too new to her. She ran her fingertips across her still-sensitive lips.

Returning to the living room, Meg moved her abandoned purse to the lamp table, then restlessly began leafing through the mail, tossing aside the usual assortment of junk and making a neat pile of things that would need attention. She worked lightheartedly, more interested in planning ways in which she could overcome her compulsive discouragement of Rob Dowell's caresses than in her mail. Then she discovered the personal letter.

Dane Bronson.

The once-familiar name on the return address screamed out at her, but she couldn't really believe she had seen it correctly. She flipped on the table lamp to verify the name that matched her own. The shock was horrifying. *Oh, God, please, No!*

The envelope plummeted to the floor like some vile thing. Meg's senses reeled as if she'd been thrown off a cliff, and she grabbed the table to steady herself. But it still seemed as if she were drifting blindly downward in terrifying helplessness. She knew what inevitably awaited her in the abyss below. Disaster. Dane Bronson, her ex-husband.

But he couldn't be contacting her after five silent years. Not after the horror with him finally had seemed cleansed from her memory forever. Meg sank to a chair and forced herself to look at the unopened envelope lying obscenely at her feet.

He stayed sober long enough to write his name legibly, was her first pained reaction.

It hurt to think, and so she quit doing so. Instead, she took off her blouse and stepped out of her slacks. Odd, what a letter could do to you. Meg found herself instinctively tiptoeing to the closet, just as she used to so many years ago when she would come home from work to find Dane passed out on their bed. In fact, she recalled, she was lucky in those last days of their marriage if he made it to the bed. Too often he would end up draped over the kitchen table or sprawled half out of one of the easy chairs. Mike and whatever current maid Meg had been lucky enough to keep for more than a few days would be caged up in Mike's tiny bedroom, hoping not to disturb Dane. Back then, he was more pleasant to be around when he was unconscious.

Meticulously Meg hung up her clothes before pulling off her tennis shoes. Memories were dogging her, and she wanted them to go away.

"I haven't done my exercises yet," she told herself in disconnected obsessiveness. Normally she limbered up every night after work, especially if she had also spent the evening out. Perhaps her brain was telling her that by doing the usual things she could not be threatened by the unusual.

She sank to the carpeting near her bed and methodically began her leg stretches. Carefully she turned the right foot far to the side, then reached with toes pointed as far forward as possible. Pain moved all the way up her calf while Meg forced her stiffened joints and muscles to regain mobility. She repeated the process twice the usual number of times, then did the left foot. The food she had so enjoyed at the dockside picnic began to taste like bile in her throat, but still she fanatically continued her usual exercise routine. Knees flexed, she raised the legs together toward the ceiling, up and down, over and over again, then alternating one at a time, then bicycling with her hips high off the floor. She began to hurt everywhere.

But overworking her cramped muscles would not stop the functioning of her brain. *What does Dane want?*

Meg was sobbing by the time she had repeated her routines twice the usual number of times. Fighting her grief, she sat cross-legged in her panties and bra and braced her forehead against her hands until she could drive back the tears.

There was no use putting it off; she'd have to face the worst eventually. With dejected fatalism she swung to her feet and went to pick up the letter. Her eyesight was blurred as she pulled out the single sheet. The message was mercifully brief:

Dear Meg,

For the past year I have managed to remain dry, and a few months ago I married another recovering alcoholic I met through AA. Maybe I should have tried to patch it up with you before looking for someone else, but I felt that I had probably hurt you too much for things to ever be right with us. Karen and I live in Baton Rouge. We are convinced that we can remain permanently sober, so I want to see Mike again. I promise I won't disrupt your lives. I thought Mike might need me, and God knows Karen and I need him. I will be anxious to hear from you.

Dane

Never! He couldn't expect her to accept that. Disbelievingly she tossed the letter aside and fell back down on the rug. The tears kept threatening, and her moans of anguish were audible as she stubbornly returned to her workout. She stretched every muscle in her body almost to the breaking point, did a brutal number of push-ups, ran in place until she was breathless.

Even if she could forgive everything else, did he think she could forget their last few weeks together, when Mike had been lingeringly ill but she could never count on Dane to help with his care? He had known that she was taking Mike to the hospital, but he had gone out drinking anyway. And during those terrifying days when their son had been fighting for his life with pneumonia, Dane had disappeared despite her pleas and not shown up again until after Meg herself had also been seriously ill. Both she and Mike had had to pull through without, or perhaps despite, him.

And he expects me to trust our son with him again? He promises not to disrupt our lives?

The questions were so ludicrous that she began to

laugh. Hadn't she heard promises before? And, yes, he should have tried to patch it up with her first. He should have contacted her sometime during those five years; she had left enough encouraging messages with their attorney in case he ever showed up. Surely she had earned that courtesy, even though he had been right that it would have been too late to repair their marriage.

Her body collapsed with overexertion and shock. She sank to the floor and cried. Cried out for years of pent-up hurt, disgust, regret, years of guilt before she had finally bundled Mike out of their apartment and them both out of Dane's life. She hadn't been able to cry then—and not for the few additional months it had taken to locate him, not when she had learned Dane was still not seeking treatment, not even when the divorce had been finalized. With some help from her parents she had made it on her own and had never let up. Maybe she should have cried long ago.

After five years, not disrupt our lives?

There were no tears left. Meg picked the folded blanket from the foot of her bed, wrapped it around her, stumbled into the living room, and sank into a corner of the couch. She huddled there staring at the ceiling—thinking, yet not thinking.

Her mental impressions were a curious mixture: Mike's funny walk when he was a baby, the feel of Rob Dowell's hand against her cheek, the new roof she needed to have installed on her house, model showings at the store, Dane's helpless smile as he drank himself into self-destruction.

At least he was never violent. Her restless mind

jumped from past to present to past. She had always been grateful that physical abuse had not been an additional trauma she and Mike had had to learn to forget—only the destitution until she had left the new baby in a child-care center and earned their living, only Dane's stupor and argumentative incompetence. Only her unbearable regret that she couldn't help a man she had once adored and respected.

So much for believing I could love again, she thought listlessly. *Goodbye, Rob Dowell. I just remembered the lesson I've painfully learned about sharing my life. I'm a terrible failure at it. You deserve better.*

The hour was quite late and Meg's soul was empty when she finally fell asleep, still huddled into the corner of the couch.

"YOU WON'T BELIEVE WHAT George Palini's manager wants to do," Meg told Susan Forsyth when the young secretary brought in morning coffee on Friday. "With less than two weeks before the trunk showing, after the publicity and invitations have gone out, she wants to reschedule."

"But our customers have too much on their calendars to guarantee a good crowd if we change the date," Susan responded disbelievingly. She eased her bulky weight to a more comfortable position in the chair at the edge of Meg's desk and reached for her own orange juice. Susan's baby was due in late summer, and she was waging a constant battle with calories and caffeine. "Do you think Palini knows about this?"

"Probably not. No reputable designer ever reschedules this late. The letter I got this morning from his manager explained that some wealthy woman in Dallas wants a private showing on our day.''

"What are you going to do?"

"Tell Palini himself that we won't accept a change of date, that I can get other designers to serve our customers dependably."

"Crafty."

"I hope it gets us his showing on the right day. I think his clothes would go over big here, especially his furs. I'd arranged for him to send in a selection of jackets and stoles and have been talking them up. It would be embarrassing for us to cancel."

"He ought to realize how lucky he is to get scheduled at our store," Susan said defensively. "You run this place so much better than the Dallas boutiques I've worked in."

"Now, Susan," Meg warned in embarrassment. She always found it difficult to accept compliments.

"You ought to see how some of those boutique owners treat their customers," Susan insisted. "Like lazy, spoiled rich women. They're unctuous to their faces and nasty behind their backs. But you act as if you think your customers' clothing needs are important."

"Their clothing needs are important. I think it's great that not everyone has to earn her own living as I do. And I wouldn't want to take on some of the social commitments these women have to fulfill for their families. Lazy they're definitely not."

While they finished their coffee and juice, Meg scrawled a letter to Palini for Susan to type. She realized that Susan was watching her with friendly concern, apparently having noted the dark circles under Meg's eyes and the weariness in her voice. But Meg tried to maintain just enough detachment to discourage personal questions. And luckily, Susan bowed to the traditional separation between employer and employee and eventually took the draft of the letter to the adjoining workroom with no comment about Meg's troubles.

Penny Sands, however, had no such reservations. "You look awful," she told Meg bluntly when she came into the office later that afternoon. "I spend five little days over at the other store and you go to pot. What's wrong?"

"Palini's manager is trying to change the date on the trunk showing, but we can't let her get away with that. Susan's typing my letter to Palini, refusing to reschedule. You might want to look it over."

Wordlessly Penny went to the workroom. When she came back, she heartily approved of Meg's action. "Good for you. Now, what's your problem?"

Where do you want me to start? Dane's drunken parties in college, which I thought were just rare weekend fun? Mike? My lousy hangups, which are losing me Rob Dowell? Explanations could take all day.

"No problem. How's Charlie?"

"I think he has some trick up his sleeve—he's behaving himself for a change. Did Mike get home from the fishing trip okay?"

"They got in from Toledo Bend on Wednesday. The folks said he almost fell out of the boat twice, but otherwise things went great. Mike needs more chances to stretch himself outdoors."

This was all so civilized, Meg thought—talking about Mike when they were both skirting other issues. She

knew that Penny would come back to what had caused
those shadows under Meg's eyes that even makeup
couldn't cover. But how did you explain how shattering
it was to have spent five years convincing a child that
his ill and absent father really loved him, only to discover the myth could soon be twisted by reality?

It wouldn't help to seek advice. What was the recovery rate for alcoholics? All Meg could remember was
that AA had the best track record and that was
only . . . what percent? Who could guarantee to her that
Dane Bronson would be on the right end of the statistics?

"Mike caught seven fish." She continued with the
talk game she and Penny were playing. "Dad cleaned
them and Mike ate some of them. Maybe I'll finally be
able to expand my menu beyond hamburgers without
using force."

"Hm," Penny murmured, no longer even pretend-
ing she found the conversation interesting. She was
one tough businesswoman and hard to sidetrack. "I'd
like to help, you know," she said.

"I'm just a little under the weather." It alarmed Meg
that she was doing it again—after five years—falling
back into the trap of lying because she simply felt too
embarrassed, maybe too guilty, to admit that her husband was an alcoholic and she didn't know how to help
him. Certainly she didn't know if she dared let him see
Mike again. She hated the dishonesty but couldn't stop
it. "Actually, you could help me locate Rob Dowell. I
need to get out of a date tomorrow."

"Why would you want to?"

"Penny, will you help or not? I need to reach him."

"If I were younger I'd jump at the chance to go out with . . . oh, all right! He usually stays at the Holiday Inn when he's in town."

Meg reached for the phone directory, but Penny didn't leave politely to give her privacy. Since she hated to wait until getting home to have all the lying behind her, she uncomfortably made the call in Penny's presence.

Rob Dowell had apparently just checked in. When he answered, Meg quickly mumbled her excuses about her son being ill and how she was too concerned to leave him with someone else tomorrow. Rob's resonant voice sounded hurt, and Meg suspected that he didn't believe her story any more than Penny did. *But don't you understand? I don't want to hurt you more.* Her hands were shaking when she hung up.

"I thought it was you who was under the weather, not Mike. Didn't you already ask me if you could slip out for a few minutes tomorrow afternoon to chauffeur him to baseball practice?"

"Penny, please stay out of this."

Her boss looked at her consideringly, then dropped her eyes to the papers on her desk.

IT WAS PERFECT WEATHER FOR BASEBALL. Shreveport was having a dry day for a change, and the sunshine was most welcome. Rob Dowell strode out of the sports store where he had bought a mitt for lefties, and thrust his mirrored sunglasses over his eyes. Bright day, too. The kids on Diego Preston's team, he thought, should be able to get in a good workout.

As he drove along the streets busy with Saturday

shoppers, his bare arm welcomed the warmth of the sun through the open window. It was the kind of day that made a man want to take off his shirt and mow the grass. If he had a lawn. Scowling, Rob absentmindedly pushed the short sleeves of his polo shirt even higher and followed the directions Diego had given him for the ball diamond.

Her child was sick, Meghan Bronson had claimed. He'd have no problem with that reason for breaking a date, if it were the real reason. But he'd listened to Meghan Bronson's voice enough throughout the year to know that she was lying. She'd had that high, strained sound she got when she was trying to cope with a problem situation. He'd noticed it a time or two in the store when he'd been doing business with Penny Sands and Meg had been nearby taking care of a difficult customer.

Her son probably felt as marvelous this sunny day as he did. Marvelous, if you didn't count your battered emotions, Rob amended. His ego felt lousy. He'd rearranged his whole work schedule so that he could fly into Shreveport yesterday, just to be available to spend as much time with Meg over the weekend as she would allow. And the minute he'd walked into his room, exhausted but thinking it was all worth it, she had announced that she wouldn't give him even one evening.

He'd have been blisteringly angry if he didn't hurt so badly. It didn't help anything to wait until you were forty-two years old to fall in love, he thought ironically. A man was just as damn-silly vulnerable as a kid.

The park was coming up on the left. He pulled into the turn lane and waited for traffic to clear. A few boys

were already on the diamonds at the edge of the picturesque park, Diego Preston was standing nearby
studying a clipboard, and cars were pausing at the
azalea-filled circular drive while more parents let their
sons out for an afternoon of practice.

"At least this ball team gives me something to do
today," he scoffed as he unfolded from the rental car
and strode toward the diamond. There hadn't been
much sense in flying back to New Orleans; he could
spend a lonely weekend in a Shreveport motel just as
easily as in his efficiency apartment. When he had
called Diego Preston to see if he'd be in the family's
way fishing at their lake house again that weekend, it
had been diverting to be asked to coach Diego's team
instead. Helping Tommy Preston and his nine-year-old
friends should pass a few hours, anyway. Rob wiped his
hands on his gray sweat pants and slipped on the new
mitt.

He should have expected Meg to back out, he
thought while he stopped in midstride to punch a proper hole in the stiff leather pocket of the glove. She was
so high-strung whenever he ventured too close to her
emotions. Those hands of hers—those slender, gorgeous hands—gave her away. They trembled when she
was upset.

Patterned shadows from the many lush trees shading
the park played across his forearms as he methodically
shaped his glove. Oh, he knew lots about Meghan
Bronson. He had been watching her closely enough for
a whole year, waiting like some lovesick kid for her to
be ready for him. Somehow the way she had vamped
him when they had unexpectedly had that dinner meet-

ing alone had given him a miscue. He was experienced enough to recognize flirting signals. True, she had backed off each time almost as immediately as she had advanced, but he had definitely felt that she would be receptive to seeing more of him. He scuffed his worn tennis shoes in the thick grass while his powerful left hand continued to batter at the emerging pocket of the glove. Apparently he had rushed her; he regretted that.

"Hey, man! I didn't see you come." He looked up to catch a relieved expression on his friend's face. "I promised the kids that we had a semipro coming to help coach today, and they'd murder me if you didn't show!"

Rob thrust Meghan Bronson out of his thoughts and loped the last few feet to join Diego Preston. "I had to stop for a mitt," he explained.

As soon as the boys realized that Rob was their awaited celebrity, lots of little bodies in scruffy blue jeans and outrageous T-shirts advertising everything from Florida to Boy George came merging on them all at once. The babble of excited nine-year-old voices was encompassing.

"Quiet, you monsters!" Diego's Latin temperament from his mother's side of the family made itself momentarily evident in his shout. Then the Preston side took over and he grinned sheepishly at the subdued kids. "This is the Mr. Dowell I told you about," he told them. "He's going to help us out today, so don't waste his time."

"Your glove looks funny," a redhead next to Rob observed.

"That's because it's new. I didn't have my own

equipment along, so I had to buy a glove, but I need to soften it up with neat's-foot oil.''

"No, I mean how does it fit your fingers?"

"Oh, that. I throw left-handed, so I have to wear it on the right hand, see?" He picked up a ball, thumped it loudly against the leather pocket a couple of times, then flipped it lightly to one of the players.

"Sir? I thought we had to throw with the hand our gloves aren't on."

A sturdy, short boy with shining black hair looked puzzled. A new glove hung awkwardly on his left hand.

"Mike, do you mean to tell me you're left-handed?" Diego asked incredulously.

"I write with it. But I've been trying to throw with my right because the glove you gave me only goes on my left.''

"Oh, for...kid! We'll see that you get a lefty's glove. It goes on your right hand so your good arm is free for throwing. Anyone else here left-handed?"

All the remaining voices were silent. Diego sent the boys out on the diamond to warm up throwing balls while he cleared his practice plans with Rob. "And I thought I was doing the kids such a big favor buying the gloves for them," he said, groaning. "That kid is one of Tommy's best friends and has been around the house forever. It never dawned on me he was a lefty. I've been wondering why he was so awkward at practice.''

"His dad should have said something."

"No dad. And I guess it didn't occur to his mother. She's a great gal and would certainly have bought him what he needed. I'm glad we found out before the season was over."

"I saw some kids' lefties' gloves at the store where I got this," Rob said. "Why don't I just run him over there now? I remember how frustrating it was not to have the correct equipment."

"Good idea. Hey, Mike!"

The boy came running up eagerly. "I can throw a lot better with my real hand," he told Rob enthusiastically. Rob could see the red marks where he had been catching the ball barehanded.

"I'll bet you can. Come on, we're going to get your glove. Then just wait and see how well you can catch, too!"

The child was not a chatterbox like Rob's little nephews and nieces. He climbed into the car and had relatively little to say until they got into the store. Then he asked Rob well-thought-out questions while they selected the right size and weight glove for him. That took a few moments. Rob was surprised at how large his hands were for the rest of him. He was a short rock of a child with hands like weapons.

"You ought to make a good first baseman," he told Mike seriously as he discarded the smallest-sized glove and selected another. "Being left-handed is an advantage there, and you look strong enough to keep runners from mowing you down."

"Mr. Preston's just been having me sub in the outfield."

"Wait till he sees what you can do using the correct hand." Rob grinned. He liked this kid named Mike. Freckle-faced, with big blue eyes, polite, but deep, too—all the things a boy should be. The glove fitted, and they bought it quickly so that they could hurry back to the field and not miss much.

Mike hovered around Rob most of the practice time. He was a quick learner, and he got the feel of his glove after only a dozen or so tosses from Rob. When the team's throwing routines were completed, Diego called the boys in for some group instruction. It embarrassed Rob that his friend enthusiastically began explaining how Mr. Dowell had maintained the best batting average in the history of the Southwest College League and had managed to play semipro ball for a couple of years before his work made it impossible. It seemed so long ago and of no interest to kids. When Diego got to the part about his turning down a major league offer, Rob interrupted and started arranging the team in two lines. He had never been one to dwell on shattered dreams.

Batting practice was where Diego most wanted Rob's help. Almost all the boys had a terrible stance, and they held the bat in a variety of ingenious but incorrect ways. Some of them picked up the instruction fast, but others needed constant reminding.

The kid named Mike seemed a natural athlete, once he knew that he could use his 'good' arm. When they started a couple of practice innings, Rob suggested that Diego give him a whirl at first base, and although the boy made a number of errors because he didn't know the position, it was obvious that he would be able to learn his skills well. He had a strong arm, his concentration was intense, and he didn't scare easily when the bigger boys came barreling down the line hoping to scare him off base.

When the practice began to break up, Tommy Preston asked Mike to spend the night at his house, and the two boys ran ahead toward the arriving cars to ask Mike's mother, while Diego and Rob followed more leisurely.

"I wish you'd be in town every Saturday. The kids have never performed this well," Diego said, wiping sweat from his brow.

"They'd get tired of hearing from me soon enough." Rob laughed deprecatingly but was tempted anyway. It had felt good to unwind his muscles on the ball diamond; he traveled too much to play on a team anymore and had had to settle for golf. Fun, but not the same kind of workout.

"You handle kids well. Why didn't you have a bunch of your own?"

"That would have been inconvenient, since I'm not married," Rob observed cynically. It was a sore point. He loved children, and while he had never been in a position where he could even consider marriage until recently, the desire for a family of his own had always been strong. Another shattered secret dream it was better not to dwell on.

He grinned sadly to himself. Those boys today had been so much fun. Cheeky. Sometimes insubordinate, sometimes rapt with attention. And, of course, muddy. They had managed to find every soggy spot on the field and roll in it. Just good old kids. He had loved it. And that boy Mike. That would be a kid any parent could be proud of. He had blossomed under just a little bit of instruction.

"That Mike of yours is going to be some ball

player," he said seriously as they walked up to a small Aries, where Mike and Tommy were apparently doing a fast-talk on Mike's mother. "It will take him a few weeks to hit his stride after trying so long to shift over to the right hand."

"Hey, sir! I want you to meet my mom!" Mike yelled out. "I told her about the glove and she wants to thank you."

Rob grinned at being addressed as sir. It was an expected courtesy of well-trained Southern youngsters toward strangers that he found charming. The slight smile was still on his face and he was totally unprepared when Meghan Bronson stepped out of the car, her long blond hair blowing about her face. Her expression was shining with courteous gratitude until she recognized him. Then she froze in dismay.

Rob suddenly didn't feel too well himself. So Mike was the little boy who was so ill that she was going to hover over him with matronly care all evening. Rob had known all along that it was just an excuse to get out of seeing him, but to have it so vividly confirmed—his cynical chagrin showed. Tommy was babbling about the practice, Mike was standing at his side announcing names, and Meghan looked as if she wished a hole would swallow her up.

I can either stalk off like an outraged high schooler— Rob tried to conquer his pride, which hurt as painfully as if he were indeed still a splotchy-faced adolescent— *or I can try to salvage something out of this.*

He decided on the salvage job. He had been waiting for Meghan Bronson for a year, and his interest in her was too deep to throw it all over yet.

"Your son has the makings of a real ball player, Mrs. Bronson." He extended his hand as if he had never met her before. "Especially after he knew it was permissible to throw with his left hand." Somehow he managed a light laugh. Meg's hand was automatically thrust into his, but it felt like a cold, limp fish and he released her immediately.

She looked anguished, yet Rob almost felt that she was suffering more for him than for herself. Her face was as red as the casual cotton jump suit she wore, and she looked so unconsciously damn sexy that it was a sin.

"I hope you're going to let Mike spend the night with us, Meg," Diego added, not noticing her stricken expression because he was getting lots of "Ask her, ask her, Daddy" signals from Tommy. "Molly thought it would be a good time to get them together, since they'll have to start back to school on Monday."

"She already said I can if it's all right with you." Mike was all grins. "But I have to go home first and clean up, then she'll bring me over."

"Run him by in time for supper," Diego told Meg. "In fact, come for supper yourself. I'm cooking hamburgers outside and Molly bought plenty of food. Old Rob here has turned me down, but maybe I can change his mind."

Rob watched every change in Meg's expression. If anything, she seemed to be growing more concerned for him, rather than less. Wondering why, he thought of an outrageous move. He would be exposing himself to more abuse, but wasn't Meghan Bronson worth climbing out on a limb for? He'd never find out what was fermenting in her mind if he couldn't get close enough to talk.

"Actually, I've been stood up on a date tonight and I have reservations for two at Malone's. Maybe I could come help drop you off, Mike, then talk your mom into using those reservations with me. What do you think?"

Mike thought it was a great idea. He was tugging at Meg's hand and trying to give her a 'say-yes' demand without getting into trouble. Meg flushed even more, and the silence grew thick. Finally she mumbled an un-exuberant acceptance.

Diego took their plans in good grace, and within minutes everyone was leaving the ball diamond, with Rob promising Mike that he would be at their house in a half hour sharp. As Rob hurried to his motel he didn't know whether to be pleased or disgusted with what he'd engineered. Either way it promised to be a tense evening, and among the many things he wanted out of Meghan Bronson, grudging politeness was certainly not one of them.

IT WAS A GOOD THING they had reservations. Malone's was packed with the racetrack crowd. Shreveport had welcomed horse racing to the community a few years earlier, and certainly the big-money crowds attracted to the ponies brought in lots of business during the season. But the thousands of out-of-town visitors made eating out on Saturday nights a pain in the neck.

The restaurant was noisy as well as crowded. Meg took her seat across from Rob Dowell at their table in the corner and wondered if the surrounding excited chatter was sufficient excuse to postpone conversation. She would have to start with an apology, and she couldn't imagine how to approach it. She watched Rob loosen the tie hugging the oxford collar that was so startlingly white against his tanned neck. Her eyes followed the movement of his throat muscles as he spoke.

"Would you like a cocktail?"

"No, thank you. You go ahead, though." She readjusted the high mandarin collar of her own rose silk dress. It was a nervous reaction that did nothing to relieve the strain apparent in her voice.

"I usually prefer a wine," he resumed with persevering good manners. "Would you like to share mine?"

"That would be nice. You select it." She studied him as he read the wine menu. His lashes were dark and thick like his hair; his mouth and jaw were almost sternly firm, yet something about his irregular face exuded kindness. Under candlelight his hands looked every bit as massive and competent as when she had noticed them in the car. The fingernails were clipped square across. No nonsense about those hands. Her regret increased. "I owe you an apology," she plunged in after he had ordered the wine.

"Not really. If you don't want to go out with a man, your only obligation is to say so in the first place. Somewhere along the line last week I must have misread what I thought were encouraging signals, so a simple explanation would be nice."

"An explanation?" She laughed bitterly. "You think I have an explanation for standing up an attractive, very nice man whom I admire a great deal? I chickened out, that's all."

"Were you afraid of me? I admit the idea of sleeping

with you has occurred to me more than once. But I'm not so desperate that I'd force the issue."

"No! It had nothing to do with you. Rob, I just don't date."

Don't ask why. My ghosts have to stay buried or I'll fall apart. Now is not the time for me to fall in love. I have no warmth to give you.

"I'm sorry to hear that. I've waited a year to go out with you. Ever since I met you, that morning your Penelope decided that she needed to increase pregnancy benefits on her insurance coverage."

Meg smiled involuntarily, remembering it well. Penny had been funny—at her erratic worst—and yet the new Mr. Dowell had patiently listened to her harangue about family planning not being what it used to be, had calmly made suggestions for the insurance care of the errant employees, and had gone away, leaving Penny mollified and Allied with a new customer.

"I do remember your handling Penny's dramatics very diplomatically."

"And I remember your wearing a blue dress with big puffy sleeves. One of your staff—Susan, I believe—came up while I was waiting near your desk. She wanted you to fill in as a blind date at a dinner party she was giving and you turned her down. Once I knew you were eligible, that was it. I was hooked."

Meg stared at him, almost afraid to believe.

"You've always held yourself so aloof, I figured I'd scare you off if I asked you out," he continued. "Last week seemed different, so I risked it."

She was both surprised and touched by his admission. "You're good for my ego, Robert Dowell."

"You're hard on my libido, Meghan Bronson."

"So that's it?" she asked hesitantly. "End of my explanation?"

"End of your explanation. You're chicken. I'm going to enjoy dinner with you and take each hour as it comes."

Her hands relaxed slightly in her lap. "Do you know what I remembered most about you? Your freebies. It's gotten to be sort of a game with me, wondering what you'll bring next."

"Some of my customers think they're silly."

"Oh, they are. That's why they're so wonderful."

Her response seemed to please him. The waiter arrived with their wine and they sipped it slowly, sometimes enjoying silence, other times talking lazily about Mike's interest in baseball, Rob's travel schedule, Meg's love of science fiction. But as nearby diners consumed more cocktails and their stories of winnings at the track became louder, it became genuinely difficult to talk together.

"We're lucky this big table next to us has been held for reservations." Meg leaned slightly toward Rob to make herself heard.

"The big group that just came in looks headed this way," he warned, glancing past her shoulder toward the door. "Our conversation may be over."

A ball of noise seemed to be surrounding the group as they moved past Meg and began fitting into seats at the large table. Apparently all of them had started their celebration before arriving at the restaurant.

Meg, with a wary sixth sense developed from long practice, noticed that one of the men was in much worse shape than anyone else in the crowd. He was thoroughly intoxicated. She picked up her napkin, re-folded it, shook it out again and rearranged it in her lap, all the time keeping her eyes downcast and hoping that the new diners would decide the arrangements didn't suit them and leave. Her hope went unfulfilled; the noise level became permanently higher as the group settled in. Meg lifted her hands to the table and tried to relax.

"The headwaiter was missing his marbles to seat that party," Rob said quietly. "I'm sorry about this."

"You can't help it." There was no point bothering to say more. Things had become so raucous that even the other relatively noisy parties nearby were looking at the new group with disdain.

"Sh." One of the new women giggled loudly and punched both men next to her with her elbows. She found the situation amusing, but was enough intimi-dated by the glares they were receiving from throughout the room to try to hush her companions. The group did quiet down slightly, but the intoxicated man seemed unable to control himself. He began shouting loudly for the waiter. A meek-looking woman next to him kept try-ing to distract his attention while reassuring him that the round of drinks they had ordered was on the way.

To Meg, the scene seemed to be taking place in slow motion like some television instant replay. The man's obnoxious behavior mixed in her mind as a repetition of remembered dinners with Dane Bronson. He wouldn't quiet down anytime soon, Meg thought. At least not if the woman were the only one working with him. *They never listen to their wives.*

The noise drifted evilly around her. A waiter began

trying to calm the group. Eventually two of the men managed to talk their boisterous friend into a trip to the rest room, and everyone nearby breathed relief. Meg couldn't separate what was real and what was being re- gurgitated within her brain.

Her salad arrived but remained uneaten before her. Her napkin was pleated into dozens of tiny, erratic folds. Rob watched her steadily. Resolutely she picked up her salad fork and lifted a small mound of greens. They looked vile and she began to feel nauseated. She carefully laid the filled fork back on the plate and in- stead reached for her wineglass. Then realizing what she was doing, she shoved it away.

"Would you like some bread?"

Rob's calm voice was like a light in the darkness of the past. She focused on his face and caught in the pe- riphery of vision a filled basket being lifted near her. Gratefully she clenched her fingers around a hard roll. *That* she could hold on to. *That* her churning stomach could tolerate. She watched Rob's capable fingers break his own roll open so that the crusty crumbs spilled out in brown flaking disarray on his bread plate. Mechani- cally she followed his motions, laid most of the roll on the china among the pile of unavoidable crumbs, lifted a small piece to her mouth, chewed it dutifully. Some- how she forced it down her throat. Rob drank a sip of water and she followed suit as if she were his clone.

The subdued men and their hopeless companion were returning. The drunk was quiet now. Meg knew the next stage as if by heart. He'd manage to stumble back to his seat, a grim expression of concentration of his still-damp face after they'd splashed enough icy

water on him to shock him into cooperating. The rest
of the men would all be looking pained, suddenly realizing the mess they were in—they still had to feed the
ladies and get him out of there. Their wives would soon
be sobered enough to resent his ruining their party.
The alcoholic's wife would be sweating cold and hot
but keeping an artificial smile on her stone face while
she pretended not to notice that her husband was
gradually slumping into a listless heap at her side.

The scenario developed as anticipated. Meg kept
breaking apart the bread, finding it more and more difficult to do so with her sweating, shaking hands. Salads
were served at the table next to them. The clatter of
forks and superficial conversation could not cover up the
great shuddering snores being emitted from the man's
slack mouth. And still the wife faced forward as if nothing was wrong, even though her eyes were diamond-
bright with unshed tears. As were Meg's own.

"Meg, I think I should take you home."

She tried to answer Rob, but her voice wouldn't
work. Gratefully she nodded her agreement. She felt
him remove the battered bread from her fingers; saw
him place money beneath a plate, then make a quiet
explanation to the waiter who had arrived with their
steaks. Her legs moved automatically in response to the
reassuring hand at her back as he guided her out of the
restaurant.

Once she was tucked into Robert Dowell's car, the
disorientation of past and present mixed with the chills
and sweating. She buried her head in her hands, moaning brokenly, "Rob, I'm so sorry to do this to you. I
don't know what happened. So sorry!"

Chapter Four

"That was more than a nice lady's natural abhorrence of a public scene." Rob spoke quietly as he brushed her hair. Somehow he had gotten her undressed and into a gown and robe, had bathed her face, and had tucked her into a corner of her couch. She leaned listlessly against his knee while he perched on the arm of the furniture and tried to loosen her tangles.

She sighed, still unable to do much for herself, yet feeling closer to control. There was nothing like the normality of freshening up to quiet hysteria.

"So who was the alcoholic in your life? Mother, husband, lover?"

"Please stop," she protested brokenly. She had never talked about it. Not to anyone.

"Who was it?" The deceptively casual questioning and the brushing both continued relentlessly. She felt the bristles move across the loose hair at her temple before blending with the mass flowing down her back.

"Husband," she whispered.

"For how long?" The brush soothed at the other

side of her throbbing head, softening each golden strand, again and again.

She tried to think. "How long?" he had asked. *Forever. Since the beginning of love and despair.*

"About five years. He drank heavily at college and had become an alcoholic before we graduated, but I was too dumb to realize it."

"I've heard teenaged metabolism is so speeded up that some previously teetotaling kids can get hooked within months."

"I've learned that, too. But understanding doesn't make the results easier to handle." She sounded as despairing as she felt.

He laid the brush aside. Her hands were still icy when he began chafing them. "You're certain you don't need to take a hot bath?"

Glancing down at her robe, she became aware of the intimate tasks she had allowed him to perform for her, but somehow she was unembarrassed. She had needed help desperately, and he had impersonally tendered it. It was that simple.

"No, I'm warm enough. I'd rather stay here. You'll need something to eat."

He turned her hands over and began massaging the fingers.

"I'll raid your refrigerator later. Is he left-handed?"

"Who?"

"Your former husband. I take it no one in your own family is, or you would have known to ask for a left-handed ball glove."

Since he acted as if coping with her whole bad scene

had been no trouble, she began to believe that she might make it through this disastrous day if she didn't let herself think about that unanswered letter. "No one in Dane's or my family except Mike is left-handed," she managed to say steadily. "Mike looks just like his father in every other way."

"He certainly doesn't look like you. I would never have guessed he was yours if you hadn't shown up at the ball park this afternoon. Is his father tall?"

Is? It seemed strange to think of Dane in the present tense. He had been dead to her so long, even before she left him. "I think he was...is only about my height."

"You're relatively tall, though. Mike might make a good pitcher, but I wouldn't recommend that you let him do it until he's quit growing. Too hard on the joints."

Her hands were becoming almost as warm as the rest of her body.

"I'll keep that in mind," she mumbled drowsily. His persistent focusing on mundane subjects had her confused. She wondered what time it was. "You must be exhausted," she murmured before closing her eyes.

Rob walked back to her bedroom to return the brush to her night table. He had been hasty when caring for her. The towel he had dried her sweat-moistened body with lay in a heap on the floor near her discarded clothes, so he began putting everything away properly. In addition to her built-in closet she had an old-fashioned wardrobe whose cherry inlaid wood matched the headboard of her double bed. The wardrobe seemed to be full of her best things, so he hung her lovely silk dress there and laid her lingerie on the antique wash-stand. The room, like the rest of the house, matched his impression of Meghan Bronson. Simple, but full of un-derstated quality.

When Rob returned and found Meg asleep he didn't even try to move her. She appeared only superficially under, and he didn't want to risk disturbing her. In-stead, he retrieved the blanket folded across the foot of her bed, draped it over her and turned off the living-room lights. In the kitchen he put together a cheese sandwich and ate it, then checked her again. Finding her still asleep, he walked toward the front door, then changed his mind and went resolutely to the other bed-room. She was not going to wake up alone in her house.

As Rob turned back Mike's spread and set aside the miscellany of books, cars and stuffed animals treasured near the pillow, it touched him how the sturdy little boy had been allowed to surround himself with things he loved. On the dresser was a picture of Meg and Mike on a Ferris wheel at an amusement park. She had her arm around him, her smiling face sharing his pleasure and softening her protectiveness. In a toy box beside his bed was a collection of sports paraphernalia—a soc-cer ball, two baseballs, a badminton racket. On a shelf nearby were other goodies. Seeing scissors on top of a crayon box, he curiously picked them up. High-quality lefties'! Grinning, he carefully put them back. So she had anticipated some of the boy's special needs. She just didn't understand about sports. He'd have to tell her about left-handed hockey sticks.

Kicking off his shoes before stretching out fully-clothed on the child's bed, Rob felt particularly close to

Mike. He glanced over at the picture again and thought how lucky that boy was. His mother would nurture his interests and do all in her power to make his dreams possible. And if his hopes had to be abandoned, she'd be there with understanding to help see him through the disappointment.

Yes, a very lucky boy.

Rob lay still and held his breath until he could hear Meg's own shallow breathing from the darkened room beyond. Then he expelled a sigh of contentment, grateful that he had long ago learned to be a light sleeper. If she needed him, he'd hear her.

"I'VE PROBABLY RUINED YOUR REPUTATION. I considered moving my car a couple of blocks away and slipping in the rear door, but I didn't want to leave you alone that long." Rob's tired voice revealed how lightly he had dozed throughout the night.

Meg transferred sizzling bacon from a pan to paper towel and turned off the flame. "I'm glad you stayed. It would have been bad to wake up alone in the house. I haven't thought about my life with Dane for a long time. Something happened earlier this week that made the man in the restaurant bring it all back."

"Maybe you should reexamine those years more often."

"And go through another melodrama like last night? No, thank you. I've never admired hysterical women."

As she put a plate of bacon and eggs before him, she noticed that his tie was gone, his shirt was loosened at the collar and his unshaven face hinted of a heavy beard. Still, Meg thought, he probably looked better than she. Although she had made an attempt at starting a bright day by changing into white slacks and a yellow short-sleeved sweat shirt, her face showed the ravages of tension and fatigue.

"About your reputation..." He seemed to have that on his mind.

"Please don't worry. I really needed a friend and I'm grateful that you stayed. Although the neighbors will know that I had a man at my house all night, they're enlightened enough not to run me out of town."

He seemed to be pondering whether or not she meant the reassurance. Reaching a positive conclusion, he suddenly relaxed and picked up his silverware. "I wish I'd known Shreveport's morals were that liberated," he said in mocking regret while he forked a generous mound of eggs toward his mouth. "I would have taken advantage of you after all. Mm, this beats motel breakfasts."

It felt marvelous to smile at his disconnected craziness. She couldn't believe that she could do it so soon after the previous night. "Rob?"

"Huh?"

She wanted to tell him how wonderful he looked across the breakfast table from her. She wanted to say how comforting it had been to lean on his strength for those crucial moments. She wanted to laugh with him again. "Oh, just...thank you."

He glanced up. "You owe me a dinner date, you know. Next time I'm in town, do you want to go to some intimate place like Quickie Chickie, where I can do lecherous things to you at our plastic table for two? Bump your knees? Pinch your thighs?"

She listened incredulously. The man was unbelievable. After what she'd put him through, was this teasing to be it? No demand for emotional confessions? No lectures?

"Yes or no? A straight answer and no backing out later," he warned mockingly.

His plate was almost empty, so she got extra toast out of the oven.

"Yes or no?" His question had lost its teasing quality when he helped himself to the seconds she offered him.

"Yes," she murmured. "If you can tolerate a very mixed-up woman."

"We'll take each day at a time, okay?"

They must have been staring deep into each other's eyes, for it was a wrench to break the hypnotic bond. "One at a time," she agreed.

THEY DECIDED ON THE FOLLOWING SUNDAY evening for their rain-check dinner together. Rob had first suggested Saturday, but since it was Meg's weekend to cover the store, they had settled on the next day, to give her a chance to rest up. That expectation had proved fruitless. Sunday afternoon found Meg at the store again, working with Penny. The Palini trunk showing, which was scheduled for the coming Thursday, continued to develop one surprise after another that required their attention.

"What fool said work is therapeutic?" Penny grumbled, not for the first time that afternoon. "They weren't talking about work on Sunday."

It's therapeutic on any day, Meg corrected mentally,

thinking that with Dane's letter to ponder, her job had been a therapeutic godsend. Her job and the expectation of seeing Rob Dowell again.

"I had thought your letter to George Palini was a good idea," Penny continued her grumbling. "But now I'm not so sure. Who would have thought the designer would come to Shreveport himself to mollify us? It makes this showing a lot more complicated."

"You adore this kind of complication," Meg retorted cheerfully, knowing acceptances were already so numerous that they would have to clear out additional merchandise racks in their south salon to make room for the guests. "And think of all your Dallas friends who are coming over. Getting Palini himself is a coup even Neiman's hasn't pulled off. Admit it, this work agrees with you! You look years younger since you've been setting up champagne catering and television coverage."

"I love the potential extra sales, not the work," Penny corrected, pushing back from her desk and stretching her tired shoulders.

"So quit complaining."

"Oh, Lord, you know what we've forgotten?"

"What now?"

"Additional insurance. I have a policy covering routine trunk showings, but with Palini here and the television crews in, plus that special selection of furs, I'll have to have a rider. Damnation! How will I locate Rob Dowell? He wanders all over the South."

"I think he's in town. Mike said he was at their baseball practice yesterday."

"Your Mike's baseball practice? I thought you weren't going out with Rob."

"Quit getting ideas. He's a friend of Diego Preston, who coaches the baseball team Mike plays on." Meg wasn't about to tell Penny she would be seeing Rob that evening. She knew how Penny's matchmaking mind worked, and Penny, unlike Charlie, adored meddling.

"How interesting."

"Is Palini bringing a model? If so, you'll have to insure for her, too." Fortunately, though an affectionate meddler, Penny was also easy to distract when business was on her mind. Meg's devious question triggered a whole new batch of arrangements that needed to be made, and they worked another hour without any more intrusions into Meg's fragile and too newly precious love life.

"I WISH YOU DIDN'T HAVE TO WORK on Sundays." Mike's wistful complaint came while Meg drove the three short blocks from her parents' house, where he had spent the afternoon, to their own.

"I wish not, too, honey," she said. "But at least we'll have a few hours together before Mr. Dowell and I drop you off at Grandma's tonight."

"You had to work yesterday, too."

Meg didn't even try to placate him by pointing out that this weekend scheduling didn't happen often. When her son complained about her work, it generally meant something else was on his mind, and if she waited long enough she would find out what it was. All in all, she felt Mike had much less to complain about than most children of working mothers. Twice a week they had an excellent afternoon maid who enjoyed having Mike home with her. After school on other days he waited for Meg at her parents' home. And Penny almost always would take over for her at the store if Mike was ill, or there was a special program at school.

"Delberta said that after you came home from ball practice yesterday, you went right outside again to play catch with Corey. How's the new glove working out?"

"Okay."

"Only okay?"

"It would be working really good if you had let Mr. Dowell practice with me today."

"Me *let* Mr. Dowell? I don't know what you're talking about."

She pulled into the carport and turned to look at Mike. He was staring sullenly ahead.

"I told Mr. Dowell he could come over this afternoon and play catch, but he said he thought you had other plans. If you hadn't had to work, he could have come."

So that was what was bothering him. Meg felt suddenly weary as she got out of the car. Yellow pollen from the huge pine trees lining her backyard had blown all over the carport. She walked through a good half inch of the sticky yellow film to the door. Mike was still pouting in the car while she unlocked the house.

"Come on in, Mike." She tried to control her growing impatience. "And be careful—the floor's slippery." Obviously he still wanted to punish her by refusing to get out. But years of being programmed to behave stood him in good stead, and he finally climbed from the car. His expression, however, was not happy as he scuffled toward her.

"What's this yellow stuff?"

"It's pollen from the pine trees. Don't kick it up so much! It can burn your skin and make you cough."

"Is that why Corey's little sister is sneezing and blowing her nose all the time?"

"Maybe. There are lots of spring things coming out right now that bother some people." She took off her shoes in the mud-laundry room that opened off the garage.

"Leave yours here, son, on the paper by mine. I'll need to clean up those favorite Nikes right away or that pollen will ruin them."

Mike plopped down in the middle of the floor and pulled at his shoes, but they wouldn't slip off without being untied. His dark hair fell across his forehead, and he frowned in concentration while his big hands, not yet having grown into mature dexterity to match their size, fumbled with the laces. Her heart softened at the dear picture he made. He was usually such a cooperative and understanding child; sometimes she felt that perhaps she pushed him too much into adulthood.

"Son, I'm sorry your weekend was boring. Next Saturday morning would you like—"

"And I told Mr. Dowell I could go out to dinner with you tonight, too, because I know how to eat in restaurants, and he said that would be up to you. But when I asked Grandma today she said definitely not."

"Why would you want to go along, anyway?" Meg asked soothingly. "We're eating at one of those clubs you always hate when Grandpa takes us. Salads and vegetables, fish with all those sauces."

"Mr. Dowell likes me."

Mike got his shoes off and came into the kitchen. While she watched him rinse off his hands at the kitchen sink, she mulled the psychological significance of what he had just said.

"Well, I like you, too. Now, what are we going to have for a snack?"

The blatant bribery to his stomach wasn't completely effective. Mike was still grumpy when they finished off the cookies Meg had made earlier that week. But he disappeared into his own room to play, apparently having decided it wouldn't do him any good to wheedle further, since Grandmother had spoken on the subject.

Meg watched with some sympathy as he ambled away. How well she remembered the intimidating way her mother could say "definitely not." Even now Meg didn't readily ignore dictums issued in that rare tone of voice. But in this instance she felt guiltily relieved that her mother had taken a stand to protect her evening out. How much she wanted to spend a few quiet moments with Rob Dowell—woman to man, no children, no past, no future. Just a few moments of conversation and laughter that could chase away the pressures that would eventually have to be tackled.

Mr. Dowell likes me. The poignant statement came back to her. So her son needed some of that man's healing charisma, too.

Sighing, Meg hurriedly cleaned both pairs of shoes, then went to her own room to change, wondering if one could ever adequately meet the needs of all the people one loved.

"I ALMOST FORGOT TO MENTION that Penny wants to see you," Meg told Rob after they had finished their meal at the country club where Allied maintained a membership and where Rob frequently played golf when he was in town.

"What for?"

She was relieved that he didn't make a sarcastic quip about being glad someone wanted to see him, as he probably was justified to make. She had been so fearful of appearing overeager that she had reactively given him a boring evening of superficial conversation.

"Thursday we're having the biggest trunk showing Penelope's has ever attempted," she related dutifully, knowing that it was too late to salvage her social graces, anyway. "I think I've told you about trunk showings. Anyway, one of the hottest young designers from New York is coming in person. He's bringing some of his summer and fall fashions, plus a special selection of furs, chosen with our customers in mind."

"And she's getting nervous about fire and theft, right?"

"Very right," she agreed. "Plus the ramifications of a bigger crowd than we've ever handled and TV coverage. Could you see her on Monday?"

"I'll be in Dallas Monday morning. But tell her I'll call her from there."

"Dallas? I thought you came here for several days of business."

"I came here this weekend to see you."

"That's all?"

"That's everything. Believe it."

His frank statement flustered her, and she couldn't

think of anything else to say while he signed for the check.

She was still bumblingly speechless when they paused on the rear porch, which overlooked the golf course.

"Mike played ball well yesterday." His hand settled lightly on her shoulder, and her eyes involuntarily followed the direction of his, focusing on a quartet of golfers coming in on their carts from the last hole just as the sun was dimming its orange glow to a pink sunset. Involuntarily she relaxed against his touch.

"He's like a different player since you got him into a lefty's glove," she said gratefully. "I can see a big difference when we play catch."

"You play catch with him?"

"Don't laugh. With two older brothers I had to learn to play ball. They always needed an extra fielder for the neighborhood games. Of course, old age is catching up with me. I figure Mike's throws will be too strong for my catching capacity in about two more years."

He smiled and his arm tightened slightly. "I know about old age catching up with you. That's why I turned to golf."

"You don't like it as well as baseball?"

"Definitely not."

"Did you get to play baseball as much as you wanted even when you were younger?" she asked sympathetically. "With your traveling job, it must have been almost impossible to fit into a regular team."

It puzzled her that he fell still instead of answering. Then he turned her just slightly and leaned his face against her cheek. She wasn't certain he had even kissed her. There had just been a sigh of a caress and a pausing of his firm jaw against the curtain of her hair along her throat.

"Meghan Bronson, you're an exceptionally astute woman."

As they crossed the parking lot Meg thoughtfully looked out over the serenity of the well-groomed course. "I guess when Mike gets an interest in golf I hunt him up some left-handed clubs. Right?"

"Wrong." He helped her into the car.

"What do your mean, wrong?" she asked when they were driving home. "Didn't you tell me he'd need a lefty's hockey stick? And—"

"Golf is different from other sports. A left-handed man has an advantage in the strength of his wrists if he can learn to play right-handed. You'll see that in the pros. And if he's serious about baseball and bats left-handed, as Mike does, it's much better for him to switch for golf. You use a different wrist action in batting than in swinging a golf club. Right-handed boys who play both golf and baseball murder their batting averages and usually don't understand why."

"I had no idea." Meg leaned her head against the seat and blurted unthinkingly. "Rob, what would poor Mike have done if you hadn't come along?"

"What would I have done if you hadn't—good Lord!"

Whatever he had intended to say was lost as he stopped in front of her house. A Cadillac filled the driveway behind Meg's car. Lights blazed all over the place in the fast-approaching darkness, and the moment he turned off the engine the outline of a man appeared on Meg's front porch.

"Is something wrong at your house?"

"Mike must have gotten tired, and my parents decided to bring him on home to bed," she said breathlessly, obviously with no conviction.

At first Rob suspected with raw hurt that she had arranged their bringing Mike home this early to discourage him. But it dawned on him as they approached the porch that her parents had no intention of doing that. They looked like nice-enough people. A little older than he had expected. The woman's hair was almost blue-white, and the man was slightly balding and stooped. Meg, he remembered, was their youngest child. They were smiling in the genuine way that said: "We're so glad you like our baby daughter and we want you to like our grandson and we want you to like us and isn't she pretty and she can cook, too." Rob had seen that look many times before when he had taken women home. This was the first time he had welcomed it.

But glancing at Meg, he realized that she certainly didn't welcome it. He drew her a little closer, slowing their advance to the house while he tried to assess the situation. All evening she'd been giving him confusing signals. Talking as politely and impersonally as if they'd never shared an intimate moment together. Then failing at the facade with a brief affectionate gesture, or a caring question. *She doesn't know what she wants from me. Or what she can give, either.*

The conclusion seemed blindingly right as he covertly studied Meg's expressive face. And her parents, eager to see her happy, were rushing her.

"You messed up by not letting me go in with you when we dropped Mike off," he warned mockingly in her ear while they still could not be overheard. "They want to check me out. Bet you money they ask me in for coffee."

She flashed him a look of alarmed chagrin, but just then the man stepped forward.

"Didn't mean to be waiting on the porch for you," Meg's father apologized, holding out his hand. "We were just coming out for some air. I'm Johnny O'Mara."

"And I'm Pauline O'Mara. Wouldn't you like some coffee, Mr. Dowell? I just made a fresh pot."

"Would you like to see my baseball cards?" Mike appeared from nowhere, fully clothed and obviously very wide-awake.

Rob couldn't help the slight sputtering. And then, to his surprise, Meg broke out laughing. A genuine, enthusiastic chortling.

"I give up, I give up! Back off, everyone, I'm going to let him come in. Please do have coffee with us, Rob."

She looked up at him in amused apology, more willing to allow herself to be embarrassed than to castigate her family, and he knew then exactly what he was going to do. Play hard to get. He'd go in there and drink the coffee of these nice people, enjoy the company of that rascally boy he wished were his own, and ignore the boy's mother. Ignore her pointedly, even though she was so gorgeous that he wished he could slowly nibble on her from her painted toenails to the top of her extravagantly beautiful hair.

If she thought she needed more time, he'd give her more time. He'd leave without once mentioning seeing her again and let her stew along with those other nice people who loved her so much. And when the reality of not having him in her life had sunk in, he'd spring. He wouldn't contact her for about a week, he decided. If he could last that long.

"Do you have time for coffee?" She suddenly seemed anxious.

He managed a casual nod. "I suppose so. Watch the clock for me, Mike. I have to leave in time to check out of the motel and catch my midnight flight to Dallas."

Chapter Five

"I know peach is in this season, but I've never thought it was my color." The tall matron with graying hair stepped inside Meg's office and held a linen suit jacket in front of her. "What do you think?"

"I've liked other colors on you better, Mrs. Belling," Meg replied honestly, tossing the plastic wrapper of the pita sandwich she had just eaten into the wastebasket. "Let me wash my hands, and then we'll take a look at it outside. Some of these colors and fabrics look different in sunlight."

Meg was accustomed to having her lunch break interrupted. Once she cleaned all the grease off her fingers, she took the suit, made a discreet explanation to George Palini, and led her customer to the private exit of the store. The designer didn't flutter an eyelash upon seeing his six-hundred-dollar creation disappearing into the sunshine.

They decided against the peach. Instead, Meg helped Mrs. Belling select a pale-green summer suit and matched it with patterned scarves in the neutral tones fashionable that season. Palini was astounded.

"I need you in my New York salon," the small Italian-American told Meg after Mrs. Belling had left. "I've never seen any dealer tell a woman something doesn't look good on her and survive! You must know your customers well."

"Our ladies live around here," Meg reminded him. "If I give them bad advice, they let me hear about it."

"You were right in telling me that the early shoppers would prefer suits and long-sleeved dresses. What do you predict for the rest of the day?" he asked curiously.

"The afternoon crowd should be younger, active women stopping on the way home. You won't sell them much daytime wear because they prefer the easy-care things, but your cocktail dresses should do quite well. And interest in furs will be steady all day."

They had decided that Palini would be the principal consultant in the store's small salon where his furs were displayed, and that Meg and Penny would work with his representative in the south salon, which featured the rest of his collection. He was soon to discover that Meg indeed knew her customers. Although patience was required to wait out the women's love of visiting over champagne and hors d'oeuvres, sales of evening ensembles were booming. And except for the time he spent with a television reporter, Palini was kept busy meeting people and talking about furs.

Susan Forsyth gave up accomplishing any office work and acted as a messenger between the two rooms.

"Mr. Palini would like your help," she told Meg late in the afternoon. "I think he wants you to advise a man he's talking to, and it could tie you up for a while. Do you want me to bring you some champagne?"

"A diet soda sounds a lot better," Meg said. "But I'd better wait to drink it until I finish with his customer. Why don't you see if Penny wants anything? She's been on her feet all day, too."

"Okay, but she was fine last time I checked. Have you noticed how radiant she's looked the past few days?"

"Radiant? Maybe it's the excitement of the showing."

"I was afraid that was it. Since her husband's health is worse, I'm worried about how she'll do once this event is over."

"Charlie is sick?" Meg paused to look at Susan in concern.

"She told me this morning that he's developed prostate trouble. Do you think he'll have to—what's wrong?"

"Ha—ah, kachoo!"

Meg choked back the burbling laughter and managed a respectable sneezing sound instead. Penny radiant? That crazy Charlie; the celibacy must be over! *Wait till Rob hears about this.*

"I suspect that radiance will last, Susan. Don't worry about her."

Still gurgling, Meg waved away Susan's helpful pat on the back and hurried toward the fur salon. So now Rob Dowell was a sex therapist! She turned radiant herself at the conclusion, then was immediately angry. For four days Rob Dowell had kept popping into her thoughts at the most inconvenient times. Very annoying, since she suspected that he didn't plan to see her again except in a business capacity—not that she could blame him after the boring evening and overexuberant family welcome he had endured on their last date. But how she wished he'd change his mind. What fun it would be to share the news about Charlie's 'ill health.'" Meg was smiling widely when she joined Palini.

"A fur wrap needs to be selected personally for each customer," the designer was insisting to a middle-aged man examining a fox cape. "The color must complement a woman's skin tones."

"I thought I'd just order her a brown one that would go with everything," the shopper said hesitantly. Palini noticeably shuddered.

"Hi, Mr. Garland," Meg greeted the husband of one of her favorite customers. "Is your wife still in Houston helping with the new grandbaby?"

"Still there, Meg." Carl Garland seemed relieved to see her. "She hated to miss this showing, so I thought I'd surprise her with a fur cape for Christmas. Every time we go to parties in New Orleans, she hints that she needs one."

"He says his wife is a redhead," Palini interjected. "But that fox he picked..."

"What do you think?" The man held up the cape he had been admiring.

"I believe she'd be more satisfied with lighter tones," Meg advised, carefully examining two other selections Palini was holding. "Look at this one. It's the same style and price, but it would be much more complementary to her hair and coloring."

"I just figured every woman wanted a dark coat."

"Let me show you what a difference matching the

color to the woman can make,'' Palini urged, horrified that the man still might select the wrong cape. ''Now take Mrs. Bronson here. We could put her in a beautiful coat...'' He slipped a neutral mink jacket over Meg's shoulders.

''She looks pretty,'' Carl Garland said.

Palini shuddered again, his thin face actually appearing to be in pain. ''But she must look marvelous in my furs,'' he protested. ''Now you shall see what is right for her.'' He disappeared into the back of the shop where his security man was guarding the selections not in use on the floor. Moments later, after subtle rustlings of paper coverings, he returned with a full-length auburn mink coat thrown carelessly over his arm.

''Oh, my!'' Meg's admiring sigh was involuntary.

''This is my masterpiece,'' Palini admitted proudly, holding it up for her to slip on. ''It is too warm for most of your weather here, but I brought it to show off.''

''You can certainly do it with this.'' Meg tucked her arms into the sleeves, shifted until the dramatic garment had settled properly around her, then loosely tied the leather belt. Tall as she was, the coat still came well below the knee.

''Now that is marvelous on her,'' Palini observed proudly.

''I see what you mean about the right color,'' Carl Garland told Palini. ''Well, if Meg thinks this other cape is best for Nan, I'll take it, then.''

''I'm certain she'll feel as marvelous in that cape as I do in this,'' Meg assured him. Reaching to adjust the collar, she couldn't help remembering the coat she had so recently noticed in a New York catalog—the one a

naked woman was modeling for her lover. Meg almost
wished Rob Dowell could see—

"Very nice." A man's warm hand brushed aside her
own and lifted her long hair free. Rob was still so completely in her thoughts that she stared at him for a few
seconds before realizing that he was actually there, re-
arranging her hair in soft waves. He hadn't given up on
her! A silly smile took over her face. "I didn't know
you were in the store. When did you come?"

"Just in time for the fun." He stepped back to admire the results of his endeavors with her hair.

"Perfect," Palini agreed. "Why don't you model that
throughout the store while Mr. Garland and I complete
his order. Maybe you'll bring me some more business!"

It was an invitation Meg didn't need seconded.
Hadn't she wanted Rob to see her in that coat? She let
her hips sink slightly forward in the model's stance before beginning the quick gliding steps that showed off
her clothing to the best advantage.

The professionalism was automatic, which was a
good thing. Because she was foolishly and completely
elated. After she thought Rob Dowell had given up on
her for good, here he was: virile in a gray jacket and
dark slacks, a hand thrust in his pocket while he leaned
one hip against a display counter and looked at her as if
she were a precious jewel. Until then, she hadn't realized how much his friendship meant to her. Meg
moved euphorically throughout the store, only half
hearing the compliments for the creation she was modeling. Rob's eyes followed her as if his thoughts might
be matching hers—as if he were thinking: *You'd look
lovely, naked, in that coat. My gift ...*

Her skin flushed and she felt the pressure of her clothing against her body as if it were sandpaper torturing her.

"Turn around again," Rob requested when she eventually returned to stand before a triple mirror near him. She complied, like some harem mistress.

"That coat would be perfect for your buying trips to New York."

Rob moved behind her to study her reflection from the triple angles. Again her body flushed all over.

"You're right. Since I could never afford it, it's lucky I only go to New York once or twice in the winter. I'd be so tempted...." When she started to shrug out of the coat, Rob lifted it off her shoulders. Briefly his dark hair touched against hers and a blaze of sensual awareness passed between them.

"Did you come to see Penny?" *Say no,* she mentally ordered, taking the coat from him.

"Yes. Is she around?"

Meg's spirits fell, but she tried not to show it. "I think she's working with Palini's representative in the main salon."

"I'll find her there. When I arranged your coverage by telephone, she seemed so worried about this showing that I thought I'd better check it out. Everything going all right?"

"Oh, sure, fine. And with you?" In view of her erotic thoughts, the ultracivil conversation was embarrassing. Maybe he didn't plan to date her again. And yet she didn't think she had misjudged the desire passing between them just then. Meg hurried to return the coat to the security man before her confused emotions could betray her into some foolish mistake. She had a terrible feeling that this beautiful day was going to twist around all wrong.

Rob spent some time with Penny in her office and later with Palini. Even after the showing was officially closed down with a final toast of champagne, he seemed in no hurry to leave. He stayed on to visit with Susan Forsyth and Penny, but left Meg strictly alone.

When she was no longer needed on the floor, Meg helped repack Palini's garments for reshipment and wondered why she did not feel a greater sense of satisfaction. This quite successful showing would add a good bit to her own bank account.

"Mrs. Bronson, are you busy? Someone wants to see you out here." Susan appeared at the workroom door.

Rob, Meg thought in sudden elation. *Finally he was ready to talk to her.* "Be right there," she agreed hastily. Handing a tunic to the assistant for its tissue-paper wrapping, she rushed over to the mirror. She was wearing lilac that day, with a wildly colored contrasting scarf used as a belt. For once she was grateful that she looked good. It seemed important. Hurriedly she readjusted the dress, ran a comb through her hair, touched up her makeup, then slid her hands along her ankles to tighten the fit of her panty hose. Rob was standing alone near the blouse counter looking at something near the door. Smiling a moment at the way he still pretended to ignore her, she started briskly toward him. She knew she glowed inwardly but she didn't care; she was too glad that it was not all over between them after all.

"Hello, Meg."

The quiet greeting coming from her left side jarred her excited thoughts. She turned in surprise, not quite recognizing the timbre of the male voice, and for a moment the pale face of the man standing beside a tiny brunette was unfamiliar to her. But only for a moment. Mike's blue eyes and dark shock of hair were so clearly duplicated in the man's features that there was no question.

"I hope we're not interrupting anything," the man continued. "When I asked your secretary where you were, she said she thought you could spare a few minutes."

"Dane."

The name sounded like a death knell on her lips. So it had not been Rob asking for her after all. Disappointment slammed around within her body at punishing force, quickly to be overridden by horrified alarm.

Mike's father was back. She stared at her former husband, almost not seeing him, so swamped was she with memories, few of them good.

"Since we hadn't heard from you we decided to come in person and let you get to know us. This is Karen, my..."

Meg later realized that it was significant that Dane had reentered her life in quiet pride, without groveling. But at the moment when he introduced his wife to her, his self-confidence did not register; all she disbelievingly noticed was that he was actually standing unswayingly on his feet and speaking rationally. Old impressions die hard.

While she acknowledged Karen Bronson, Meg forced a swallow down her paralyzed throat. "You were serious about seeing Mike, then,'' she eventually said to her former husband.

"We realize you have justification to question that." Dane Bronson's observation seemed sincere enough, but Meg felt her own indignation rising.

"Justification?" The word squawked out, and Meg promptly tried to control her voice as well as her thoughts. *No scenes,* she ordered herself. What was to be gained by pointing out that Mike had endured neglect and incompetence from his father in babyhood and that five subsequent years of absence and nonsupport had hardly indicated paternal love?

"We thought perhaps you could talk with us over dinner." Karen Bronson's voice was poignantly eager. Meg drew a deep breath, knowing that if her coloring reflected the icy coldness she felt she must be deathly white.

"Well, I don't know, I do have plans," she lied, trying to think. Her brain didn't seem to be working properly.

She wondered if they would insist on trying to see Mike that night. In no way could she allow that to happen. Mike was at too vulnerable an age to be confused by a comatose parent wedging into his life once every few years. She had to be certain Dane Bronson could be trusted again. Yet her basic morality reminded her that a boy needed to know his own father. Her mind whirled. She wasn't up to this situation yet, not alone. Out of the corner of her eye she saw Rob Dowell watching them.

Oh, Rob, please! Come!

Silently she sent out her most urgent, pleading vibes,

forgetting completely that he had been ignoring her most of the afternoon. She needed him too much even to consider that he might fail her. As if in answer to her thoughts, he began ambling casually toward them. She grabbed his arm just before he could move past.

"Darling, look what a surprise," she exclaimed. "You remember I told you about hearing from Dane after all these years? Could we possibly change our dinner plans to include him and Karen?"

THE GUY HAD TO BE MIKE'S FATHER, Rob realized as he was introduced to Dane and Karen Bronson. The eyes, body size, even the big hands matched up. But the woman with him—sister, wife? Hard to say, because contrary to Meg's brash statement, she had told him relatively nothing of her former husband except that alcoholism had been behind the divorce.

Remembering the warmth Meg could share with colleagues, and her panicky rigidity when a man crossed the line from business to emotion, Rob had trouble managing a civil greeting to Dane Bronson. He kept comparing the sophisticated Meghan Bronson he had so frequently seen handling difficult business problems with the huddled Meg whose empathy with the wife of a drunk in a restaurant had tipped her beyond self-control. *What this man has done to the woman I love....*

"Darling, if you'll entertain Dane and Karen a minute, I'll let Delberta know we won't pick Mike up after work," Meg gushed, patting Rob's arm possessively. "Since we want time to visit, I think I'll just tell her we'll stop by for him tomorrow after breakfast."

Watching her walk unsteadily toward her office, Rob

mentally manipulated her intimation that they regularly slept together. He wondered what role he was supposed to assume in this charade: live-in lover? Fiancé? Husband? Selfishly he didn't appreciate her empty boast. Her claim of fulfillment wrenched tauntingly at his repressed desire.

They talked about the weather. By the time Meg came back she had arranged to leave work early, said her good-byes to Palini, and was obviously anxious to avoid making any introductions within the store. She slipped her hand into Rob's, and he felt keys pressed against his palm. Of course. If the Bronsons saw the logo on his rented car, they would realize how temporary he was in her life. He closed his fingers around the keys and hoped she would lead him to the car she wanted him to drive. He didn't like the situation but loyally decided explanations could wait.

"WE BOTH WORK AT THE TELEPHONE COMPANY, but in different divisions," Karen Bronson was explaining to Rob over dessert. They had plowed through the quiche and salads popular at the tearoom Meg had chosen, and for Rob it had been an awkward meal. Nothing seemed to come out in the open and he could not decipher the nuances. Conversation focused on sports, high fashion and the continuing corporate adjustment of AT&T. It skirted the issues of the delicate blond woman who was scarred so deeply within that she could not open herself to love and of her son, whose eyes and body matched those of the man sitting across from them.

Rob's periodic clenching and relaxing of fists was the only visible sign of his personal torment. Meg, on the other hand, showed her nervousness through nonstop polite conversation, just as she had when they had last eaten at the club.

"Being employed by the same company must be convenient for transportation to work," she was saying to Karen Bronson. "Poor Rob flies all over the country. I'm of no help to him at all in that department."

Rob lit a cigarette and watched her calmly. It was only one of many possessive innuendos she had dropped— dropped discreetly enough, he supposed, if one called telling the whole world you were living together discreet. He had refuted none of them because he could sense her desperation. And he had not shaken off her hand, which frequently rested on his forearm in apparent affection when she wanted to make a point. But he was festering deep within.

"What is my son like?" Dane Bronson's quiet question took Rob by surprise and he momentarily wondered what to do. He didn't dare look to Meghan for directions; that would give away her whole ploy. And yet he sensed an eagerness about the man that he could identify with. It would be frustrating to have a son to love and yet not know him.

"He's a fine boy, as I'm sure you know," Rob hedged, his first loyalty still to Meg.

"I'm sorry to say I don't know. I haven't been a good father. I hope, of course, to change that."

Rob believed him. They measured each other levelly. "Meg's done a good job with Mike. Any father would be proud of him."

"Mike likes baseball," Meg cut in quickly. "Of course, he's doing much better at all sports since Rob's been working with him. I didn't know how to adapt for being left-handed.''

"Left-handed, is he?" Dane seemed surprised. "I didn't remember that."

Karen began asking Meg about Mike's preferences, and Rob leaned back to draw heavily on the cigarette. Although not a regular smoker, he thought there were times when an occasional cigarette came in handy. You weren't necessarily expected to talk when you were smoking, and Rob could use a few moments' respite. He felt in cultural shock. The erotic vibes going on between him and Meghan Bronson in the store had been electrifying. His game plan had seemed to be going so well that he had been ready to move in with a dinner invitation, which he had fully expected she would eagerly accept when suddenly she had plunged him into this mysteriously critical charade. His body actually hurt with the strain of confusion.

He noticed that it took Meg only a few seconds to turn the conversation away from Mike and back to superficialities. While they discussed the changes that had taken place at LSU since they had graduated, he curiously studied Dane Bronson. He was pale and slightly underweight for such a stocky build, as if he had been extremely ill and was only recently on the mend. Signs of troubles lined his eyes, and he looked much older than his years. The woman who was apparently his wife was a tiny thing, but seemed quite healthy and happy. Given any other circumstances, Rob would have wondered how two such ordinary people could have prompted Meg's extremely cautious behavior.

He wondered if she were facing a child-custody case.

If so, she was unwise to intimate she and Rob were living together. Lawyers could focus on all sorts of supposed problems in a custody case, and a live-in lover was a likely one. He inhaled deeper on the cigarette and watched the smoke curl above their heads. They were talking about gardens now. In Biloxi, Mississippi. He decided to intervene. It was time to get things out in the open.

"How long is it since you stopped drinking?" he asked Dane Bronson. Meg's gasp was audible.

"A year and a half. It took me six months with AA to get dried out enough to believe I could make it. I would have contacted Meg sooner, but I wanted to be sure that I wouldn't just be dumping the old problems back in her lap."

"That makes sense," Rob agreed, wondering if the sober behavior would last. Meg said nothing. She was staring at the ceiling.

"Frankly, by the end of our marriage I was so out of it that I have no idea specifically what problems I did cause," Dane Bronson continued thoughtfully, the slight scraping of his coffee cup as he ringed it around the saucer the only sign of his stress. "I don't expect her to be able to forget those years quickly."

Rob nodded, feeling a grudging rapport with this man. He was trying to be honest, at least.

"Dane, I'm glad things are going better for you," Meg managed to say, although her voice was thick with hurt.

"But not enough to trust me with Mike?"

She didn't answer.

Karen Bronson moved restlessly. "Don't rush things, Dane," she cautioned.

"You know of course that you could legally attempt to see him," Meg told her former husband stiffly. "The fact that you haven't threatened that makes me believe you have Mike's best interests at heart." The veiled implication that she would fight him with gloves off under those circumstances was there.

"I have several younger brothers and sisters," Karen Bronson said stiffly, but with determination. "I guess I must have been a terrible influence on the younger ones during my worst times with alcoholism, but I'll never know what I did. I only know that after three years of success with AA, my family still hasn't trusted me enough to welcome me back. I suppose their feelings are understandable."

Rob watched Meg restlessly pleating her napkin.

"You've made out all right financially, Meg?" Dane Bronson asked.

"You're worried after five years?" Meg seemed to regret the sarcastic words immediately, for she shook her head apologetically, her eyes glistening suspiciously. Rob either had to hit the man or leave. He stood up precipitously.

"Look, why don't I go take care of this check and give you three a few minutes to—"

"No, Rob!" Meg grabbed his arm. Noticeably controlling her voice, she continued beseechingly, "Darling, there's nothing Dane can say that you shouldn't hear." Standing beside him and clenching his hand, she turned toward her ex-husband. "Mike and I are doing all right. My parents helped during those first couple of years while I got reestablished.''

Dane stood up, too. "I'm able to help a little now.''

Meg clutched Rob's fingers with inhuman strength. Her consternation was apparent.

"It's time we headed back to Baton Rouge," Karen Bronson intervened hastily as she took her husband's arm. "We'd like to come and talk again.''

"I...I'll get in touch with you," Meg compromised. They settled for that.

Rob took care of the dinner bill, knowing the gesture would establish that he was there to intercede for Meg's interests. It was undoubtedly, he thought, the impression that she wanted to create. They drove the Bronsons back to their car in the mall parking lot, with no further things being said about Mike Bronson.

Once the couple had driven off, Rob started to get out of Meg's car himself. But it annoyed him unspeakably that with her need for him now over, she was staring listlessly out the window as if he didn't exist. His stored-up resentment overwhelmed him, and he shoved the key back into the ignition. The klink of the delicate metal against the inner tumblings sounded ridiculously fragile in the charged atmosphere. Meg still would not look at him. His loins tightened aggressively as he saw how her hair draped to hide her tragic expression, how her breasts lay soft and vulnerable beneath the clinging dress, how her hands, only short moments before constantly stroking his arm in open possessiveness, now were clenched tightly in her lap, shutting him out.

When Rob pulled her car out into traffic, she didn't even ask where they were going.

Chapter Six

"What are we doing here?" Meg stared through the windshield at the rows of colored doors with black numbers. She wasn't pleased to find herself parked in front of Rob's motel.

"We're finding a private place to talk."

"I'm not going in there."

"You can either come into my room, where we can hash this out alone, or you can air everything at your house in front of your son. But make no mistake, it's one or the other."

When Meg didn't answer, Rob walked around the car and opened her door with the key. She got out reluctantly, knowing that she owed Rob an explanation, but at that moment she was incapable of being cooperative. Despair weighed her down as she strode toward the anonymously numbered doors, then preceded Rob into a room that was like every other motel room she had ever been in. Practical, clean, impersonal.

As I want my life to be!

The thought seemed significant. She was trying to puzzle out its meaning when she became aware of a noise behind her. "There's no need to flip the night lock," she objected. "I'm not running off."

"Habit with a traveling man. You can open it whenever you want." He made certain the door was secure despite her complaint.

"All right, I apologize. Is that what you want to hear?"

He walked past her to the interior of the room. "No! It isn't what I want to hear."

"I panicked. I used you and I'm sorry. Is that better?" With Rob studying her so intently, Meg couldn't help bungling on: "I don't owe you anything!" That brave statement was a lie, after the way he'd allowed her to use him as a buffer with her former husband, but her body seemed programmed into a self-protective course that she couldn't stop.

"Why?" His question sounded ominous.

She leaned against the edge of the desk near her, a hand bracing on it for the support that her confused mind couldn't seem to offer. "Why don't I owe you anything? Because..."

"Meg, I'm a grown man and I won't play these delusive games. Have you analyzed *why* you pegged me as a lover?"

"If I thought through my motives for doing things, I'd be well-enough adjusted not to make such stupid mistakes!"

"Then start thinking. Now."

He took off his jacket and tie and threw them on the desk. Buttons clacked against the plasticized top with that artificial sound only motel furniture can produce. Unnerved, she watched him loosen the collar of his shirt, then his cuffs.

"I'm not paying you back by going to bed with you."

"That's among the more senseless remarks you've made today," he snapped. Systematically he rolled each sleeve into a neat cuff below the elbow. "Normally when I get in from a disaster of a day like this one, I peel out of my shirt and shoes. I'm compromising my comfort for you."

"Don't let me stop you."

"Meghan!"

His concern, showing through the impatience, undid her. She collapsed into the desk chair and buried her face in her hands. "What's happening to me?" she agonized.

His warmth radiated over her as he angled his lanky body against the desk and waited. Near her, yet not invading her space with touches to comfort. She appreciated that.

"Rob, I am genuinely sorry I used you so suggestively tonight," she said brokenly.

"And I genuinely want you to understand why you did it."

She looked up. "Because you were there."

"Penny was there, too. A much closer friend."

"I needed a man."

"Why?"

"To keep Dane from hurting Mike!" The words burst out without her knowing where they came from. She listened to them and let them tumble around in her brain.

"Now we're getting somewhere. How do you think Mike could be hurt?"

After that it was as if a big ear were in front of her,

demanding to be spoken into. Rob Dowell became the vehicle to purge the past. Meg's mouth opened obligingly, and thoughts that had never been shared with anyone poured out. The words came fiercely—because Meg was angry with Rob for making her dredge all the ugliness up, angry with herself for being unable to face the problem alone, angry at the whole world for letting irrationality exist.

Her years with Dane Bronson could be covered quickly. It didn't take long to capsulize disbelief, concern, failure, loneliness, despair or to relate the most terrible feeling of all—that if she weren't alert every minute her baby son might suffer, for certainly his father couldn't watch over him. Dane couldn't even care for himself. Agoraphobia! She spat out the explanation of how, for months at the end of the marriage and afterward, she had fought that terrible compulsion, making every moment away from home traumatic. Eventually, with time and distance, she had been able to understand that her psyche was falsely telling her that someone needed her. Once she had finally admitted that she was unable to help Dane and had created a new life in which Mike could be safely cared for, she was able to conquer the phobia. But it had been another hell to endure.

It was pitiful enough, she finally concluded to Rob, that Dane—a once-healthy, talented young man—had allowed his illness to ruin ten years of his life. Tragic that he had neglected his son. Terrifying that he expected to be trusted with that son again.

"You don't believe he's cured, then?" Rob asked.

"How can I take that chance? Can't you understand

how excited Mike will be to learn that his father is well and wants to see him? But what about when—if—Dane can't stay sober? Will Mike have another five years of never hearing from his father? Or worse—seeing him become nonfunctional? Mike is old enough to perceive things now. You don't know what it's like to be unable to prevent someone you love from going down the tube!"

Rob unfolded from his perch on the edge of the desk. "Meg, let the situation gel for awhile. You can face it later. They're giving you time." His hands settled soothingly over her forearms, but she shrugged them off almost in panic. Human comfort was terrifying to accept. It offered hope, which was always shattered.

"Don't touch me!" There was more to tell and it was the most horrifying, for in it was no hope at all. She felt hysteria spiraling much too close.

Again Rob took her arms, this time gripping her so firmly that she couldn't break away. He drew her to her feet and against his chest. "Meg, I love you. Let me help."

The moment her body felt the strength of him, Meg fell apart. She had needed assurance too desperately for too long, and it had never come. She didn't dare trust. Wildly she struggled out of his arms.

Perhaps if he had given up on her then she would have regained her control. Perhaps. But he didn't give up. Although her reaction obviously astounded and worried him, he approached her with concerned determination. She struck at him, and he captured her hand and firmly drew her toward him. When her kicking and

hitting became so uncontrolled that he had to lift her
off the floor to break her leverage, she resorted to panicked flailing that was even more difficult for him to
handle.

"Meg, stop this!" He had to set her back on her feet.

She cried out, beyond stopping herself. Then Rob
did the only humane thing possible. Shook the breath
out of her. His face was white as he manacled her
shoulders; the merciless treatment hurt them both, but
it worked. The hysteria passed.

When Meg's body finally sagged limply, he tucked
her head against his and groaned his own distress into
the softness of her hair. "Darling, let me help," he
repeated. He was swaying her in his arms as if she were
a precious baby.

"I've never done this before," she mumbled with
alarm, trying to gather her life back into herself. "It's
not your problem." Her breathing became a little
steadier, but her skin felt as icy as her soul. She tried to
step away from him, but her hands remained captured
in his and she could feel the heat of his caring through
that small contact.

"Quit shutting me out, Meg. I've earned the right to
be in your life, just by going along with your obscene
innuendos tonight."

"Obscene?"

"Telling your former husband we are lovers? Yes,
obscene! You've made the most private, meaningful
feelings a man and a woman could share into empty
brags." He spoke quietly, but his voice was hoarse with
distress. At her guilty shudder he drew her hands
against his chest and began stroking her fingers.

"Rob, I never intended..."

His eyes were filled with pain when he leaned his forehead against hers. "Hush, Meg, give me a moment."

The stroking continued—on the backs of her hands, along her wrists, up to her fingertips. It seemed strange to her that now it was he who was tense, he who was hurting and trying to collect himself. Somehow Rob Dowell had taken on part of her burden, changed it, and was suffering with it in a new way. There was more of her past he didn't know about and couldn't share, but he was trying. She slid her cheek along his jaw until her head could tuck into the hollow of his shoulder.

"Rob, what have I done to you?"

Loosely he folded her to him, but still she could feel the beating of his heart against her own. "Practically emasculated me," he said with wry pain. She stiffened protestingly at that statement, and his arms tightened.

"Do you have any idea," he murmured against her ear, "what it's like for a man to want a woman as much as I've wanted you and know he shouldn't take her? To know that she's sorting out so many personal problems that he can't risk making her life worse by rushing things? Each trip into this town, all I look forward to are the few moments I can be with you. Then, inevitably, I come back to a lonely motel room alone and hurting, because you still aren't ready to open yourself to a man. That I could live with. But when you glibly tell others we've been sleeping together—Lord, Meg!"

He was making no pass, no preludes to one. Blindly Meg reached for him and began stroking in kind.

"I didn't mean to do this to you."

"I know, darling, I know."

"Rob, my soul is a mess." She pressed her lips urgently against his throat. "You can't get mixed up with me."

"I *am* mixed up with you." He was pressing his own lips against her ear. Nuzzling. Cherishing, yet needing to be cherished, too.

The change happened gradually for Meg. For a time she was confused and touching him and moving so that he could better touch her, and wondering how life could be so bleak. Her hysterical despair had been conquered with this man's help, but its cause still lay raw under the surface. Moaning, she clutched him closer, forcing the burning hurt to a more manageable state deeper within. Relief flowed in to fill the welcome vacuum.

Feeling suddenly restricted, she kicked off her shoes, and in response, he managed to heel his own off, too. It pleased her that she was helping him get comfortable as he had earlier indicated that he wanted to do. Meg knew about needing comfort after a disaster of a day and reached to soothe him more. Again they touched to hold despair at bay for just a few precious moments. But the moments extended longer and longer. And eventually a mindless sensation, as familiar to women as eternity, yet never known by her before, overrode everything else. Meg no longer was dominated by the past. Only this pleasant instant in time existed. The sensation grew from inside and reduced her to jellied, moist trembling.

So this is how it is with Rob Dowell!

She had forgotten so much about being with a man. She began rubbing her mouth against his, not really kissing yet exchanging much goodness, letting him turn her face at angles so they each could better find every lonely hollow. They moved, sank, then steadied. Male weight was pinning down her body, but she knew with timeless feminine instinct that she could carry that burden. Softness cushioned her while she lay still beneath him. As she felt a large male hand shift against her palm she gripped her fingers around it. Then her hands moved restlessly on until she could stroke the coarseness of his hair and roughness of his bristled jaw. She strained toward Rob, needing so very much again his lips against hers to fuel the new world of rightness forming within her.

Moaning in a different way, Meg opened her mouth to his and invited entrance.

SHE WAS OBVIOUSLY STUNNED. Rob knew she didn't realize what she was doing, but he didn't care. They had had enough of life's ugly reality. He sensed that something was still repressed in her mind and preventing her healing, but if lovemaking could blunt its evil, he would do his utmost to fulfill her. Recriminations could be faced later.

He thrust his tongue inside her welcoming mouth. Their hungry kiss was deep, and it excited him that in passion she tasted just as he imagined she would— sweet and maturely ripe.

Lustful need, too long repressed, tore at his loins. But she still seemed so vulnerable that he didn't dare risk jarring her by separating for the brief time it would take them to undress. And so in frustration he pressed against her, fully clothed. They caressed each other feverishly, rolling over, entwined with each other, then actually laughing in delighted pleasure.

"I didn't know it could be like this." His shock at the sheer fun of their lovemaking, despite all the trauma they had just endured, tumbled out in urgent murmurs against her throat.

"I don't know where we are." She sounded confused, yet couldn't seem to get enough of running her hands through his hair. She caressed his face and circled his mouth, letting him kiss her fingertips each time they passed his lips.

"We're in my bed, darling." The fingers came by again and he captured them.

"That, too. Ah, beautiful!" It seemed to please her when he sucked gently at her hand, and his body responded deep within. He had desired her so long that he was fast reaching his limit, and he tried to slow it down by lifting her away from him. But she insistently struggled back against him and then hugged him so tightly that he wondered at her strength. Undressing them both became desperately necessary and ridiculously awkward.

"Don't do that—your arm is stuck." He tried to ease off the dress he had earlier thought so gorgeous but now hated because it kept her from him.

"I want to hold you."

"Meghan, let go of my shirt."

He couldn't get the dress off because of some sash thing tied around her waist. "What is this?" He fumbled and tugged at it and she was no help at all, constantly trying to pull him closer.

"A Gloria Vanderbilt scarf."

Not just a scarf—a Gloria Vanderbilt? It was the most irrational lovemaking he had ever been involved in. And the most urgent. "Kiss me and untie this thing!"

She seemed more interested in tugging at his own clothes, but finally he managed to get the dress off. Knowing by then that she needed constant body contact for reassurance, he rolled to his back and continued to kiss her while somehow pulling off her panty hose and his own shirt. When he flipped her beneath him, she stroked his bare back while he managed to pull from his slacks pocket the sheath he needed to prevent her pregnancy. He worried vaguely that she might be offended that he was this prepared to take his woman.

"I've wanted you so long, darling." He tried to explain that for months he had loved her too much to trust himself and had kept ready to care for her at any opportunity—like a lovesick boy. But they were adults and their needs overpowered explanations. His words were lost in excited murmurings of love and loneliness as he finally managed to complete their undressing.

"Rob, hold me."

They fitted wonderfully well. She was almost as tall as he and, lying against him, left very little of his lonely flesh untouched by her own. She pleasured him beyond belief.

"It's so good with you, Meg."

Her mouth swallowed his words. But much as he enjoyed her kisses, they soon weren't enough. Dragging away from her lips, he licked his way along her throat toward the firm, nippled globes he was kneading gently. Her small breasts were ready for him, pointed and swollen when he arrived to love them. Pleased, he drew back to admire how beautiful they were—just right to play with. And taste.

"Oh, yes—Rob!" She gasped and shaped his head with her hands.

Later, in her own explorations of him she seemed shy and perhaps inexperienced, content to hug him close and lightly stroke him. He wanted so much to make her happy that he didn't ask for more; he had no desire to be a teacher, only a lover who shared whatever she was ready to offer. When at last she encouraged him to lift her hips against his thighs, he hoped she knew what she was doing, for if she was not softened enough to receive him he would still be unable to stop.

"Rob, I need you. Ah!"

He didn't know if the sighs were hers or his own. He only knew that when he entered her, it was as if he had finally found the way home.

Meg was floating. She was damp and soft all over, filled with the man who had made her soar to this place and who still formed the mountaintop over which she drifted.

She tightened her body around him and he groaned. Smiling in smug satisfaction at this unexpected power over him, she tried it again. He stirred with pleasure, but she was too weak with the wonder of having his strength within her to experiment more. The moments they had just shared kept recreating their own beauty—the whirling sensuousness that had swept her body and gone on and on until she had thought she would die, the release that had come when that cycle had burst and she and Rob had been crying hoarse, ecstatic encouragement to each other before floating into this heaven. Meg smiled and thought she felt his own thankfulness curve against her cheek, where he rested his mouth. She dozed, but her satiated body still responded to the occasional brush of his lips and tightening of his arms whenever he reassured himself that she was still with him in that enchanted world.

When he later took care of freshening them both, it didn't occur to her to object. Everything about what he did for her seemed natural and welcome. But once he left her bedside, she did try to struggle to a sitting position and find her clothes. She was holding the sheet around her breasts and staring about the room at the confusion of garments slung all about when he returned from washing his hands. He walked toward her, magnificently naked and unashamed—slender, holding his age well.

She tried not to stare. "I should go. It's already getting dark."

"Not yet. You said your Delberta was staying the night with Mike. Let me hold you just a while."

"Rob..."

He slipped in beside her and the temptation was too great. She turned into his arms and drifted down to his side.

"Mm, this was a good idea."

"Wonderful idea. Don't talk." His hands came around her breasts and she snuggled into him, letting him curve his thighs up tight against hers.

"Can't I talk about how wonderful I feel?"

"Only if you give me all the credit." He chuckled against her and her laughter matched his.

"All the credit," she teased, turning to peck kisses on his face.

When he stroked back her hair, his expression held such tenderness that she was spectacularly touched. "You've made me so happy. It seems unbelievable after today."

"Most especially after today?" he asked. She thought his expression clouded.

"Maybe. I didn't think I could ever enjoy being with a man again after the last few months of my marriage, and seeing Dane brought all that back."

"Let's get back to today." His voice held a note she couldn't quite decipher. She touched a finger to the edge of his lips, then ran it up along his jaw, silently studying the change in him.

"Meg, you have to go a little deeper, you know."

For a moment she thought he was talking about her lovemaking. But even before that insecurity could completely register, she realized from his solemnity that it was more than that. "Not confessions again!"

Violently twisting away from him, she tried to slither to the edge of the bed. He captured her at the hips before clamping his hands around the sharp indentation of her naked waist to drag her into his arms.

"Meg, I want you healed. Listen—"

"No! Leave me alone."

"What did his family say?"

She tensed beneath him, wondering, almost with hate, how he could bring this up now.

"It's because I love you." He answered the question

that had never left her mind. "What are you holding back? Wouldn't his family help?"

"Why should they," she wailed, "when it was all my fault?"

"Your fault? Meg—"

She clutched his shoulders desperately, sobbing in grief. "Rob how can you do this to me after, after—"

"You caused him to be an alcoholic, right?"

"Yes. Yes!"

"By dating him when he was in college?"

"Yes! I should have seen what was happening. I should have stopped him from drinking too much."

"And when he was working, too?"

"Yes! He took that sales job to support me." Her hands gripped tighter around his shoulders with each new claim of guilt. "I should have known three-martini lunches would be an occupational hazard with that job."

"His parents gave up on him?"

"And his friends. And his boss."

"But why did you finally give up, too? You were his wife."

"Every way I tried to help made him worse. And there was Mike."

"But it was your fault if you kept making him worse. You shouldn't have given up."

He was propped above her like an inquisitor. Suddenly her guilt and grief changed to rage. "No!" She pounded at his imprisoning body. "It wasn't my fault, and I had to leave him. He wouldn't get help as long as I kept him from hitting bottom."

The minute the shrieked words left her mouth she

fell motionless against his bed in shock. Utter silence surrounded them. Rob Dowell was holding himself above her with exquisite care, as if he knew that the slightest wrong movement might destroy her. Her body was limp, while tears of relief poured down her cheeks. She could hardly mouth the words.

"It really wasn't my fault, was it?"

He carefully lowered himself against her, then rolled to hold her on his chest, letting her tears soak over him while he babied her in his embrace. "No, darling, it was never your fault," he soothed. "Ask any medical expert."

"It wasn't my fault," she sobbed out again in wonder, laying her cheek on his damp chest and melting completely against his supportive body. Her broken voice sounded awed at the escape from a great and horrible burden. In a few moments she was asleep in his arms.

THE NEXT TIME THEY WAKENED from their dozing state it was completely dark, and they both felt the pressure of time. Meg approached the inevitable first. "Rob, it must be close to midnight. We have to go soon."

"I know."

She had been lying close to him, her hand against his chest. He placed his own on top of it and slid over until he could feel her all along his side. Meg sighed in contentment. "I don't think I'll ever fall apart again. Something happened to me tonight."

"Something sure happened to me." He sighed. "I don't think I'll ever be able to move again."

"Mm, what a marvelous idea."

"Are you through talking now?"

"No—yes. I want you to talk. Tell me about your freebies."

He twisted a strand of her hair around his finger and curled it up tight. The frosted ends caught little beads of moonlight. For a while he watched the reflections play among the blond tones, then he let the curl bounce loose.

"What about my freebies?" He started on another strand.

"Why do you give out so many? I used to think you believed people would forget your name."

He chuckled. "Nothing that meaningful. I just like junky souvenirs. When I was a kid we rarely took a trip, and if we did we never had money to buy anything. Now I can share souvenirs with lots of kids, little and big."

"Some people who've had it rough growing up want huge houses and yachts."

He chuckled again. "I don't think that big. Junk satisfies me."

"You mean junque."

"Huh?"

"J-u-n-q-u-e. Give yourself some class."

"Meghan Bronson, I love you!" He swung her onto his chest and patted her rump. Then, as if on second thought, he touched her there again, caressingly. "Meghan Bronson," he corrected huskily. "I want to love you."

"Again?" Her response was a mixture of surprise and eagerness.

"Again and again."

THE RECRIMINATIONS HE HAD ANTICIPATED began the next time they awakened. Rob was alone in the bed and he could hear her fussing around in the darkened room.

"What are you doing?"

"Don't you mean, what have we done?"

The despair in her answer was not what he had wanted to hear. He was clutched by gnawing fear.

"Come back to bed, Meg."

She flipped on a lamp and he scrunched his eyes shut against the harsh glare. "I have to get home to Mike. I've never had Delberta stay all night before. And she has to work for someone else tomor—today."

He was still lying within the cold sheets, his body feeling the shocked loss of her soft cushioning, when she began thumping around in the bathroom. Visualizing her pulling her bra over her tiny breasts, he wondered why she bothered to wear that lacy thing. At least he thought it had been lacy; he had been too eager to pull it off to remember much except that roughness threaded against his fingers before he had slung it aside to get to what he was more interested in.

Knowing that he had to face losing her, at least temporarily, he rolled to his side and looked around the room. She had piled his things in a heap at his feet. Even from there he could tell that his shirt was torn at one top button. Grabbing it, then sitting on the edge of the bed, he grinned in satisfaction as he dressed himself. So he had not dreamed some of her eagerness, shy though she had been. His mood was not completely grim when she eventually came out of the bathroom.

After what they had done to each other, he found it funny that she couldn't look him in the eye. Her gaze fastened on a fly speck over his left shoulder as she addressed him.

"I can drive myself home, Rob. I'll have a couple of the mall janitors bring your car over to the motel first thing tomorrow. They're discreet and—"

"To hell with being discreet." He put on his jacket and tucked her car keys into his pocket. "I'm seeing you home."

"It isn't necessary."

"It is to me. We'll stop by the mall and pick up my car and I'll follow you to make certain you get in. Wait!" He had taken the lock off the door and she was trying to brush past him. When he held her around the shoulders, she stiffened defiantly. "We're not parting like this. Kiss me."

"Rob! This was all a mistake. I was upset and foolish and I can't imagine why—"

"Meg, we needed each other. What's so hard about admitting that?"

She hesitated, pain in her expression. He knew she wanted to deny it, and he was proud of her that she finally nodded her head. "All right. I needed you. So much so that I dragged you into this mess with Dane, besides practically forcing you to make love to me."

"I wasn't exactly protesting."

"But now I—"

"Now you must get back to your son. It's that simple. We'll take this as it comes, but you're not leaving without kissing me." She looked stubborn about the idea. He grimaced. "Frankly, my body is feeling a little shell-shocked. I need a quick fix."

She stared at him a moment. Then she totally surprised him with her reluctant smile. He wanted to hug
her; she had actually smiled. "A kiss is a fix? Rob
Dowell, you settle for mighty little in life."

"Kiss me. Tomorrow's another day."

She needed a quick fix, too. He could feel it in the
way she drifted stiffly against him, then suddenly softened with a shudder, letting her whole body droop
against his. He staggered a moment to balance her
weight before drawing her close.

Their lips nestled pillow-soft together. Warm, like
the hollow they had just slept in. Moist, like the love
sweat that had coated them in the heights of passion.
He nibbled gently at her, and she nipped him back. He
could feel the sad curve of her lips. She genuinely believed that it was all over for them. But he wouldn't let
it be. He'd find a way. Tears gathered at the edges of his
eyes.

Sensing something wrong, she pulled back slightly,
staring at him in tragic confusion. "Oh, Rob, I'm so
bad for you." She brushed at the moisture with her
fingertips, then framed his face in her hands and kissed
him deeply one last time.

When they opened the door, their senses were as-
saulted by the neon garishness of the motel sign and
laughter from a party in a room nearby. The real world
waited relentlessly. Rob thought about that real world
as he drove her back to the deserted parking lot at the
mall. She had gotten lots of thoughts out in the open.
Thoughts she needed to put into words so that they
could be examined and cleansed. And yet she was far

from purged. Despite the pleasures they had shared, she was staring listlessly out at the gray emptiness around them.

Probably trying to justify everything.

"I'd like us to get married."

"That's hardly necessary, Rob. You made certain I wouldn't get pregnant."

So she had noticed. Or at least been aware after the fact.

"I've been prepared to make certain I wouldn't get you pregnant from the second time I came in your store."

"You're very efficient." She said it sarcastically.

He wondered what would have pleased her. She was certainly in no emotional condition to have another child. Not yet. She had her hands too full with unresolved problems. "Not efficient. Just very much in love. It's never happened to me before."

"I wish you'd quit saying that, Rob. This isn't going anywhere, and you know it."

"Meg, we could make a good life, even if you don't love me as I do you. We've been together intimately enough to know we wouldn't wear on each other's nerves around the house. I'd be proud to have Mike as our son. Obviously the chemistry between us is very right, and—"

"I don't know how you can say our chemistry is right. Any man would have been right for me tonight. It's been more than five years—"

"You're more inexperienced than I think if you believe that."

"Oh, beautiful," she said bitterly. "We've just been to bed together and I'm supposed to appreciate your making cracks about how inexperienced I am?"

"Lord, Meg!"

"You told me your car's on the back side of the lot."

"I know where my car is. Or hope it is, if the police haven't hauled it off, thinking it's abandoned. I've stopped here so we can talk."

"Then I'm getting out."

He captured her hand on the door release.

"We're in your car, remember?"

She shook off his restraining grip and folded her hands in her lap. "Rob, this evening you probably saved my sanity. I can't thank you enough. Oh, that sounds so awful. You meant everything to me tonight, but I don't want it to go further. I'm not right for you."

"Meg, don't do this to us."

"Quit talking about 'us;' there is no 'us.' And would you please get out?"

He shoved the car into gear and drove around the mall complex. His familiar rented automobile was still there, a lone mystery among the marked slots where by day hundreds of vehicles had joined it. Thinking dispassionately of the comparative symbolism to his own solitary state, he opened the door and stepped to the pavement. Meg quickly slid into his place. He caught the car door before she could slam out his good-byes.

"Next week I will be tied up in Houston. But I'll be back here that next Saturday and I'll expect to see you and Mike. I'm staying in your life because we both need me to be there."

She did manage to close the door on his last "I love

you," but he'd give her credit for one thing—she knew him well enough not to try driving off before he could get into his car to see her home. He would have followed her right into her bedroom if she'd tried that. He wanted to do that anyway, even while he waited outside her home until she was safely inside. But he didn't. For he was making plans.

She had said she wasn't right for him. Rob knew that it might take her some time to realize otherwise. Her self-confidence had taken a terrible battering in her marriage. But he vowed he'd soon convince her that at least he was right for her, even if he had to storm her bedroom, or worse—refuse to enter it.

Chapter Seven

The doorbell interrupted Meg's second cup of coffee. For a moment she felt an uneasiness because it seemed so conveniently timed, coming just after Delberta and Mike had left, but before Meg had to be at the store. She knew that it couldn't be Rob; he had an early flight to Houston. Then she relaxed. Mike, she decided, must have forgotten something. With school well into its last month of the year, he was fast losing his concentration.

"What did you leave at home this time," she teased wearily as she threw open the door. "Oh! Charlie?"

"Are you all right?" The old man looked concerned as he stood before her in a rumpled white shirt and crisp trousers.

"I'm fine. What's wrong? Has Penny—"

"No, nothing's happened to Penny. I just—is that coffee I smell?"

"Get in here, Charlie." Affectionately she tugged him inside and led him into her kitchen. "Lots of sugar and no cream," she verified her memory as she poured him the final drops warming in her coffee maker, then set the sugar bowl before him. He nodded and quickly spooned several mounds of sweet stuff into his cup.

"What's happened, Charlie?" Meg knew that he wouldn't drop in on her just before she was due at work without a reason. She sat across from him, expecting to hear some complaint about Penny, but his answer came as a complete and unwelcome shock.

"I figured Dowell had taken good care of you last night, but I wanted to be sure."

Meg couldn't stop the embarrassed flush.

"Now, now. It was just that Mall Security called me around midnight when the Shreveport police were planning to haul off Dowell's car from the parking lot. They thought it had been abandoned."

"They knew whose car it was?"

"They knew it was rented from the airport agency. I figured it must be Dowell's, so I told them to lay off. Then I drove by the motel I remembered his saying he usually stays at, because I figured something was wrong."

"You saw my Aries there," Meg deduced.

"Don't look so embarrassed. At least you didn't have to drive him to the police station to get his car."

"That would have been awful. Some of his business associates would never have let him live it down."

"Not so easy for you, either, girl," Charlie said gruffly, patting her on the shoulder.

"I knew he shouldn't be going out with me. I'm a jinx."

"That's dumb."

"Charlie, don't you think that some people are just wrong for each other? That there's nothing they can do to work it out?"

"I think you're making a lot of trouble over nothing. If you want something, go for it."

"Go for it? Just like that? Even if you mess everyone else up trying?"

"Sometimes messing up is fun." His craggy face broke into a grin. "I remember the time Penny tried to lock me out of my own house. Made me so mad I climbed a tree and crashed through our bedroom window to get in. Cost me twenty stitches and a broken leg."

"And you call that fun?"

"Penny makes a mighty solicitous nurse."

"You're an old reprobate." She laughed. "But I owe you one for taking care of that car."

"You owe me nothing. Except maybe a little more spunk. I only came by because I didn't want Penny surprising you with some gossip about an abandoned car. I didn't expect you to tuck your tail between your legs. If you like that man as much as I think you do, work at it. He's worth making a few mistakes for."

Meg stared pensively at her hands. Suddenly she looked up. "Why did Security call you?"

"Huh?" He was hiding something. She could tell by that ultrainnocent look masking his dear, craggy face.

"Why did they call you about the mall?"

"Because I own it, dammit. And don't tell Penny."

"But I thought the Charles Corporation owned... oh, Charlie!"

"I'm trusting you. Penny will get all hurt and mad if she thinks I've been helping out her business."

"Have you?"

"Only by making certain any tenants coming in will be compatible with Penelope's. Don't look at me as if I've been keeping big secrets from her. We'd divorced and weren't speaking when my manager told me she had applied for tenancy at my new mall. I knew she'd back out if she learned that I owned the place. Penny's not a very good listener when it comes to her stores."

"She's going to have a fit when she finds out. None of us dreamed the mall's manager was a front man for you."

"That manager makes all the business decisions. I just stick my nose in once in a while, like last night. Penny hasn't found out for three years. I'll take care of it when it happens."

"You sound like Rob Dowell. It must be wonderful to be able to face problems head-on."

"Indecision doesn't help anything," Charlie warned, pushing back his chair. "You take care, hear?"

CHARLIE WAS RIGHT about indecision not helping anything. While Meg managed some appearance of normality throughout the day at work, she realized that all indecision did was make her feel worse. She was so mixed up about whether she should see Rob Dowell again that the contentment she should have been experiencing after spending a night in his loving arms never surfaced. Moreover, she caught herself glancing nervously about the store every once in a while, as if Dane and Karen Bronson might again spring themselves on her. It infuriated her that despite the churning in her stomach she was no closer to knowing what was best for Mike.

By evening she had determined to do something about it. *So I take one day at a time,* she thought while sitting at her kitchen table with a box of stationery at her elbow. *And I do something about my problems instead of letting them fester for years in my subconscious.*

The supper dishes had been cleared away, and she could hear thumping from the back porch. There was a letter still to be written, and she knew she had to get on with it. Mike would not be satisfied much longer with tossing balls into the big laundry basket she had taped to the porch railing. Decisions! She was at work on the first one and it didn't come easily.

Meg grimaced at the two crumpled papers already littering the table, drew out a fresh sheet and wrote:

Dear Mr. and Mrs. Bronson
   It occurred to me you might like to see this report Mike

She frowned at the "Mr. and Mrs. Bronson." It was like writing to herself. The paper joined the other crumpled discards. "Dane and Karen" hadn't felt right either, for they were strangers to her yet shared something so intimate—her son.

"I need a basketball hoop for Mike," she thought disjointedly, half listening to the boyish sounds going on outside while her pen again sought the paper. She decided against any salutation at all. A note could be just that, a note. She wrote:

I thought you might enjoy seeing this report Mike wrote about France. His class is practicing library research and he seemed to learn quite a bit doing it. Mike is a slightly above-average student, but his teachers indicate he could do even better if he didn't daydream. On rainy days he likes school, but if the weather is clear his mind obviously wanders to the moment he can be free to go out and play. Here is a snapshot of him on his bike.

She signed her first name only, stuck the note, one-page report and picture in the envelope and addressed it before she could change her mind. A big part of her didn't want to send that letter. It would be so much simpler to go back to how it had been before, when Dane and all the bad memories and regrets had been repressed out of her life.

The thumping on the back porch stopped. With a mother's intuition, she listened for the sound of footsteps in the mud-laundry room. Her estimate had been about perfect. She was nodding her head for the first slap of Mike's tennis shoes upon the vinyl floor at exactly the moment that her ears picked up the sound.

"Hey, Mom, there's nothing to do."

Instinctively she tucked the envelope under the stationery box.

"I have to mail a letter at the corner; then we could stop at the park and play catch for a while," she told Mike with more energy than she was feeling. "It shouldn't get dark for another hour or so."

"I wish Mr. Dowell were here. He *really* knows how to play catch," Mike complained, delving into the toy box for his new glove anyway.

"Thanks a lot." Meg tried to tease him out of his bad mood.

"Tommy said he won't even be at our practice tomorrow. Why didn't you let him come?"

"Mike, I had nothing to do with Mr. Dowell's coming. He has business in Houston."

"When will he be back?"

"The Saturday after this one." She answered without thinking.

"Oh, good! Then he can teach Tommy and me how to steal."

"Steal!" She knew what he meant but looked jokingly stern and grabbed him by the shoulders anyway, hoping to divert him from his obsession with Rob Dowell.

"Steal bases, Mom." He giggled, suddenly miraculously happy.

She loved seeing the smile on his face and wished she could keep it there all the time. But she felt uneasy that her son's happiness hinged on someone beyond their control.

"Mr. Dowell might not have time next weekend to work out with your team, Mike," she warned gently once they began the walk to the corner postal box.

"Oh, he'll be there if he's in town," Mike bragged. "He promised."

"People can't always keep their promises," she said. More worry. But it was so hard not to worry. She'd seen Mike as a toddler live through too many broken promises with Dane. She wondered if he had any conscious memory of that.

Her steps slowed while Mike ran ahead to open the box.

"Who's that letter to?" he asked innocently when she dropped it in.

She hesitated. *It's time to put yourself on the line, Meg. Do you believe Dane wants to get well or not?*

"Your father," she murmured. "Your father," she said more firmly. "He's been asking about you."

"I thought he was sick." Mike let the box snap shut.

"He has been. He is. But he's getting better."

"Is he going to come live with us?" Mike didn't seem too enamored with the idea. She studied him out of the corner of her eye as they strolled on a block farther toward the small neighborhood park.

"No, he has a wife now and they take care of each other." Meg swallowed. "He just wants to know how you are. I sent him a picture of you on your bike."

"Mr. Dowell says I need to put the seat up. On my bike. 'Cause I'm getting tall."

She looked at him with misty eyes. How easy telling him about Dane had been after all. The hard part would be later, when Mike got used to the idea and actually wanted to see his father. *Let that take care of itself when it comes.*

"You are getting taller. I hadn't noticed. We'll look at your bike tomorrow."

"Let's wait till next Saturday when Mr. Dowell can help me. I'll probably grow some more by then anyway."

"You probably will," she agreed thickly, wondering how she could stand to see the hurt in her son's eyes if Rob Dowell didn't show up. She didn't dare confront the disappointment she herself would feel.

ROB DID KEEP HIS PROMISE. He arrived in town the next Saturday just in time to make the baseball practice and was getting out of his car at the park when Meg dropped off Mike.

"What about dinner tonight?" he asked, leaning over her open window.

"I wonder if you'd like to eat at our home," she offered shyly.

"I'd like that very much."

She was grateful that Mike had been called over to Diego Preston's car to help haul the bags of equipment out to the diamond, for Rob was looking at her longingly as if he were remembering every secret detail— the mole under her left breast, the bruise on her thigh where she had bumped against one of Palini's packing crates, the shiny tint on her toenails.

She felt as if they were making love again right in front of the whole world. Her gaze drifted to the ground. "I wasn't certain you'd come this weekend."

"How could you doubt it? I love you. I want us to be a family."

She looked up at him in confusion. He was going too fast for her. The decision to ask him to dinner had seemed a monumental-enough step.

"Hey, Mom, are we all going to eat at home or what?" Mike had returned to shadow Rob eagerly. And the we-all hadn't slipped past either her or Rob.

"At home."

"Hamburgers! We'll cook 'em on the barbecue and you can do all the inside stuff," Mike suggested.

"I like cooking out, and I don't get much chance," Rob volunteered.

"It looks as if it's going to rain—oh, all right, Mike! Quit making those pleading faces. I'll stop by the store before I pick you up." She laughed with her son, sharing his excitement.

"You don't have to come back," Rob said. "He can ride along with me to the motel while I change."

"No, I'll come for him." The refusal snapped out instinctively. Then Meg gasped in contrition, realizing what she had done. Mike's few rides with Dane had been such dangerous nightmares that she had necessarily developed a habit of driving him almost everywhere herself.

"Aw, Mom," Mike objected.

"We'll do as your mother says, Mike," Rob told him. "Now run on along and warm up. I'll be out on the diamond in a minute."

"You talk about being a family," Meg told Rob brokenly after Mike had gotten out of hearing. "And yet, see what I just did? Panicked at the thought of letting him ride in your car. Rob, give up on me."

"You come for Mike as you planned. I'll be over as soon as I've showered."

THEIR BARBECUE GOT RAINED OUT and they had to cook inside. Or, rather, Meg cooked while Rob and Mike huddled under the soggy shelter of the carport and adjusted the bike seat. After dinner they spent the rest of the evening on the floor of Meg's living room playing Monopoly and listening to the heavy splatter of rain on the windows.

"Mr. Dowell, what do you do in your work?" Mike asked after he had passed "Go" for the fourth time without managing to land on "Boardwalk."

"Are you trying to distract me because it's my turn, and you don't want me to buy that place if I land on it?" Rob teased, rolling the dice.

Mike looked guilty.

"What exactly do you do, Rob," Meg asked semiseriously after he had safely landed on the "Luxury Tax" spot between the two pieces of prime property Mike so coveted. "I haven't known many commercial insurance agents who travel as much as you do."

"I have to cover such a wide territory because I specialize in big-business insurance. I have the policies for several of the Charles Corporation shopping centers, but it's one of my smallest accounts. Most of my work is in analyzing company trouble spots and tailoring insurance for them."

"Then why do you handle Penelope's?"

"You should be able to figure that out, Meg."

"Mom, it's your turn," Mike said impatiently.

"Hah, you were trying to distract me." Rob ruffled Mike's hair. "Now you're in a big hurry to get around to 'Park Place' again and don't want to hear about my job. Traitor!"

Meg was feeling distracted herself.

It was a feeling that did not go away the whole weekend. Rob made the most touching indirect declarations of love right in the middle of ordinary activities—little statements such as the revelation about Penelope's, which only she could understand. He was patient, impatient, tender, tough. Each time he left her, she had a curiously mixed feeling of relief and frustration. If he had initiated lovemaking she would not have turned him down. But he rarely touched her in front of Mike, and in the few moments they found alone he seemed to be banking his fires, waiting for her to make some move. Unfortunately, she did not have the confidence to do so. It was a standoff that could not continue.

THE NEXT WEEKEND was rainy, too. Rob arrived on Friday evening and found Meg at her office in the store, studying a packet of papers.

"What are you doing, working so late? I thought you usually took Friday evenings off."

"I do. I'm planning a new project to hit Penny with on Monday, and I want all my data together to make the best impression."

"You must be expecting a fight."

She laughed. "Not exactly. But Penny's a topnotch businesswoman. I have to prove that this idea will make her money."

"What do you want to try?"

"A career woman department. We've never gone in much for working clothes for women. We've emphasized high fashion suits, furs, cocktail wear and designer casuals. I think there's a new generation of women coming along in the South who will be pursuing professions outside the home. We're going to start losing customers unless we meet that need."

"I would think Penny would be in sympathy with working women."

"Oh, she is. She just thinks they'll go to the department stores for wash-and-wears. I think they want some style, too, and are willing to pay a little more for it. But only a little—not nearly what they'd invest in social wear. We'll have to locate some good designers who can give us both style and easy-care fabrics at a competitive price."

Rob stood over by the window, watching the rain continue to pour down as Meg finished her paperwork.

"So finding the right designers is the key?"

"That's it. I want to talk her into letting me make at least two extra buying trips to New York and California this year, plus financing a speculative opening inventory."

"Maybe you could get a backer."

"Have you been talking to Charlie?"

"What does Charlie have to do with it?"

She laughed self-consciously. "Oh, never mind. What do you want to do tonight?" She didn't even question that they would spend the weekend together. Somehow that had become an accepted axiom in her mind.

"Stay home," he said immediately, turning from the window. "It's a mess out."

"Is it still raining? Poor Mike. He's not accustomed to staying inside three days in a row. I'd hoped I could at least walk with him down to the park tonight."

"You won't even want to walk to your car with an umbrella and raincoat. I tell you what. I'll read him a pioneer story. I just happen to have along a collection of freebie pamphlets for kids to read on vacations."

"Are these your latest Robert Clark Dowell handouts?" Meg asked enthusiastically, looking over the little stack he handed her. "Where did you get such a marvelous idea?"

"When I was a boy, every time it rained—which admittedly wasn't very often in western Kansas—my mother read to us."

"What fun!" She was delightedly thumbing through the titles of classics and historical biographies. "But I would have predicted you'd pick sports stories for your freebies."

"Do you think I'm a philistine?" he accused depre-catingly. "I care about a few things besides sports. History's good anytime, but pioneer stories go best with heavy rain."

"I think you're a very classy man." Meg gathered up her things. "And I'm glad you got in tonight instead of tomorrow. Charlie brought us some fish this morning, and I want to show off how well I cleaned them."

"Braggart," he teased, wrapping an arm around her waist as they left. "I'm more interested in how you cook them."

Both the fish dinner and the pioneer story went very well that rainy evening. And the next rainy morning when Rob came for brunch, a tale of a Revolutionary spy filled another hour. But when the rains continued that afternoon and baseball practice was canceled, neither Rob nor Meg dared risk another reading session. They took Mike to an afternoon movie and spent the evening again playing Monopoly.

Luckily for all their tempers, the sun emerged hot and apologetic on Sunday morning. Mike and Rob headed to the park with their gloves and Meg didn't see either of them for several hours.

"YOU LOOK LIKE little Red Riding Hood." Rob enjoyed watching Meg's skirt hike up over her thighs as she slid into the front seat of his car. He had never considered himself a leg-and-ankle man, but she had on high-heeled strap shoes of some kind that were sinfully provocative. She was so lovely to him that, in his mind, she seemed to match the freshness and charm that the warm Sunday afternoon had brought to the soggy city.

"You must be color-blind." She rearranged her white wraparound skirt and apricot knit top more modestly. "Did you talk Diego and Molly into inviting Mike out to their lake place this evening?"

"I did not. Is his going somewhere else the reason for the what-big-eyes-you-have-Grandmother-look?"

She was smiling contentedly as he fitted himself in behind the wheel and glanced over his shoulder for traffic before pulling away from the curb.

"It just seemed very convenient, after Mike has been hanging on your arm all weekend, that the one invitation that could tempt him away came while you still have a few hours in town."

"I won't say I'm not delighted to have you alone, but actually it was a coincidence. Diego doesn't know we've been together except that evening after the first practice. I figured that our relationship is our private business."

Meg shifted slightly, and he wondered if she felt, as he did, a need to relieve the sensual tension building up within.

"I don't think we should go to your motel," she blurted unconvincingly.

So she was aching as badly as he was, he thought triumphantly. Good! Let her ache. It might bring her to a more agreeable state of mind about marriage. "Neither do I," he lied. "We're going for a walk."

"A walk?"

He laughed. "Walk and talk, how about that?" Whistling a nothing kind of tune, he drove through the sparse evening traffic past the National Guard Armory and large Veterans Administration Hospital to the picturesque Veterans' Park. The recent May deluge had had its typical catalytic effect on Shreveport flora. When they got out to explore the narrow rock path leading up along the bluffs overlooking the Red River, the world appeared an unreal, aggressive green. Living things seemed to grow instantaneously and reach out to tug at their feet.

"Sometimes I think naturalists who believe the environment is fragile have never seen Shreveport in the spring," she said, grabbing for his arm when her high heels wobbled dangerously on the moss-encroached walkway.

"This is wild undergrowth. Have you been here before?" he asked, taking her hand to help her over a washed-out hole.

"No. I usually choose playgrounds because of Mike, and I didn't know this had that one we passed down near the parkway. What's up here?"

"Fort Humbug."

She threw him a look that said she was certain he was teasing. As they continued a short way farther, occasionally her ankles wobbled slightly. And although he enjoyed slipping an arm around her waist ostensibly to assist her balance, it occurred to him that those shoes were totally impractical for such a difficult climb, so he led her back down toward a relatively private picnic area they had passed. Undoubtedly those shoes, he thought, were designed simply to drive a man crazy, wanting to take them off a woman. He quashed the appealing fantasy. There were deeper things than sexual gratification that he urgently needed to establish between them.

"I want you and Mike to come to New Orleans the weekend after his school lets out." He plunged right in, knowing that he had to take advantage of the few minutes they would have alone. "I already have your plane reservations and tickets for that first Saturday in June."

"Why New Orleans?" She settled more comfortably on the wooden bench.

"To meet my sisters. They are primed to tell you what a good cook I am, how easy to get along with, and in what terrible shape my prostate gland is."

She tried to look stern, then couldn't help her grin. "You and your sisters have a lot to answer for. Have you noticed how radiant Penny has been looking lately?"

"I have. You look a little radiant yourself."

"Rob—"

"All right, all right. You know why the top of this bluff is called Fort Humbug, don't you?"

His absurd question obviously caught her off guard, which was exactly what he had in mind. That way the New Orleans trip could percolate in the undercurrent of her thoughts, and she wouldn't refuse out of hand.

"I've never heard of there being a fort in Shreveport."

"Who taught you history? These were the Confederate Fort Turnbull fortifications, according to one of my clients who is Shreveport old-family. Back in the Civil War, when this city was the capital of Louisiana." He gestured down toward the meandering Red River, which had once been navigable but long since had been allowed to fill with the muck of upstream flooding, while railroads and trucks took over its duties. "A good location, don't you think?"

"Was there actual fighting?" she slipped her hand into his and looked sadly out at the tangled, wet undergrowth that cast a sweetly pungent smell around them. Rob cursed himself. Sadness was not at all what he had intended to inspire.

"This client claims the Confederates were greatly undersupplied here," he continued his story hurriedly, "when they learned the Yankees were coming upriver to attack Shreveport. All along the bluffs they simulated cannons by wiring together wagon wheels and charred logs. When the Yankees paddled around the bend of that river, the Confederates shot a couple of warning shots with the few real cannon they had."

"What happened?"

"Nothing. The Union troops thought the place was too well fortified, exchanged a few token shots and turned back."

"No battle at all?" She seemed relieved.

"That's what my client claims. It was Shreveport's great victory, but the city didn't dare brag about it until the war was over. And the name Fort Humbug stuck."

"I'll have to bring Mike up here sometime and tell him that story. Of course, he'll probably be more interested in running along these bluffs than in listening to me. This vegetation must be as wild and unkempt as it was a century ago."

"Bring him up here after we see New Orleans together. I can start him on the War of 1812 there."

"About New Orleans, Rob..."

He hadn't planned what happened next. He was afraid that she was going to refuse to come, and he didn't want to hear that answer, so he leaned over and kissed her. He had only meant to shut her up with a light caress, but when their lips met she gasped, then startled him by ardently kissing him back as if she had been dying for him. Her response was overwhelming fuel to his own tightly reined desire, and he opened his mouth to probe for more satisfaction even while his hand plunged inside that apricot blouse and he began fumbling around like some schoolboy.

"Someone might come." She breathlessly mumbled the warning even while she elevated herself enough so that her little breasts rolled into his searching fingers.

"They won't. Hold still."

She felt wonderfully round and soft to him. He quieted her with one hand at her back while the other burrowed hungrily under her clothing, stretching the neck of her blouse and giving him too little gratification. Her nipples hardened under his fingers. He started to nuzzle open her sweater, but he could hear the confusion of people tumbling out of a car in the parking lot nearby.

I'll mortify her. She earns her living in this town.

Cursing his lack of control, he fumbled her lacy underthings back into place and drew her to her feet. She looked so disheveled that he hurriedly led her into the shielding privacy of the shrubby trees.

"You see how it is with us?" He smoothed down her hair and straightened her clothing while the newcomers passed the picnic spot to rush on up the bluffs. "We can't even trust ourselves out in public."

"We've both been lonely so long."

"Do you know how much I missed you all week?"

She shook her head. "Tell me—no, don't!"

"Make up your mind." He laughed, tracing her lips with his fingers. He liked the way they plumped against

his flesh. He leaned forward to kiss her, then not trusting himself to stop once he started again, drew away. Giving in to his desire was simply not in his game plan.

Her eyes were big and wondering. "Rob, maybe this is just mid-life crisis for both of us. Maybe we have— stop laughing!"

"Mid-life crisis?" he grunted. "Then God bless middle age!"

"Stop that!"

She drew his teasing hand out of the waistband of her skirt, but he grinned unrepentantly, then sobered. "I've waited so long for you to come into my life, Meg. You're the magic I thought I could never have. Come to New Orleans. Meet my family."

"Rob, I'm not certain I have anything to give a marriage. I've become aware of so many hang-ups that seem to take over my actions at the most unpredictable times. Like bad dreams I can't control. It's not fair to you."

"I've never lived with a woman. We'll probably find I have worse hang-ups. And terrible habits."

"And there's Mike—"

"Come meet my family."

"No commitments if we come?" She seemed to want to make a decision.

"No commitments," he agreed reluctantly. "You and Mike can have my apartment and I'll bunk at Helen or Patty's house."

"Well, if you really mean no commitments..."

While they walked back to his car, he wondered if even for a moment she believed that any more than he did.

Chapter Eight

"If Charlie and I had spent only weekends together, we'd probably still be married," Penny Sands told Meg one June morning. "It's having my own routine upset every day that gets me. Tell Rob never to quit his traveling job."

"Penny, we're not getting married. I'm just taking the weekend off to visit his sisters in New Orleans."

"The worst thing about living with a man every day is his shaving. You find little bits of hair all over your sink when you want to wash out your lingerie."

"If it's not convenient for you to switch Saturday duty with me, don't worry about it."

"Of course I plan to trade this Saturday with you—how can you go otherwise? Another thing I don't like about marriage is meals. It's one thing on holidays to eat anytime you're in the mood. But Charlie could live like that every day. And what he considers a meal—"

"You've told me about Charlie's eating habits."

"I have? Well, when you're in New Orleans, eat at Brennan's, of course. Everyone says you should have Sunday brunch there, but if you do, get a sitter for Mike.

You'd be wasting your money taking a child to Brennan's. I took Charlie's nephew there once and it cost me fifteen dollars for him to pick at one strawberry."

"I'll keep that in mind."

"And while you're there, go to the Bar Association's monthly meeting. I called my friend Cara Robidoux, and she agreed to take you."

"What?"

Penny tossed a scrap of paper across the desk to Meg. "The Bar Association. You know—lawyers. Here's Cara's number. She'll be expecting to hear from you when you get in Saturday morning. I think the meeting's about one o'clock."

"You've lost me."

"If you're serious about starting this career department here, you need to talk to career women, don't you? What better place to start than women lawyers and paralegals?"

"Penny, you've actually looked over my proposal? Why haven't you said anything?" Meg couldn't quite contain her excitement. For all she knew, the packet explaining her idea had sat unopened on Penny's desk for more than a week.

"I'm still only thinking about it, understand. I'm afraid you're about ten years ahead of your time; Shreveport doesn't have enough well-paid professional women yet. But go ahead and collect your ideas on the clothes and we'll keep looking at it."

"Penny, that's marvelous. I can't ask for more than that."

"I do want you to talk to Cara. She dresses like a million in the courtroom."

Thoughtfully Meg tucked the phone number away in her purse. There would be Rob's plans to consider. "I'll at least call her," she promised. "But I'll have to see about that meeting. It depends on Rob's family."

"Although in marriage there are some nice things about having a man around all the time," Penny continued reflectively with no concern about maintaining continuity in her conversation. "Sex, most of all. And Charlie listens to good music. I've never understood how he can have such bad taste in clothes and such good taste in music. What kind of music does Rob like?"

"Penny, we're just visiting his sisters."

"Sure, sure."

THEY HAD STOPPED at Rob's apartment near the New Orleans airport to drop off their luggage, and he was showing Meg where everything was while Mike arranged his treasures in the bedroom.

"Do you spend much time here?" She was having trouble hiding her distress.

"Rarely more than a couple of days a week, to do laundry and sleep between planes," he explained easily. "Looks too much like a factory, does it?"

"Looks too much like a motel," she retorted loudly, trying to make herself heard above the roar of a jumbo jet gaining altitude over the building. "Where are all your personal things like souvenirs and family pictures that make it a home?"

"At my office. You sound like my sisters. They don't like to come here. I keep telling them that it has all I need to survive."

Meg glanced around. He was right about that. Coffee maker, utilitarian furniture, radio, a small TV, queen-sized bed in each bedroom and a full magazine rack. Easy to maintain because it was so bare and unfrivolous. But she agreed with his sisters. A man deserved more than merely surviving in his home environment.

"It doesn't look as though anyone lives here," she said bluntly. "Would you mind if I got you a plant? Maybe a blooming one to keep you company."

He seemed pleased at the idea, but grinned teasingly. "Will I have to talk to it?"

"Of course. It will want to hear all your boring stories. And I'll be careful to pick one that will let you brag about your golf scores."

He laughed heartily. "You're on. I'll even get my landlady to water it when I'm not home."

"Mom, I put my suitcase in the corner as you said—" Mike ambled out of the bedroom at the sound of their laughter, apparently afraid he might miss something interesting "—and I got my toy bag cleaned up. I didn't lose a thing when I dropped it on the airplane."

"That's good. I had visions of your favorite Matchbox car being crushed under some pilot's heel."

"Can I take my cars with me to Mr. Dowell's office?"

"Sure." Rob answered.

"No!" Meg responded simultaneously. Then she tilted her head warningly at Rob. "You don't know how many he brought along."

"One in each pocket, then. Okay, Mike?"

"All right!" Mike dashed back to hunt out his favorites.

They ate lunch at a downtown grill near Allied's headquarters, then walked a few blocks so that Rob could show Meg the nearby building where she would be attending the women's caucus of the Bar Association.

"You're certain it will be all right for me to leave Mike at your office while I'm gone?" she asked anxiously. "Cara Robidoux said I could bring him with me. I'm just dropping in on their hospitality hour after their meeting."

"You'd better leave him," Rob said convincingly. "I've met enough of all my staff's family members. Now *I* want a chance to show off."

Family? Meg's hand tightened on his arm. He sounded so proud that it was almost frightening to think of living up to his hopes.

But after they had wandered through the nearly deserted lower floors of Allied's large office building to an upper floor that housed the corporate policy division, she understood better what Rob meant about showing off. And about why he kept the things he loved at his office. People were what made a home. And there was affection and respect surrounding him at his work.

Allied kept a skeleton crew of two secretaries and several agents working in the corporate division on Saturdays because so many emergency situations cropped up in big businesses. And those people were all obviously delighted to see Meg and Mike.

"We wondered what was going on in Shreveport

when Rob started sending through those policies for that little dress store," the older secretary, named Grace, admitted to Meg after Rob took Mike off to the executive washroom. "He hasn't handled a policy that tiny for years. Now we know!"

"It looks as if you people keep him plenty busy." Meg tried to hide her embarrassment.

"Too much so," one of the agents seconded. "I have several messages to pass on to him. I'm sorry."

"He warned us that he would have some work to do. I'm headed out briefly for a business appointment myself. I hope my son won't be in your way while I'm gone."

"It will be fun to have him," Grace assured her. "Rob has certainly entertained enough of our staff's families up here on Saturdays. It's about time he brought his own child by."

His own child? Meg felt a pang to realize that with Mike he would not be getting his own child, unfettered and free of loyalty demands from others. He would be getting a wonderful little boy with a mixed-up mother and an untested father in the background. It didn't seem fair, and she felt guiltily selfish to even be considering the possibility.

The feeling remained when she returned from her meeting a couple of hours later, carrying a potted red geranium and a small gift box. Another stack of messages was on Grace's desk, waiting to be delivered, and Rob and Mike had disappeared.

"I think they were going to check out the vending machines," Grace told Meg.

"No. Mr. Dowell took the boy to see the computer

room," an agent called from his desk behind the framework half-walls favored throughout most of the floor.

"We really have interrupted his day, haven't we?" Meg asked Grace regretfully.

"Yes, thank goodness. We're glad someone can keep him from overworking. Oh, they're back now."

"How did your meeting go?" Rob asked, dropping an affectionate arm over Meg's shoulders in the most natural way.

"Mom, can I type on the computers?" Mike asked at almost the same moment. "Mrs. Grace said I could, but I thought I'd better ask you first."

"If you're careful and do exactly what she says."

"Take good care of him, Grace," Rob instructed his secretary, tightening his arm around Meg's shoulders.

"You have some more messages," Meg warned, motioning toward the stack on Grace's desk. With a grimace he picked them up before guiding her into his own office, which was one of the few fully enclosed rooms on the floor.

It pleased her to see that paintings lined the walls. They were pleasant things, light and airy, but with just a hint of genius that made them nice to live with. She didn't need to look at the signatures to know they were his father's. A battered set of encyclopedias and old storybooks tumbled all over in a place of honor on the bookshelf behind his desk, and clear plastic modules containing colorful piles of his freebie collections brightened one corner behind a work island holding a computer terminal and several other pieces of office equipment. So this was what Rob Dowell substituted for a home, she thought.

Better, but still not good enough for a man like him.

"Are those presents for me?" Rob asked eagerly, watching as she set them both down on his desk.

"Yes, but you're supposed to take them to your apartment and not open the box until we've gone back to Shreveport."

"I won't last that long unless I know what it is."

Meg believed him. "You're as bad as Mike. No! Don't open it now—it's a Pet Rock. They're almost passé, but I adopted one for you anyway. It's to keep your plant company when you're on the road. They both need to sit in a sunny window."

"A geranium that likes golf and an orphaned rock," he said huskily, running the edge of his finger along the bright red bloom of one of the flowers. "If I catch them talking to each other, I'm calling you to complain." His face was vulnerably softened for just a moment before he turned to her.

"Now, how did your meeting go?" He closed the door behind them.

"Marvelously! Those women gave me lots of ideas. I'm ready to order unlined suits, tissue-thin skirts, polyester designer blouses and to forget about wool." She started to explain more, then remembered the messages he held. "Rob, I ought to wait outside. You have work to do and I'll bother—"

He eased her into one of the comfortable overstuffed chairs near his desk. "You distract me, but you don't bother me," he said suggestively, leaning over to peck a kiss on her open mouth. He probably had intended a teasing greeting before sitting down to work. But when she surprised them both by instinctively stretching upward to eagerly meet the gesture, his determination wavered. Groaning, he wadded the messages in his hand and drew her into his arms.

Her breath expelled in a soft "oooof" of surprise when he hugged her high against his chest. She tried to reach his mouth, so he slowly let her slide to her feet while he turned his lips to hers. Loving it, Meg shut her eyes and kissed him with the pent-up ardor of weeks of waiting. When they at last drew breathlessly apart, she turned her head slightly and could feel the brush of his lashes against her cheek.

"I'll never be understanding about your going to meetings again," he said, sighing deeply. "How I missed you this afternoon."

"Mm. Me, too. Don't kiss me that way!"

"What way? Ah . . ."

Meg wasn't making much sense, telling him not to open his lips over hers in warm sucking motions when at the same time she was sliding her hands beneath his jacket and pulling him closer.

"I agree with Charlie," he said thickly, going back to the kisses she had so ineffectively objected to. "Celibacy is for the birds." They staggered a bit, trying to tangle their legs and press their hips together in the most suggestive and satisfying of motions. Once they regained their balance, their movements were well matched and almost impossible to stop. It was Rob who tried to pull away and restore some sanity to the situation.

"And you dare say we don't have chemistry."

"Quit talking," she urged, shamelessly slamming at his shoulder beneath the jacket to force him back against her. His delighted laugh was lost in the mating of their mouths.

It was not until Meg felt the crumpled papers drifting all over her feet that she jerked guiltily out of his arms. "Rob, you have work to do. Oh, look at this mess I've caused!"

She fell to her feet and began gathering up the debris in almost frantic haste. "Grace will be upset with me."

"Grace isn't the boss here." He ran his hand lingeringly over her buttocks until she swatted his caressing fingers away. "You're the one who let this kissing get out of hand," he reminded her, tossing the papers onto his desk.

"I'm trying to keep from hurting you," she said urgently, thinking of how already most of his office staff seemed to assume they would marry.

"Mr. Dowell." The voice preceded a light knock.

"Come in, Lila." Rob began tugging his tie looser.

Meg straightened up, immediately recognizing the sultry feminine voice as belonging to the woman who had inquired for Robbie so many weeks earlier. She watched with interest while the secretary crossed the room to Rob's desk, living up to all her telephone voice had promised. She was as tall as Meg, but brunette whereas Meg was blond, full where Meg was skimpy, younger. And obviously very much infatuated with her boss. Hostility bristled between the two women like static electricity.

"You haven't met Mrs. Bronson yet, Lila." Rob spoke with impersonal courtesy. Meg wondered if he were really as unaware as he appeared to be of the blind adoration on the woman's face. "Meg, this is one of my secretaries, Lila Faloney. She's just come in for the late-afternoon shift."

"I believe we've talked on the phone." Meg held out her hand for a limp greeting.

"I'm sorry to interrupt you two, Mr. Dowell, but the director of inorganic research at the Bailey Labs just called."

So he did have a talk with her about the "Robbie."

"They're taking delivery on some toxic chemicals on Monday and realized that their coverage is inadequate. They insisted that you have this data."

Rob groaned uncharacteristically after glancing at her notes. "This will mean another hour or so," he apologized to Meg. "Do you mind waiting here, or ..."

"I'll check on Mike," she responded, absurdly jealous that Lila Faloney remained hovering possessively by Rob's desk.

There was a subdued hum of activity when Meg returned to the outer office. Grace was apparently working elsewhere, but Mike was installed at one of the empty desks near hers, fiddling with the word processor. He was so engrossed in pecking at the keyboard that he didn't even notice Meg approach. Interested, she peeked over his shoulder and saw:

Michael John Bronson, Shreveport, Louisiana.
Michael John Bronson, New Orleans, Louisiana.
Michael John Dowell, Shrevep

Immediately realizing that she had inadvertently invaded her son's private dreams, she drew back, but it was too late. Mike's open little face reddened guiltily when he realized that she had seen what he had created. He tried to delete the words, but in his haste fumbled the directions, and instead, the series of names and addresses began to repeat themselves in scrolling fashion over the screen.

"Can I help?" Just at that moment Rob had come out of his office with Lila, and upon seeing the scrambling on the CRT, walked toward them. Mike jumped up, looking mortified, and tried to hide the screen with his body. Protectively Meg joined him.

"We'll work it out, Rob. You finish what you have to do."

"My dad wants to know how I am." Mike stretched his shoulders broader in front of the repetitions. "Mom wrote him about me."

Rob looked startled at the irrelevant remark, and his eyes flicked behind the boy before softening with instant understanding.

"Of course he wants to know how you are, Mike." He turned slightly away as if he had seen nothing. "I have a new Polaroid camera. You get that computer to behave itself, and when I've finished this work, we'll take a picture of you working at it. I'll bet your dad would like to get that in the mail."

Meg sank to a chair beside Mike, shaken by what had happened. It was the first reaction he had shown to the news about his father. But how terrible to have its only use a feint because Mike didn't want Rob Dowell to know how much he loved him, how much he wanted

him for his own. It seemed to make everything so
much more complicated.

Mike had managed to clear the computer screen by
the time Rob had collected his information from Lila's
files and returned to his office.

"Will Mr. Dowell be much longer?" Mike asked his
mother.

"Probably, son."

"He's an important man, isn't he? I've been hearing
the secretaries take lots of messages for him."

"I suppose he is. We'll both need to be patient while
he finishes his work."

Her words proved to be prophetic. Rob started to
join them twice, when more calls required his attention.

"This is terrible," Grace apologized to Meg when
the work had stretched into a couple of hours. "Especially the first time Mr. Dowell has ever brought a
friend up here."

Even Lila Faloney began to look concerned that the
calls for Rob continued to pour in. She and Grace vet-
ted them, decided what could wait until Monday and
summarized what they had done when Rob eventually
emerged from his office with his jacket over his
shoulder and a Polaroid camera in his hand.

"If anything happens that absolutely has to be taken
care of, we'll be at my sister Helen's this evening."

"It will have to be an act of God," Grace snapped
protectively. And surprisingly, Lila nodded her agreement.

"All right, Mike," he said, "let's get a good picture
for your dad. You remember how to turn that word

processor back on?'' With the resiliency of childhood, Mike had recovered from his mortification and happily posed for two Polaroid shots before the phone rang again.

"You'd better get out of here,'' Lila Faloney snapped, apparently genuinely wanting Rob to get his break from work, even if it was with another woman.

"Right.'' Rob tucked the Polaroid camera under his arm. "Hold down the fort.''

He took pictures in front of some of the stately old New Orleans trees draped with Spanish moss. He took pictures throughout their late afternoon stroll in the French Quarter. And he used up three rolls of film on Mike playing with Rob's five nephews and nieces.

"My father won't need this many pictures,'' Mike finally told Rob at bedtime when they were looking through the many facets of his happy face caught in the stack of photographs.

"I was hoping maybe we'd have a few left for your mother and me,'' Rob said easily.

"You can have any ones you want!''

"Good! I'll put this one of you and your mother on my desk. And this one on my kitchen windowsill with that talking flower and my Pet Rock.''

Mike giggled at the nonsense of adults.

"I'VE NEVER FELT MORE RELAXED in my whole life.'' Meg rolled over on her back and floated lazily beside Rob's sister in the warm water of the backyard swimming pool. "I could get addicted to a morning dip like this too fast.''

"I'm glad you haven't minded staying around our

houses so much," Patty Kirk said, swishing her four-year-old daughter in a rubber ring near Meg. "Helen and I figured that if you went to LSU, you'd driven up from Baton Rouge to do the usual tourist things dozens of times."

"This is better," Meg agreed. "I've loved getting to see both your homes." She let her feet sink to the bottom and began checking, as she did frequently, on Mike's whereabouts.

"He's still playing with the girls over on the grass," Patty reassured her.

"It's astounding that he'd rather do that than be in the pool. He hasn't been around babies much, and I wasn't certain how good he'd be with your children."

"Well if he likes them as much as they seem to adore him, there's a real love affair going on." Patty laughed. "I've never seen those two cousins plop right into a stranger's lap the way they did with him last night. I thought they'd have a fight over who got to stay there longest."

Patty's daughter had gotten bored with the rubber ring and wanted to paddle on her own. So her mother moved with her over to the shallower water, where Helen and both their husbands were trying to teach their toddler sons how to swim. Meg took another lap around the pool, then returned to the lazy floating on her back.

Twisting her head slightly, she could see Rob lying on his stomach along the edge of the deep end, lazily enjoying the warm morning sun. His whole body, visible except for the swimming shorts, was tanned and freckled. The freckles were a surprise to Meg. She hadn't noticed them when they had made love. Floundering a little, she sputtered, then again watched him longingly. With the children all momentarily occupied, Meg was tempted to swim over there and splash water on him. But as immediately as the flirtatious idea occurred, she abandoned it. His sisters were already watching their every moment together too eagerly. She didn't want to raise any false hopes, for they obviously wanted Meg to adore Rob.

That had been such a surprise. Meg had nervously dreaded meeting Rob's sisters, expecting great resentment because the two had had his affection all to themselves for so many years. It had astounded her to find, instead, that they were nervously anxious for her to like them. The way they had tried to get acquainted, to please her, to make her comfortable, had been touching in the extreme.

"Don't put your feet down. You've floated out too deep to reach bottom."

Rob's voice nearby startled her, for she had not noticed him slip into the pool. Treading water, Meg felt a stir of excitement as she watched him approach. Erotically the water carried waves of caressing warmth from his nearly naked body to hers. Behind him she could see Patty and Helen getting out of the pool with their children. Apparently they were getting ready to serve the final meal they would all have together.

"I guess I'd better be drying my hair," Meg said reluctantly.

"Probably so. Your plane leaves in three hours."

Both of them continued to tread water and stare at each other, wanting so much more. Meg didn't even try to hide her unbidden desire. It was safe to want, she thought ironically, when there were so many people around, that you could not do anything about it. Not like the previous night, when she and Rob had so awkwardly said their good-byes in his barren apartment. They had both wanted then, too, but Meg had kept her cool distance, knowing that if she went to bed with Rob again it would be a commitment of sorts. And that decision she was not ready to make.

"Everyone here loves you," she blurted out.

"Present company included?" His brown eyes darkened.

"I mean your family. Your colleagues. Even Miss Sultry Voice. Did you know that Lila loves you?"

"Meg, I have never had an affair with anyone in my office. That would be business suicide, even if I were interested in the woman. Which in this case, incidentally, I have never been."

"I didn't ask if you had an affair with her. I asked if you knew she loved you. She wants you to be happy, you know."

"Who? Lila?"

They were still treading water, and it made the conversation tiring. Or maybe the subject was old and dead anyway, Meg thought in disillusionment. She began to swim over to the nearest ladder. Rob matched her strokes and caught her arm before she could climb out.

"Hang on here a minute," he urged, hooking an arm around one side of the ladder. Reluctantly she followed suit. Mike and the children were still playing noisily on the grass, but the husbands were up on the patio nearer the house, helping with the meal. A strange sort of public intimacy enshrouded their hesitant words.

"Meg, I have never had an affair with Lila Faloney." He seemed to think she had that on her mind. She smiled sadly.

"I know. It's just that everyone wants happiness for you. They know you deserve it. Last night your sisters told me about Kansas."

"What about Kansas?" he snapped, flipping back his head to shake the water off as if he needed that preparation to do battle.

"Oh, just about those history stories your mother would read to you on rainy days. And the aunt who read the encyclopedia aloud during snowy evenings. They claim you know ten years more of the encyclopedia than they do."

"We had lots more snow than rain in Kansas." Rob laughed, his expression relaxing a little. "And by the time the girls came along, Aunt Sophie's eyesight was bad enough to slow her down." His shoulders dipped under the water, then out again, and little pools remained in hollows along the muscled arm gripping the ladder. Pensively Meg reached a finger over to begin scooping the moisture out. He fell quite still, watching her.

"Ten years of Aunt Sophie's reading accounts for *A* through *L*," he said thickly. "If you need to know anything about the 1930 *Encyclopaedia Britannica* up to *L*, ask me, not the girls."

"Love."

He twisted his sun-bleached brows in confusion.

"What does the 1930 *Encyclopaedia Britannica* say about love?" she clarified.

"Nothing. That's a dictionary word. Encyclopedias only deal with tangibles."

She had all the water off his shoulder. But still her hand rested there. "Is your Aunt Sophie the one who's still alive?"

"Uh-huh." He tilted his head so that he could rest his lips briefly against her knuckles. "She was the eldest, and after mother died last year, she was the only sister left. Ninety-one years old."

"You're doing a very special thing, letting the girls help pay for her nursing home, you know."

"They told you about that, too? Do we have any family secrets left?" He sounded annoyed.

"Rob, it's not every man who would understand that they needed to help. Even though you could afford to take care of that aunt yourself, you've done a lot for their self-esteem by not doing so. Helen said that they're just beginning to realize how much you gave up, supporting the whole family all those years and putting her and Patty through college."

Rob twisted toward the ladder, grabbing it with both hands.

"Rob!"

Reluctantly he sank back into the water. Grimacing, he began to trace the little droplets his splashing had left behind on her body. "You women dwell too much in the past."

"They think the hardest part must have been that no one, not even your father, realized what dreams you were giving up."

"They make too much of that pro-baseball contract. If a man misses one dream, he goes for another."

But he deserves a chance to reach at least one, Meg thought.

"Don't you see? Everyone wants you to have something of your own for a change. I do, too. But look what you'd be getting with me. A retread wife and someone else's son. I've already failed miserably once when I tried to make a man happy. And I still haven't resolved how Dane can be fitted back into Mike's life. It's selfish of me even to consider marrying you."

"Oh, Goddamn!" He lunged out of the pool in a swell of water and quickly pulled Meg out beside him. If they hadn't been at his sister's home he would have taken her right then and there. Meg could see it in the anger and frustration enveloping him as he stared at her near-naked body dripping with the pool water. "You'd better get dressed."

Disturbed, she began walking toward the dressing cabana.

"Meg."

She turned at his soft entreaty.

"Quit thinking so much. Just follow your heart."

Chapter Nine

Dear Dane and Karen,

Mike has discovered word processors, as you can see from this photo. I understand that next year his school will begin some computer instruction for fifth-graders. I hope he will enjoy that, too—it seems to be a necessity for the future. His life now revolves around baseball, fishing, swimming and being outside for any excuse. In the summers I cut my work schedule back to four shortened days so we can do our share of entertaining and transporting friends. About your last letter—yes, Mike is late losing his baby teeth. I didn't realize you had been, too, Dane. Since I don't hear from your parents, I would appreciate your letting me know any other potential health quirks Mike might encounter.

Meg listened idly to the store conversation humming outside her office, then looked back at the letter. Charlie had said that she should make decisions. Rob had said that she should quit thinking so much and follow her heart. The two bits of advice seemed incompatible.

She still hadn't brought Dane any closer to seeing his son. But the very thought of her and Mike's being around her former husband brought a wave of nausea, matching what she had suffered constantly the last few months of their marriage. She had never known then what condition Dane would be in from one moment to the next, and that tension had taken its toll on her health. Meg drew a deep breath, realizing that she could not handle this reunion. And that reality made the decision clear. Saying no was a decision, too, wasn't it? Nevertheless, her pen remained poised above the paper, her heart urging her to encourage Dane's recovery. Were there other possibilities than an outright refusal? *"Later?" "I'm working on it?" "Soon?"* Yes, of course there were. And surely Dane could read that pending decision between the lines. She added one final sentence to her letter:

I have told Mike that you are recovering from your illness, now live with your new wife, and that you have been asking how he is getting along. He posed for this picture to send you.

Meg

She felt it significant that she had not mentioned where the picture had been taken or by whom. Surely it was a sign of her coping that she did not use Rob Dowell as a crutch this time. Encouraged, she sealed and addressed the letter and took it in to the stack accumulating on Susan's desk.

"We ought to quit giving you mail duty in this hot weather," Meg observed thoughtfully as she noticed how cumbersome and bulky her secretary was becoming.

"The postal branch is just across the mall and I need the exercise," Susan assured her. "My doctor says I should walk at least a mile every day."

"Well, if it ever seems too much for you, just say so. We can always wait and let the afternoon delivery man pick it up. We'll have to do that when you go on leave next month anyway. Has Penny come in yet?"

"She's out on the floor somewhere."

Meg went to look for her, was buttonholed instead by some customers seeking advice on summer jewelry and didn't get back to her office for another half hour. This time Penny was there.

"You're just who I want to see." Meg perched on the edge of Penny's desk. "I've received confirmations for informational showings of those two young designers we talked about in California. If you're still willing to pursue this career department, I should get out to L.A. early in July."

"After all the encouragement you got from Cara's friends, I want you to keep at it. I'll probably only inventory one rack at first, while we test out our market. But treat these showings just as if you're buying for a whole department. We need all the pricing and discount information we can get. Is Rob going to be in town much this summer? We could work that trip around his schedule."

"That's nice of you to think of, Penny. He hopes to stop by today, but after this it will be every other weekend at best. He said that throughout June and July he's going to be involved with some big reorganization at Allied."

Meg started to go back on the floor to visit with customers, then thoughtfully returned to Penny.

"Are you feeling all right?"

Penny was staring at some things on her desk. "Hm? Oh sure."

"Anything I can do?" A pensive Penny was always of concern to Meg.

"Ship Charlie off somewhere. He's thinking about marriage again. I can just tell."

Meg leaned against the door frame. "Is that so terrible? I assume you mean marriage to you."

"Who else? Lord, he's been a part of my life since I was fifteen."

"You're kidding!"

"Fifteen. We met when he was working on a ranch near the west Texas town where my grandmother lived. I went back home from my visit with my virginity gone and him stuck in my mind so much I could never get him out."

"How soon did you get married?"

"He made me wait for fourteen damn years—until after his first well came in and he felt he could support me in the way I was used to. I was twenty-nine and he was forty when we finally eloped. That's probably what's been wrong all along. We both got too set in our ways."

"Fourteen years is a long time to wait." Meg could not even visualize such a thing. Here Rob was getting impatient with just a few weeks of indecision on her part.

"You'd think by now it would be easier to know what to do."

Meg thought about Penny's observation as she wandered throughout the store, assisting customers and salesclerks. For her it had been so simple when she had married the first time. *Do you love him?* Certainly. *Do you want to get married?* Oh, yes! The only problem had been fitting the wedding in between the semester's final exams, the church's bookings and the starting date for Dane's summer job.

Now, some ten years later, love seemed an intangible that could be applied to so many relationships, none of which demanded the wisdom marriage did. Even the encyclopedia couldn't handle "love," so how could she be expected to?

"If we got married, I'm afraid I'd miss the challenge of this job," she told Rob later that day when he stopped by to see her. They had grabbed a hurried lunch at a cafeteria near the mall, and she was idiotically trying to carry on a serious conversation in front of the store before he had to rush to his appointment.

"Then keep on working." He swooped forward to kiss her on the mouth despite the gawking shoppers and seemed unworried that she was not jumping at the chance to spend the rest of her life with him.

His patient, supportive attitude continued throughout June and July.

"Mike hero-worships you right now, but it would be different if you were around every weekend," she told Rob a couple of weeks later after the three of them had been to a movie together. "He can be overactive and demanding like any other child." Rob took her into his arms in her living room and told her that he had some overactive and demanding things in mind himself. Since Mike was dozing in full sight of them from his bedroom, she had not learned the full extent of Rob's deviant thoughts, but she had certainly never got back to discussing childrearing.

"I'm just not fair to you," she told him mournfully in early July, after he had managed to spend two full days in a row with her and Mike. "Some flashback from the past that I can't control keeps popping up in my behavior. Take this weekend. When you stuck a few beers into my picnic cooler of sodas, I immediately snapped at you."

"I won't be the first man who's learned to tune out a nagging wife."

"Would you quit joking about this," she insisted.

"Haven't you ever wondered why you didn't immediately refuse to marry me?" He rubbed his thumb along the third finger of her left hand as if measuring how their wedding band would fit there. "Sort that out in your mind, and we can get on with the happily-ever-after."

He was saying good-bye on his way to the airport, and she was frustrated with the whole situation: with Mike living for the days Rob would be in town; with herself for letting the past complicate the present; with Rob and her never having enough time alone to talk things out. And most of all, frustrated beyond bearing from trying to stay out of Rob's bed until she decided if she could manage the kind of commitment he wanted from her.

"I haven't said no right off because you're comfortable to be around," she objected angrily. "You have no noticeable bad habits. You never argue. You're virile. You're interesting. And you're too perfect to be true."

"I like you, too," he teased before giving her hand one last squeeze.

It was not until the end of July that the answer finally became shockingly clear to Meg.

She had left Mike in the care of her parents and spent three days in California sounding out two young Hollywood costume designers on their plans to go commercial. Their projections had paralleled Meg's expectations for her career line, and the possibilities of making the idea work for Shreveport seemed closer than ever. Meg left Los Angeles exhilarated and anxious to relate her experiences to Rob, who planned to arrive in Shreveport the same evening she did.

While her parents and Mike brought her home from the airport, she contentedly half listened to their stories of how they had spent their time and wondered if Rob would mind picking up fast food for dinner. She had so much to tell him that she didn't want to spend her time cooking. Once he got to her house she wanted to put her feet up and have a totally one-sided conversation at the expense of his always-agreeable ear.

Then gradually she realized a significant explanation had slipped past her consciousness. "He's not coming at all this week?" She was certain that she must have misunderstood her mother's message.

"That's what Rob said when he called early this morning. Something about being held up in Atlanta with all-day meetings and having to see bankers in Houston on Friday. He didn't know where to reach you to tell you himself.''

"I wanted to talk to him, but Grandma wouldn't let me," Mike complained. He said it eagerly, as if he had been waiting hours for the opportunity to tattle.

"Mike, I explained that he was calling from his company's office in Atlanta." Pauline O'Mara's voice was overly patient and smooth, a dangerous sign that she was contemplating a full-scale lecture. "I could hear men talking in the background. He was too busy."

"He told me once he was never too busy for me," Mike argued.

Meg placed a warning hand on her son's knee to stop the conflict that apparently had been raging since the call had come. She didn't think that either Mike or she needed one of her mother's well-intentioned lectures at that moment.

Mike lapsed into pouting silence.

Out of the corner of her eye Meg noticed how his lower lip puffed up and ballooned forward. She wondered if pouting helped lessen the disappointment when your expectations fell through. She felt like puffing out her own lip.

Rob's not coming this weekend? The ramifications were shockingly dreary. She wouldn't be able to tell him about that lady with the pink-and-green hair selling candy firecrackers in front of her hotel. Or about the easy handling, casual elegance of these new career collections and how both designers were willing to give Penelope's a fantastic special discount in exchange for promotion. Or about the soda machine near the taxi stand that had spouted mountains of change at her like a Las Vegas jackpot.

How she hurt. She felt just as she had when she was fifteen and had leaped off a high board and confidently floated in graceful form for the perfect swan dive. She had landed in a belly flop, and in that horrifying instant her unprepared body had been slapped all over with hot pain. Yet the worst had still been to come. She had had to struggle to the surface and climb out of the draggingly engulfing water in front of her friends as if nothing had happened.

"You and Mike could have dinner with us tonight," Meg's mother was offering pleasantly. Given some quiet time, she wouldn't take long to get over being miffed.

Mike shoved his elbows into Meg's rib and shook his head. Setting aside anger was a slower process for him.

"I think we'd better stay home." Meg marveled that words would come at all. "I'm tired and I do have to work tomorrow."

Her parents stayed at the house awhile, visiting about her trip. She mentioned seeing California's expected quota of fascinating people, but although they listened politely enough, they seemed more eager for their turn to tell how much help Mike had been in finishing some painting work at their house. She had wanted to hear all that, too, of course, but it had been a disappointment that the conversation never again came back to her trip. Later she started telling Mike about things she had done while she was away, but he had looked at her blankly until she paused; then he had asked her why she hadn't gone to a baseball game instead of the theater.

"It would have been the same with Rob," she tried to tell herself as she got ready for bed. "He wouldn't have wanted to hear all my ramblings, either."

But somehow she knew that wasn't true. She tossed restlessly, thinking about him, regretting so much that he wasn't there. Just when she began to doze, the doorbell rang. She bounded out of bed and ran through the living room in her nightgown, certain that he had come after all. Only when she started to turn the door handle did she come to her senses.

"Who is it?" she asked tentatively, expecting some distraught neighbor in trouble.

"Don't be afraid. It's just Rob."

"Just Rob?" She threw open the door like a wild woman.

"I couldn't stand not seeing you at all for a whole month," he explained sheepishly from the darkened porch. "I have to catch another flight out of here in four hours."

And that's when the decision came. Crystal clear. *I shouldn't marry you—I have too many scars. But I must. You fill my life with something beautiful no one else can give me.* The thought was urgent and final. But Meg couldn't express it in words.

"You weren't here for me to talk to," she wailed instead, jerking him inside and throwing herself into his arms.

SHE WAS NOT HOLDING BACK as she usually did. Rob wondered at it, even as she draped herself against his chest, fumed at him in a garble of accusations about no one listening to her, and planted wet kisses all over his face.

He figured that something had gone wrong in her day to drive her to him so uninhibitedly. But never one to overlook a miracle, he half lifted her to his side so that she could still feverishly spread her kisses all over him while he closed up the house and led her past Mike's open door. In between bestowing exuberant hugs she was jabbering about things like pink-and-green hair, slot machines and baseball theaters. He locked her bedroom door and undressed them both in a comic attempt at quiet.

And that was when he knew she was going to marry him.

It wasn't verbalized among all the words she seemed impelled to spout in whispered doses between their ravenous caresses. But he knew it. If his physical needs hadn't been so pressing he would have insisted she say "Yes, I'll be your wife, Robert Clark Dowell," just to hear how musically wonderful it would sound. But he was hurting like a roped stallion near its favorite mate, so he let her answer his proposal through the heat of her body, interpreting in the silence, *I'm yours. Help me!*

And help her he did as best he could—with the stroke of his tongue and the praise of his words and the fire of his hungry touch.

This time she seemed to want to please him and he taught her how. She became so instinctively good at it that when she eventually guided him into the privacy of her body, he could wrap his loneliness in hers and go with her closer to heaven than he had ever believed possible for mere humans to venture.

"Do you know how much I missed you?" she asked later, lying spent by his side with his hand clasped in hers.

"You gave me a little hint," he quipped, wearily raising a hand to brush across her naked breast. She was still hardened, and he turned to his side so he could leave his hand resting there to help soften her into rest. She moved more comfortably into his touch. "What happened to you in California?"

Her silent laugh raised her chest against his fingers. "Lots of interesting things that don't seem so important right now. It was just not having you here to tell them to."

He slid his hand over to soothe the other breast, easing closer against her side. "You know what I think? The day you can throw yourself into my arms like that without any reason at all except that you love me, we'll have it made."

She closed her eyes lazily, knowing as he did that they did not dare drift into the restoring luxury of sleep; the specter of Rob's necessary flight schedule hung around them both. And so they lay quietly together, happy with what they had shared, but greedily wanting more. Wanting to move on to that special enervated bliss of sweet sleep known only by lovers, wanting everything but the separation that was facing them.

Finally Rob made himself stir from her bed.

"It was crazy for you to stop in Shreveport," Meg fussed while she lay in bed and watched him dress. "You'll be worn out later this morning."

"I'm worn out right now, thanks to you."

She laughed in smug satisfaction. He pulled on his shirt, meticulously buttoned it up, fiddled with the cuffs. It bothered him that the words were still unsaid. "Am I to take it that this means you will let me make an honest woman of you?" he finally managed in a casual tone while he zipped his slacks.

"If you still want to," she agreed shyly.

"That's a hell of a way to finally accept a proposal, but I'd be proud to make an honest woman of Meghan Bronson." His voice was husky, and when he looked into her eyes he seemed so vulnerable that she wanted to leap out of bed despite her nakedness and comfort him. It was almost frightening how trustingly he placed his happiness into her safekeeping. Meg sighed when he perched on the edge of the bed to pull on his shoes, and the moment for comforting was gone.

"Why did you have to stay in Atlanta so late? Did something go wrong?"

He tied one shoe and reached for the other.

"No, things went right. I accepted a promotion."

She popped to a sitting position, dragging the sheet with her. "I thought you'd just turned down one. The one your sultry Lila wanted to talk to you about."

He laughed. "Still jealous?"

"No. Yes! What promotion?"

"The first offer I turned down was to establish a branch division, probably in Miami. Not an office. A new division."

"But wouldn't that have been a challenging opportunity?"

"A marvelously challenging opportunity, not to

mention a lucrative one. It would also have tied me up in Florida for months. I wouldn't have been able to chase you.''

Her responsive groan of anguish was genuine. "Rob, this is like Kansas repeating itself all over. I won't be responsible for wrecking your life!"

His other shoe was on. He stood up and looped his tie under his collar. When Meg scrambled out of bed and went searching for something to wear, he was distracted by her nudity; but once she had slipped into her robe, he deftly finished the knot.

"Rob, we'd be fools to repeat what your father and mother did to themselves.'' She stood flat-footed in front of him, belting her robe about herself as if she were a boxer readying for a fight. "You shouldn't have—"

"My job is not what gives meaning to my life. If I can enjoy whatever I do to earn a living, then I'm satisfied. I don't need status, and I don't need artistic fulfillment. But I do need you. After I felt that there was a genuine possibility we would marry, I still couldn't see uprooting you and Mike right now, even if you would agree to it. There will be enough adjustments for the three of us without throwing you into a new city.''

Even before he finished his long discourse, her hands against her lips were trembling in that characteristic way she had when she was worried. He smiled reassuringly.

"Besides, I'm not exactly a lousy businessman after all these years. I convinced Allied the new corporate services division should be in Shreveport instead of Miami. The business climate is favorable here, it's in a central location for our fastest-developing marketing area, and it's Southwestern enough in culture to be amenable for my key personnel, most of whom will be Texans. We signed the architectural contract this week in Atlanta, and I'll be finalizing the financing in Houst—"

"You'll be based in Shreveport? You're going to be through with the traveling?"

"That's right. I'll be bringing these ears home every evening and you can talk and talk and—"

"Rob, tell me!"

"They offered me the same promotion again, but this time with the division definitely being located in Shreveport," he started to explain. Once the implication hit her, she didn't give him a chance to tell the rest. She threw herself into his arms.

"You'll really be here? Oh, Rob! I don't care if our meals are any old time of the day or night."

"You're about to knock me over."

"I don't care if your whiskers get all over my lingerie!"

"I think you've lost me—Meg!"

She began hugging him and crying and laughing so excitedly that Mike woke up and came running in to see what the ruckus was about. Rob had to watch the clock and hunt for his briefcase while fielding kisses from both of them.

"How long have you known this was a possibility? Why didn't you tell us before?" Meg hung onto one arm and Mike seemed permanently attached to the other as Rob worked his way to the front door.

"I figured if you knew I'd be around all the time, you'd put off deciding to marry me."

"Are we marrying you?" Mike asked.

Meg smiled at the "we," and Rob picked him up high in his arms before answering solemnly. "Yes, Mike, you two are marrying me. While I'm in Houston you both decide when and where, and I'll be there."

"Tomorrow!"

"Wonderful," Rob agreed.

"Mike, we can't get married that fast. We'll have to make some arrangements."

The clock was pressing. Rob eased out the door, spreading his kisses and his love as he went.

"We'll take care of everything," Mike confidently assured him.

THE WEDDING PLANS got out of hand, of course.

Meg set the date for the second Sunday afternoon in August and had planned to have the most minimal of functions, with just Rob's and her immediate families. She regretfully didn't even plan to include Penny because she knew if she made any exceptions it would be hard to draw the line. Then Charlie fouled everything up.

When he heard about the upcoming marriage, he made one of his rare storming appearances into Meg's office.

"Are you marrying him because of the boy?" The old man spoke gruffly as he stuffed some tobacco into his battered pipe but did not light it. Meg was not offended by his inquisitiveness. The question seemed important to her, too. Rob deserved more than acquiring an instant stepson.

"No, I'm being selfish," she said slowly. "This is for me. I just hope Mike and I can make him happy."

She watched Charlie sink into the big oak armchair they kept there especially for him. Her answer seemed to have satisfied him. "Aren't you going to invite me to the wedding?" he barked. She couldn't help smiling at the thought of what a storm she would create if she invited Charlie and not Penny.

"What's so funny about me wanting to come to a wedding? Despite what Penny has probably told you, I do own a suit and I do know how to behave in church if I have to."

Meg couldn't resist. She knew Rob would be charmed to have Charlie there, and all along she had wanted Penny to come. And so she had made those two exceptions to family only. Then Penny had, in typical autocratic fashion, invited the whole store staff. Mike had invited Molly, Diego and Tommy Preston; Meg's parents had included their two favorite neighbors; several of Rob's staff in New Orleans assumed they would be coming; and some of Meg's best customers began to drop hints about attending. The list grew.

What Meg had originally thought she would easily fit into her work schedule had become an event that took much too much of her time and energy. She chose a new dress—blue, because that was the color Rob had first seen her in and she sentimentally wanted to please him. She talked Mike into a tan suit. She ordered a boutonniere and small nosegay. She planned an early supper reception for who knew how many people, as family and friends kept inviting more to come.

She was exhausted as the wedding day approached.

And frustrated. She and Rob had had almost no time alone since they decided to marry. In order to arrange for a week's vacation together both of them had been busier than ever at their jobs. And during the time Rob could fit in being in town, Mike had hung onto him like a leech.

On the Saturday morning before the wedding, Rob pulled up at her house in his own car with his entire wardrobe, the geranium and his Pet Rock. Just minutes later her two brothers and her sister swooped into town with their whole families. Rob's sisters and their families arrived in the afternoon, and after that, chaos reigned. People of all ages and sizes were dropping in and out of Meg's house. She did her best to help Rob's family and her own exuberant siblings get acquainted amicably. But occasionally difficult moments nevertheless occurred.

Helen's husband saw Mike throwing balls into the laundry basket Meg had taped to the back porch railing, and he offered to install a basketball hoop on the carport facing. Meg's brother Tom had gotten in on the act and the two disagreed on the best way to proceed. Finally Rob smoothed it all over by suggesting he put it up himself after the wedding. Wives on both sides gratefully insisted on that solution.

And there was the debacle over Susan Forsyth. Not that it was Susan's fault. She had stopped by with Meg's veil, which had been designed by their alteration specialist to match her dress. With her baby due in less than a month, Susan had been uncomfortable and quite self-conscious about her appearance. Meg had been trying to reassure her that she looked fine enough to meet Rob's sisters, but as they walked toward Helen and Patty, Susan had said tiredly, "Just wait until you're eight and a half months pregnant again. When your husband tells you you're beautiful, it isn't so easy to be convinced."

And Meg had teased unthinkingly, "You make me believe Rob and I are lucky we're too old to be thinking about having a family."

She hadn't consciously meant a thing by it. And yet with Rob, Helen and Patty hearing every word, she realized she had publicly served notice she did not plan to have Rob's baby. Done it automatically without ever realizing that reservations about starting a new family had been lurking in the back of her mind. She was aghast.

Rob managed some intervention that smoothed over the awkwardness. But the incident became just one more nagging, unsettled pressure building up within her. She worried more and more that she simply might not have the resilient capacity to make Rob happy. And the confusion that night of the two blending families made the situation seem even worse.

Their wedding day dawned with Meg wishing she and Rob had eloped like errant teenagers. That way, she thought in desperation, they might at least have had a chance to make a go of their marriage.

"I haven't even had time to make room for your clothes in my closets," she whispered to Rob while they waited in the minister's study to walk into the chapel together. "And we'll have to set up a desk for you somewhere in the laundry room until I can arrange things in the den. Oh, Rob, things are such a mess!"

She was probably not the first bride in history to go into a ceremony with her eyes puffy and her mascara less than perfect. Nor was Rob the first groom in history to wonder why so many people seemed to enjoy attending weddings. But like all brides and grooms, they made it.

The peace of the church settled about them as they walked hand in hand past all their loving family and friends to face the minister. And something about the afternoon sunshine filtering softly in through the stained-glass chips in the lofty windows centered their concentration on essentials. They wanted to be together. Everything went serenely from then on.

They said their vows with sincerity, greeted every single guest at the overflowing reception with genuine affection, and managed to slip away before Meg's brothers could tie cans to the back of Rob's car.

They had told everyone they would be vacationing in northern Wyoming. And actually that had been their plan. They needed to be alone in a picturesque environment. But when Charlie saw how exhausted Meg and Rob both looked the night before the wedding, he had taken them aside and told them that if they didn't want to face a trip, they could hole up at his lake place. They had been doubtful that they would change their plans, but he had given them a key and guaranteed to have the house stocked with food if they decided to take him up on the offer.

Once they were man and wife and driving to the airport to catch their flight to Wyoming, they had looked at each other tiredly, and by unspoken agreement, turned around and headed to Cross Lake instead. Within a half hour they were splashing in Charlie's swimming pool, washing away the dripping mascara and the spilled champagne and the hurt feelings. Laughter and exercise provided the necessary safety valve that restored them. And then their loneliness and passion took over.

Meg decided she had had enough sun and went inside to dress. She was standing at the door of the guest bathroom, wrapped in a towel and brushing her sunbleached hair, when Rob stepped into the cool, deeply carpeted bedroom to get a change of clothes. Instantly she trembled before him in undisguised longing, and his tanned body was drawn toward the softness of hers.

"Meg, darling," he breathed against her shoulders as his swim trunks dropped to the floor and his hands found the tucks of the towel, "I love you so much."

For five days after that they alternated exploring each other with boating or lying lazily in the sun. They subsisted on love, fish and Charlie's provisions of bologna, V-8 juice, chocolate bars and canned lima beans.

It was a magical honeymoon. Not once did either admit to pondering the responsibilities and adjustments they both would have to face when they returned to the real world.

Chapter Ten

They discovered one thing right off. Meg's house would be too small for them. The room she optimistically called a den was actually a tiny third bedroom, probably originally intended as a nursery. The previous owner had opened it up to the living room and lined the walls with bookshelves, making it even smaller. It had served as Mike's winter playroom, and Meg's sleeper-couch was the only furniture in it. They had to move that out to the laundry room to make space for Rob's desk, but Rob insisted that Mike's toy box remain, even though it meant a tight squeeze to get into his chair.

By the weekend after they returned from Charlie's, when they got around to unpacking Rob's business wardrobe, they discovered how inadequate the closet space would be. "I could pitch some of these suits, now that I'm going to be in town most of the time," Rob told Meg when they reached the end of hanger space in her bedroom and still had two garment bags to unpack. "I probably won't need so many, since half of them won't be at the cleaner's while I'm traveling."

"Don't you dare. You look great in every one of those suits. We'll do as Mike suggested—put one of those rolling racks out in the laundry room to hold winter coats. That will leave the entry closet open."

"It's a good thing I didn't move all my things from the office, too," Rob said. "We'd have to sleep out in the laundry room." On their way out to tackle the coat closet, he absentmindedly patted the little brown-and-gray rock nesting by his geranium in the bedroom window.

Meg was touched by the unconcious gesture, for it told her better than words what her silly gift meant to him. "I want you to have all your things here," she said huskily. "I want this to feel like home to you."

"My home is where you and Mike are." He probably would have kissed her then, but Mike came tumbling in from playing at his newly installed basketball hoop, bringing to Meg's attention another inadequacy of her house.

Privacy.

Any couple needed that occasionally. And for newly-weds, having a nine-year-old son rambling underfoot and sleeping only one thin wall away hindered the growth of deep affection nurtured by spontaneity.

They didn't actually talk about moving to a larger house. But as the lazy summer days rolled on toward fall, Meg noticed that Rob seemed to spend as much time looking over the real-estate sections as she did.

For the first few weeks Rob was not home as much as he had hoped to be. There was still traveling to be done in preparation for the new division. And the hours working in Shreveport were long, too. He located temporary office space in a downtown building and brought in a skeleton staff. Meg was pleased that Grace, a widow, had opted to make the move to Shreveport. And although she kept very quiet about it, Meg was delighted that Lila Faloney had apparently accepted the inevitable and remained in New Orleans.

For Meg's part, daily life went fairly much as usual. Delberta had developed a great fondness for Rob and agreeably managed to clean around the crowding his joining the household created. Mike continued to stay with his grandparents on the days that Meg or Delberta were not at the house. Of course, having Rob around in the evenings was an adjustment for Meg, but a pleasant one. Even though the togetherness in their small house dampened the potential of play in their lovemaking, Meg found great satisfaction in going to sleep each night with Rob's warm presence next to her.

Her contentment in her new life grew steadily, yet she sensed that for Rob, at least, their relationship was not complete. He seemed to be waiting for something *transforming* to occur in their marriage. And she felt helpless to understand what new element it would take to convert them from two affectionate individuals into the lasting unit that he apparently envisioned.

ROB STAYED HOME late from work on Mike's first day of school. During the waning days of August the boy had seemed so alternately wary and excited that Rob had identified closely with him. Well he remembered each new start of the school year in Kansas, when he would be eager to see all his friends again and to get back to team sports. But he had always been apprehensive about meeting his new teacher and doing the school-work. Now, as a supposedly mature adult, he thought perhaps an extra presence at home that opening September morning might make Mike's trauma easier to overcome.

"What time do I have to be there?" Mike asked the question for the third time while looking anxiously at the new wristwatch he and Rob had shopped for only a few days earlier.

"Eight-thirty. Same as last year," Meg said calmly, clearing her son's breakfast dishes off the table. He had eaten very little, which was unusual for him, but Rob was relieved that Meg realized the boy had enough on his mind and did not reprimand him.

"It's almost eight o'clock already. Corey will probably be late coming by." Meticulously Mike rearranged the little pile of tablets, pencils and crayons in his back-pack to make more room for his lunch box. Then that went carefully in on top. He looked at his watch again. "We'll probably be late getting to school on our very first day."

"Corey was never late last year," Meg pointed out reasonably, knowing Mike's friend from next door was predictably prompt. "And you boys only have three blocks to walk."

"But this would probably be his first time. I'd better go over there and get him."

The leave-taking involved the expected hustle: the reluctant brushing of his teeth, an adjustment of the backpack on his shoulders, a hasty kiss to Meg and a serious wave to Rob, a trip back in to get the lefty scissors he had forgotten; a request to Rob to help him adjust his watch, which he was convinced was running one minute late; then the amazing silence.

"And so another year begins." Meg refilled both their coffee cups and sank into the chair opposite Rob. "Do you feel as worn out as I do?"

He laughed. "You got off easily. On each first day of school, my mother always spent at least five minutes going through my pockets confiscating marbles and rubber bands."

"I should have checked him for Matchbox cars," she admitted, sipping contentedly from the steaming cup. "He was brokenhearted last year when the teacher impounded one of his favorites."

"With that having happened, he'll know better than to have a favorite with him this time," Rob predicted. He felt in no hurry at all to leave. It had been a long time since he and Meg had had much time just to chat. "Have you heard how Susan and the new baby are getting along?"

"They've been home from the hospital two weeks," Meg told him, and the doctor says that she can start taking the baby out for short trips. "Penny and I gave her one of those wonderful canvas collapsible strollers our customers like so much. We told her now she doesn't have any excuse not to bring her new daughter to see everyone."

"She's not planning to come back to work, then?"

"Only part-time, I think. Penny's pretty adaptable if she finds a good employee. They've worked out some deal where Susan will come in a few mornings a week and do a good bit of the bookkeeping at home."

"Doesn't that leave you without enough help?"

"I have to have some daily secretarial coverage. Right now we're using someone from a temporary service until we see what Susan decides to do."

"Could you ever work anything like that out for yourself? I mean, if we got a bigger house and you wanted to cut back your hours a little. Say, like keeping your summer schedule all year long?"

Meg looked surprised. She obviously hadn't considered the possibility. "I don't know how Penny's health would hold up if she had to share the managerial duties in the winter, too. Are you hinting that I should quit?"

He noticed some hostility there and regretted that he had brought the idle conversation up. Especially on such a pleasant morning. "No, in fact, I think it would be a mistake for you to quit. You're good at your job and you obviously like it, so why give it up? You just seem to get such a kick running around with Mike, puttering in your yard, and cooking special things—I thought you might enjoy having a little more time for those interests, too."

Meg seemed to relax. "I suppose there are some aspects of the work that I don't necessarily have to do at the store on a set schedule. Like setting up this career line. Most of that is *thought* work: looking through the professional fashion publications, contacting designers, talking to prospective customers about their needs."

"How is all that going? I haven't heard you talk about it lately."

"You shouldn't have asked." She laughed, looking at the clock. "Do you have to get to work anytime soon?"

He shoved away his cup and stretched lazily, wondering why he hadn't thought of poking around after breakfast with her before. It was marvelous fun. "Not too soon. How is it going?"

"Oh, Rob, it's been fascinating to work on! That crafty Penny was right on the button about the city not having enough professional women yet to justify the type of department I had originally envisioned. But we've come up with some compromises for a smaller inventory catering to working women. After I get back from this buying trip to New York next week, I'll know exactly what I'll want from there and can complete my orders from those two California designers."

"I didn't know you were going to New York next week."

She looked stunned. Then horrified. "I haven't told you, have I? Oh! I'd kill you if you pulled that on me. I'm just so accustomed to making these arrangements by myself, I forgot."

Rob supposed her embarrassed explanation made sense. But how could she have forgotten? A buying trip like that would have been in the works for weeks. He wondered if she had subconsciously postponed telling him.

"So what arrangements did you work out?" He couldn't help it. The hurt showed in his tense voice.

"Penny's taking me out to the airport Monday noon, and I'll get home Saturday morning in time to go straight to work."

"Now I'm going to have to mimic Mike. What time does he get out of school?"

"Three-thirty, but—"

"I could arrange to get home that early for a week. Delberta will still be here on Monday and Thursday, won't she?"

"You don't have to worry about all that; I've already taken care of everything. Mike's going to stay with my parents."

"You mean after school?"

"No. He'll live there while I'm gone, and they'll go on a fishing trip over the weekend. Rob, don't look that way. It's what I've always done."

He didn't know how he was looking, but if it was anything like the way he was feeling, she should be alarmed. He'd never experienced such pain. A greasy scum was forming on the remaining cold liquid in his coffee cup, casting the iridescent rainbow colors that reminded him of an oil spill he had seen once in the ocean. Thousands of living creatures had died in that mess. He stared at it in sick fascination. Silence and tension hung heavy over him. Finally he scraped back his chair.

"Rob, don't go. Aren't you going to talk about this?"

"What am I supposed to say? 'How nice that your parents can take Mike, so I won't be bothered with the brat?'" Discouragement mingled equally with hurt as he slipped into his suit coat. "You couldn't have picked a better way to force a wedge between Mike and me. Is that what you intended? To convince him that I don't want him, because you can't trust that I do?"

"No!"

"Then what, dammit?"

She had no answer.

"What did Mike say about this arrangement of yours?"

"I haven't told him yet, but why would he say anything? This is what we always do when I'm out of town."

"And your parents didn't find it strange, now that you're married?"

First she looked surprised at the idea. Then embarrassed. He suspected that she had only then realized her parents had assumed Rob would be out of town, too. He grunted his disgust.

"How are you going to explain to Mike that although I have managed to make it home on time for dinner every evening since I relocated in Shreveport, I won't do it when he needs me? Or that although I've installed computer terminals here so I can access my files and take care of all emergencies through this house, I prefer to go to the office instead of being with him? Why don't you just tell him I don't love him?"

"Loving him doesn't mean you have to care for him. I've learned the hard way to take full responsibility for my son."

"I'm Robert Clark Dowell, not Dane Bronson! You might do well to quit confusing the two of us."

He paused for a moment, hoping she would offer to change her plans and let him keep Mike as if the boy were his own son. But she hesitated just the fraction of a second that told him all he needed to know. She hadn't managed to bury the past yet.

It seemed unbelievable that in the matter of an instant one of the most pleasant mornings of his life had turned into a disaster. They had had their first real argument and he needed a hell of a lot of space before he could sort it out. For the first time since they were married, he left for work without kissing her good-bye.

Rob didn't fight her arrangements. That night at the dinner table when she told Mike he would be at his grandparents' in her absence, it obviously astounded her that Mike exhibited the very resentment Rob had predicted. He had looked over at Rob as if he had been betrayed, later turned down Rob's offers to play catch and offered good night only to Meg when bedtime came.

"You were right. I've made a terrible mistake," she told Rob brokenly that evening when they were in bed. "I'd better call Mother and tell her Mike will be staying home instead."

"Leave it—the damage is done. Mike doesn't need further confusing signals sent his way right now." Rob rested his head on his crossed arms and looked at the ceiling. A great sadness dominated him.

"Rob, I'm so sorry." He didn't doubt that she really meant it. And perhaps if she had touched him, even just laid a hand on his shoulder, it would have been all right. But when she stayed stiffly on her back, saying her words to the same ceiling he was studying so intently, he couldn't bear it.

"So am I," he said wearily, turning away to his side.

Later, in the dawning of a new day, he couldn't help himself. Things should not remain that way between a man and his wife. He had turned to her, and she had responded almost gratefully. But their silent lovemaking had a desperation about it that frightened them both.

MEG WONDERED, A WEEK LATER, as she was walking the corridors of her Manhattan hotel to a welcoming cocktail party put on by the fashion industry, if she had expected Rob to talk her out of it—to throw a big macho fit, tell her how much he loved her, how much he loved Mike.

The conscious idea was repugnant. Why should Rob have to prove himself? What did it take to convince her that a full marriage such as he envisioned was really possible for her?

She did know that she wanted no more of the tension that had filled their house the week before she got off on her trip. Up to that time things had been going so well. Then with one thoughtless gesture harking to the past, she had turned everything around. *If I don't watch out I'm going to foul up this marriage.*

Meg tried to shake the gloomy thoughts as hour by hour she went through the motions necessary to transact her business in the Big Apple. Luckily she was an experienced hand at these buying trips and knew how to sniff out the old and new designers who could offer the combination of trendy selections and financial discounts Penelope's needed.

On Tuesday she called Rob in between a mandatory dinner and a style show. He was at home, but said he had just been at the O'Maras' house and everything was fine. She had learned long ago that calling Mike every evening only made him miss her more, so she asked Rob to let her parents know she had arrived safely.

It had made her feel better to hear Rob's voice and to sense that, despite all, he wanted things to go well for her. But at the style show Rob haunted her thoughts. As she watched countless emaciated models stalk across the stage in the newest fashions, it seemed personally significant that "stalk" was the approach for models that season. Feminine "floating" was out; even the unisex movement of the seventies had moved on to the competent, assertive look of the eighties. Each model's aggressive stance revealed self-containment that was supposed to depict American working women.

Meg wasn't certain she liked it. The absorption with self struck too close to home.

She had the same reaction on Wednesday during appointments at various salons. *Is this what I'm trying to make of my life,* Meg wondered idly while she studied one designer's choice of women's business suits. They were harsh, broad-shouldered, no-nonsense. A Keep Off sign on the back would not, she thought, have been inappropriate.

"Just like me. I can let Rob into my life so far, but there are definitely keep-off areas." There had to be some way women balanced competence with sharing.

When she got in from dinner and entertainment thrown by one of the big fabric houses, it was much too late, even with the time difference, to justify a casual call. Her disappointment that there was no message for her was heartfelt.

"He's getting too close to me," she thought uncomfortably as she took a quick bath and slid between the harshly starched sheets, which were not at all soothing to her skin. Everything about the lonely bed irritated her.

There was a trade show of accessories on Thursday.

Meg spent the better part of the day tromping around the huge meeting centre, examining the displays, negotiating with representatives on discounts for Penelope's, and being barraged with free gifts for the store to distribute. Her shoulder tote was heavy with perfumes, leather telephone coin cases, rain bonnets, shoe buffers and other samples to pass on to her customers. She didn't know if her customers would be impressed with her collection of freebies, but she fully expected Rob to be. On the way back to the hotel she stopped by a souvenir shop and carefully selected for him a marvelously garish ashtray and a miniature Statue of Liberty.

This time when she got back to her hotel room there was a message that Rob had called. With trembling fingers and wrenching knots in her stomach, she dialed him back immediately. He answered on the first ring.

"I'm sorry I missed your call." Her voice was as shaky as her hands.

"How are you getting along?"

"Fine. All I have left tomorrow is brunch with George Palini and an afternoon with the shoe people." *I'm miserable. I miss you so much it scares me.*

"I've stopped by your folks' every evening to see Mike. He misses you, but I think he's looking forward to their fishing trip to Toledo Bend tomorrow after school."

You've been seeing him every day. Oh, darling, what am I doing to us?

"I appreciate your looking in on him." Cursing herself for sounding so stilted, she rubbed the base of her stomach, trying to relieve the ache. But there was no relief. She hurt all over with loneliness.

"I'll be at the airport Saturday to meet your flight."
His deep, resonant voice sounded marvelous. "If I
have any trouble getting past security, I'll wait for you
at the Delta desk."

"That's not necessary, Rob. I always take a cab if the
folks are tied up."

"We're going to start some new 'alwayses' in this
family, Meg," he warned with a levity that didn't mask
the underlying seriousness. "If you think I can wait to
see my wife till she gets off work, you're crazy."

She smiled mistily. "So you haven't given up on
me?"

"Never! And don't you give up on me, either."

ROB THOUGHT MEG LOOKED a little tired when she approached him from the plane. And apprehensive, too.
But he didn't care. He needed her in his arms so much
that he didn't even try to hide the jubilance in his expression. Forgetting his pride, he crushed her against
his chest in a tangle of arms, magazines and carry-on
luggage. He hugged her, pressed his head against her
soft hair, kissed her, hugged her again.

"Rob!" She was laughing and trying to look busi-
nesslike at the same time. He grinned at her confusion.

"Welcome home!"

"You've gotten along all right, then?"

"Sure, if a little lonely." *A little?* His detachment was
shot to hell, he was so glad to see her back. He took her
shoulder tote, grunting momentarily at its surprising
heaviness before hitching it around his side out of the
way so that he could peck another kiss on her cheek.
"What do you have in this thing?"

"Wait until you see all the freebies I've brought back. You'll be so jealous. And I brought you two souvenirs."

She didn't seem to mind his public demonstrations, so he plumped another kiss right on her mouth.

"I think you're getting frisky," Meg whispered, her face flushed.

"Damn right." He hid his surprise at her suggestive comment. She had never loosened up enough to have playful sex talk with him before. It occurred to him again, as it had when she had returned from the California trip, that if she could ever sustain such open seduction, even verbally, many of their problems would be over. For by so doing, she would be admitting that she loved him and that they irrevocably belonged to each other. If she could make that step, he thought, everything else would fall into place.

She seemed uncomfortable that he was staring at her hopefully.

"Have you heard anything from Penny?" As always, her moment of brave flirting passed quickly. Disappointed, he took her elbow as they walked to the baggage depot.

"She and Charlie are getting married again."

"Really?"

"Next month. They want us to come and Mike to be in the wedding. Charlie apparently enjoyed our church ceremony so much that he's decided he wants one, too."

Meg began to laugh. "Now that will be a wedding to see. They may have a fight halfway down the aisle."

"Penny doesn't seem to have any bridal nerves yet.

She's anxious to have you come to the store today. The Palini shipment came in yesterday.''

"Oh, good. He asked me if we had gotten it yet. I guess you'd better just drop me off there instead of stopping at the house. We'll be swamped getting everything unpacked and sorted for pickup. Penny can bring me home.''

"I'll come in with you and wait. I have to pick up my own order anyway. Penny said it was ready.''

"You ordered something from Palini?'' She looked at him in surprise, more interested in that remark than in the bags that were starting to appear at the depot. "For Helen or Patty?''

Studiously he watched for her bag to show up. "Actually, it's your wedding present.''

"But the Palini showing was before we were even considering getting married.'' She began to flush, and he strongly suspected that she, like him, was remembering that the showing had been the very afternoon before they had first made love. He felt so stirred by the memory he didn't elaborate on her unspoken question.

MEG WISHED SHE HAD BOUGHT HIM the gold cuff links she had admired in the jewelry display at the hotel. They had a golfer in high swing engraved in beautiful detail, and they would have been perfect for him. She had been so tempted. But she was afraid he would think it was a bribe to make up for taking Mike from him all week. Which in a way it probably would have been. At least the souvenirs were selected with unquestioning affection.

She waited awkwardly by his side, not even paying attention to the arriving luggage.

When she eventually got to the store, however, things were so harried that worries about presents and loving husbands were necessarily shoved aside. Not that she literally shoved Rob aside. She did make certain that he got the place of honor in Charlie's massive wooden armchair in the corner of her office. And she supplied him with magazines and a Danish left over from the brunch snack someone had ordered. Then she got down to business.

Everyone who was not on the floor with a customer was in the large back workroom helping unpack and sort Palini's collection. Momentarily the work was slowed because they all also wanted to hear about Meg's buying trip to New York.

But she soon managed to get into the swing of their routine and swap a few stories at the same time. She could see Rob through the open door of her office. He read a magazine part of the time, visited with employees who drifted in and out, and seemed perfectly contented.

She didn't worry too much about him as she unwrapped from tissue paper item after item their customers had ordered from Palini. Not until Susan Forsyth arrived with her baby. Then she wondered if he would feel too surrounded with women's interests. Predictably, everyone, including Meg, was having a fit over the infant.

"My baby-sitter couldn't come at the last moment," Susan explained to Penny, "so I didn't know what to do except bring Melanie. I figured I'd stay as long as she can be satisfied dozing away in her stroller. But I may have to take all the book work home this first time."

"Stay under any circumstances," Penny said breathlessly between jobs. "Are you certain you like being a mother? I could use you sixty hours a week."

"So could Melanie," one of the salesclerks quipped.

"Melanie is going to get lots of confusion here," Meg warned, eagerly taking the baby into her arms. "It's been a madhouse. The word has gotten out that the Palini things have come in, and people keep coming in, wheedling for their orders."

"Are you giving anything out yet?"

"I don't know." Meg reluctantly passed the baby back to Susan.

As she did, Penny, who always swore she was not the least motherly, absentmindedly tickled Melanie's chin while waving her order book in the other hand. "I don't dare let anyone have anything until I verify the complete shipment. That's why we're in such a hurry. I just know I'll have a swarm of people coming in the door first thing Monday morning."

Since Penny wasn't giving things out yet, Meg went to tell Rob there wasn't much use for him to wait around. But Melanie began to cry at that moment, and Susan followed Meg into the relative quiet of her office.

"Would she be in your way?" Susan asked Rob before Meg could speak. "I think she's getting too much noise out there."

"So this is Miss Melanie Forsyth." He was on his feet and peeking toward the wriggling bundle as eagerly as all the salesclerks had. Susan proudly peeled back the blanket.

"Only a month old," Rob said reverently as he touched the tiny little fingers clutching blindly at the air. "I remember my nephews and nieces when they were this age. They would just about fit in the curve of your arm."

His big hand gently shaped the downy head of the tiny girl, and he seemed not at all bothered by her lusty little cry.

"She must be getting hungry," Meg said, wanting to spare Rob from dutifully having to ooh and aah over a squalling infant, even though she personally thought the child adorable.

"Feeding her I can do," Rob said, then grinned at Susan. "Unless, of course, she's nursing. If so, I'll step out."

"I've brought her bottle." Susan laughed. "If you're sure you don't mind, I'll just let you take care of her and I'll go back and help Penny."

"Rob, do you know what you're doing?" Meg asked dubiously.

"Are you this lady's mother, or is Susan?" Rob obliquely corrected her interference as he sat down. In astonishment Meg watched him plop the clean diaper Susan handed him over the shoulder of his immaculate fall suit, then take Melanie in his arms as comfortably as if he had handled infants all his life.

Susan went back to work as if she didn't have another thing to worry about. But Meg couldn't get over the competency of her husband. She pushed the little canvas stroller into position next to him and set the brake, so that he could put the baby down to rest if something went wrong. Then she went back to the unpacking, but got very little done because she kept tiptoeing to the corner of the worktable to get a better glimpse of Rob with Melanie Forsyth.

She watched the little girl suck her bottle contentedly while Rob safely cradled her fragile body. She was peeking when he fitted the baby over his shoulder and patted her gently. Meg made herself unpack more clothes, then was again peeking when he cuddled the well-fed little girl with one arm while he delved around in Susan's diaper bag. Just as Meg decided she should go help him, he triumphantly retrieved a pacifier. Once it was properly inserted in the baby's eager mouth, Melanie lay quietly against his chest, staring happily up at him. When next Meg peeked, he was rocking slightly in the sturdy old chair and the little girl's eyes were drifting shut.

Meg only got one more dress registered in before the compulsion to look came again, and this time she watched while Rob easily slipped the sleeping Melanie back into the stroller, strapped the waist belt and made certain that she was safely situated out of drafts and traffic. Most of all, during all her interested spying, Meg watched her husband's face. Never had she been more aware of the man's capacity to give undemanding love.

I could trust this man with my very soul.

Suddenly Meg was thunderstruck. Her knees buckled, her skin felt damp and she had to clutch the worktable to brace herself. All because she suddenly had supreme confidence in her husband.

It was such a relief to experience. But so long and painfully arrived at that she wanted to sob for all the time she had wasted. Now she could love him completely because she knew she could trust him. Knew in her heart and the hidden recesses of her soul, not just in her reasoning. And it made all the difference.

Rob was aware of none of this. He had been concentrating so on his task at hand that once the baby was settled he relaxed in the chair without once noticing Meg's observation. She took one last fond look at what a wonderfully masculine island he made in her woman's world, reading a magazine with his legs crossed at the knee so that one pant leg rode up and his dark sock showed. Then she thoughtfully returned to her work.

IT HAD TURNED SURPRISINGLY COLD by the time they arrived home. "They must be having an early blizzard across southern Colorado," Rob said as he pulled her close to him against the force of the chilling wind while they ran from the carport into the house. "I probably should have brought you straight home instead of stopping for dinner. You're not dressed for this."

"It's never been this cold in mid-September." Meg shivered while he turned the key in the lock. "We must be setting records."

Rob hurried her inside and made a couple of trips back outside to bring in her things.

She had just dug the two presents for him out of her suitcase when he walked into the bedroom carrying a huge, beribboned box. His Palini selection. She had forgotten all about it. "I didn't think Penny was letting anything go out today."

"I threatened to cancel her insurance," he joked, setting the box on their bed. "Are those my presents?" He was looking at the two little newspaper-wrapped parcels in her hand.

"I'm almost ashamed of them now."

"Give them here!"

It did embarrass her to hold out the two souvenirs, but she hoped that he would understand with what love they had been chosen—love she had only that afternoon fully understood.

He took the packages with that slightly lopsided grin that made his face even more irregular. Hesitantly she picked up her own gift. The box was shiny white and tied with a fabric bow boasting Palini's golden logo. Meg loosened it meticulously, drawing out the moment, listening as he carefully unwrapped the newspaper taped around his own presents. He slipped out the tissue-covered Statue of Liberty first and set it on the floor while he finished unwrapping the ashtray.

He looked so boyishly eager she couldn't bear to watch. Fearing he would be disappointed, she looked down at her own present. Judging from the size of the box she guessed that he had gotten her a complete outfit. Some sort of suit, perhaps, with blouses. Penny had seen her admire several things and could have advised him. She lifted the lid of the box. Mounds of creamy tissue paper protected its inner contents.

Meg plunged her hand in, expecting to touch the edge of several garments. Instead, the soft, clinging, unmistakable texture of fur greeted her. Immediately she thought of the coat he had seen her model—the outrageously expensive one that had reminded her of that equally outrageous advertisement. Then she squashed the thought. Never! She wouldn't have wanted him to. She ran her hand around farther. There was so much of it. But he couldn't have...

Carefully folding back the paper, Meg stared in astonishment. Indeed, there, nestled in deceptive simplicity, was the very coat she had modeled at the trunk showing.

Rob was chortling enthusiastically, "I like this, Meg." She couldn't believe it. He was actually admiring that black glass ashtray with its red logo: "I Love New York" while she held a full-length mink coat on her lap.

"But we're going to have trouble with the great lady here." He had also finished unwrapping the Statue of Liberty. "My Pet Rock will be jealous."

"Rob, I think you're crazy."

There was no way to hide her delight. It was a coat any woman would cherish, but her pleasure was more than that. She would have been as overcome with a simple blouse, for she knew he had chosen it with love long before she had made any kind of commitment to him.

"I know a man should let his woman pick out her own clothing, but after seeing you in it, I didn't think any other coat would ever do for you." His quiet explanation was almost apologetic. "You looked so beautiful."

"It's...it's..." Words completely failed her. She slid her hands underneath the fur and lifted it up against her face as if it were a live object.

"I know it's too warm for Shreveport, but I worry

about you in New York during the winter. And I wanted to take you with me on a business trip to Denver." Her eyes misted as she listened to his continued explanation of how useful the coat could be. *Darling, there's no way you can find a practical reason for giving me this coat.*

She regretted that she had made it so impossible for him to give her an extravagant gesture of sheer devotion. A fear suddenly gripped her. Why couldn't she have shown him earlier how much she loved him? No matter what she said tonight, would he ever know how completely she was now his? Or had she hurt him so permanently that he would think she was just trying to go through the polite motions of thanking him for his gift? She racked her brain for answers.

"I'm going to have to work for just a few minutes," he explained as he turned to leave the room with his presents. "This is the fifteenth of September, and it dawned on me at the store that I haven't mailed in our quarterly income tax estimate. I'll have to get a check made out and run it to the main post office for postmarking before midnight."

"Rob, thank you so much for the coat. It's...just wonderful, as I'm sure you know." Words were so horribly inadequate.

"I'm glad you like it." There was the lopsided smile again. "Well, I know you want to unpack, and I'd better get that check written. It shouldn't take me long to run it over to West Shreveport, if we don't have snow by now!" He grinned at his own joke.

She felt panic set in as he walked out of the room.

Standing, the coat in her hand, she wanted to cry. He hadn't even asked her to put it on.

The picture from the catalog flashed through her mind again. *No!* The fantasy was too outrageous. A desperate idea. *You wondered what it would feel like to be naked in a fur like this one.*

She rushed to the bedroom door. He was entering the den.

"If you can just give me a minute," she said shyly, the coat draped crazily in her arms, "I'll ride along with you. As cold as it's gotten, it will be a perfect time to break in my present."

Apparently pleased, he nodded his agreement.

Chapter Eleven

"I never dreamed you could use that coat in Shreveport in September. A midwinter trip to the mountains would have been more likely." Rob looked up at the glaring red stoplight. Inside the car he was comfortable in his suit coat, and he wondered if Meg wasn't too warm wearing his gift in a maiden run to please him. Glancing over at her just as the light changed, he decided that apparently she was not. She clutched the high collar around her neck as if she were freezing.

He pulled on across Texas Avenue to their destination, a modern brick building set back from the street beyond a landscaped parking lot. "You look so beautiful, it's a shame all we're doing is stopping at the post office. Wouldn't you like to go somewhere for a snack, a drink?"

"No! This drive is a big-enough event for me." Meg's voice was muffled. "Aren't you using the outside box?"

He pulled into a parking place. "I'd better take it inside to the main chute to be certain it gets postmarked before midnight. Lock your door. This will only take a second, but some idiot might drive up."

When he came back, she was still gathering the coat high to her throat above the belted waist. After she released the lock for him, he slid in hastily and tugged the door closed against the increasing gustiness of the cold winds. "Meg, you look as though you're freezing. I'd better turn on the heater." He had started the car and was reaching for the dashboard controls when she stayed him with a hand over his.

"Don't turn that on, Rob. I'll get too hot."

He twisted his head to look at her. The coat had drifted open when she reached for his hand, and upon seeing the slight separation of her delicate breasts before the fur closed around them, he wondered how he could not have noticed that she had been wearing a low-cut dress. No wonder she was cold.

"You're certain?" His eyes traveled along the dashboard to the switches that controlled the heat, and in his peripheral vision he saw the outline of Meg's long legs. She had on a pair of those shoes again—the strapped, ridiculously high-heeled kind that made him think like a dirty old man. Even as she assured him that she was not cold, he wondered why he had never been all that taken with any other woman's legs. Maybe it was because Meg had such delicate ankles. Her feet were long and slim and the toenails peach-colored and shiny.

When he released the heater switch, it seemed natural to let his hand drift down to her naked leg nearest him. *Naked leg? In weather like this had she taken off her hose?*

Curiously he let his hand drift upward to check how warm the fabric of her dress was. But only soft femininity greeted the rough texture of his palm. For a moment he remained almost paralyzed against her flesh. Disbelievingly he stroked higher along her thigh, forcing aside the clinging weight of the coat as he explored. A long expanse of gorgeous leg and hip came into view. No dress—nothing—hindered his journey upward.

"Meghan?" The car motor seemed to be roaring in his ears.

"It will be very embarrassing to me if you have a wreck." Her voice was husky. "My mother always taught me to wear clean undies in case I should end up in the hospital, but..." Her wriggling around to pull the coat back over her knees had let it slide open all the way from the collar to her waist, and there was no doubt that her body was bare as a newborn baby's. Rob actually stared dumbfounded, his hand still warm against her inner thigh. Modestly she tipped her head forward, letting that gorgeous, long blond hair nestle against the curves of her breasts before she drew the collar closer.

"I—I'd better get us home." He thought he might explode as he pulled his hand out from under the clinging heaviness of the fur. Sluggishly the car moved away from the curb. But in no way could he dare rush and risk an incident. He stopped for every green light that even thought about turning yellow. He cut five miles per hour off his normal speed to make certain no policeman had an excuse to flag him down. His eyes felt strained beyond endurance as he watched for every possible hardy motorcyclist, pedestrian or errant driver who might be out on such a blustery night, aiming for an accident with his car.

Meg began laughing quietly at him. "I didn't expect you to notice until we were back home."

"I'm middle-aged, not dead," he croaked.

It was building for a chilling rainstorm when he finally pulled up behind her Aries, just beyond the carport. He was in such startled euphoria by then that the record-setting weather patterns were of minimal interest. He lowered his head to the wind and ran arm in arm with Meg to the shelter of the porch, aware that somehow they were making personal history much more important than the weather—making a real beginning for their marriage.

"You know, of course, that this drive home has aged me a decade," he whispered while thumbing the door key to the edge of the ring jangling in his hand.

She smiled in satisfaction at his confused ardor and tipped her face, letting the rain blowing across the porch cool her own feverishness. "I doubt that. You'll be young and virile forever." Her playful voice broke off when he left the door only cracked, drew her into his arms, and began licking the icy droplets off her face.

Soon she was doing the same for him, her tongue raspingly stimulating against his stubbled jaw. Cold and night swirled around them while they cleaned each other like tiny kittens. But their enthusiastic efficiency so exceeded the rate of blowing rain that before long they were making no excuse of doing anything other than loving each other.

"We'd better get inside," Rob mumbled thickly.

He couldn't resist holding back and watching the

movement of her feet in those tempting shoes while she preceded him into their living room. Each time her bare heels lifted up slightly from the high platform, the tiny strap moved a little, leaving its mark on her skin. He wondered if the rubbing hurt her. It would be unfair if anything that fascinating to watch would cause her pain.

"What are you doing?" She glanced over her shoulder at him anxiously, as if worried something had gone wrong.

Thinking thoughts I can't discuss in public. He was stimulated at the thought of taking those shoes off her, and he felt ridiculous to be aroused by such an ordinary prospect. People put shoes on and took them off several times every day. He had watched Meg do it for herself dozens of times. But he hurt anyway and couldn't wait to get his hands on those shoes and on the lovely feet within them.

"Locking up," he said aloud, reaching behind him to fasten the night latch. The sound of metal against metal, breaking so forcefully into the sensuous hush, was oddly stimulating. He remained motionless by the door, watching her. "I feel like a boy trying to figure out what to do next on his first attempt at necking," he admitted.

Smiling mysteriously, she belted the wide leather sash tighter at the waist, then walked across the darkened room toward her little mock fireplace. He loved the way she moved: shyly, yet with a new yearning and self-confidence that glowed from within.

"Do you have a match?" she asked.

"A match?" She couldn't see his grin, but it was

there, reaching out to her as he fumbled in his pocket. "You ask for a match, dear wife? I just happen to have three different, colorful match folders for you to choose from. They all say Robert Clark—"

She laughed aloud and sank to her knees on the deep-piled carpet in front of the hearth. "Give me one of those wonderful things!"

He sat down beside her and watched her lean forward to light the gas logs. An orange flame leaped high, emitting the peculiar odor of newly torched methane before settling back into the sweet-smelling, soft glow that, while not like the roaring natural fires he had known in Kansas, was a pleasant sight that he had grown accustomed to in the South. He pulled off his shoes.

"You'd better take off that damp coat, too," she said huskily, straightening up to help him slip out of it. He was removing his tie when she stood. "I'll hang this up."

He stopped her with a gentle hand on her ankle. "Aren't you going to take your coat off?"

"Not yet."

His hand caressing her delicious leg became damp with growing passion. He wondered if she could feel the change. In concern, he tightened his loins and closed his eyes, trying to slow his aching need. Events were moving too fast for him. He wanted so for them both to savor every moment of this surprise she was offering him. Breathing deeply, he regained control.

"Just toss my jacket on one of the love seats." With one hand he slung his tie there while still gripping her ankle.

She looked down at him tenderly, her hair draped modestly about her face, before she did as he suggested. "I missed you terribly in New York." She was fiddling with the knot of leather at her waist.

He watched the orange glow of the gas flame play across the movements of her hands as she loosened the belt. The coat slipped looser until a narrow line of her shadowed white body showed beneath the edge of the dark fur. His hand ran over her ankle, up to the knee, then back down to trace the outline of the shoe straps around her bare heel.

"Come here."

The belt fell to the floor when she stepped closer.

Being in love is like watching a sunset, he thought as he looked up at her. The coat now hung open several inches along the length of her naked body, and her shadowy curves were bathed in a wavering glow of orange mixed with blues and reds. She began playing with his hair, making little curls of the wiry gray strands at his temples while he stared lustily at her. *You never get too old to be awed by a sunset.*

"I don't see how you women can walk around in these things." He leaned free of her caressing fingers and lowered his gaze to her shoes.

"I couldn't walk right now if my life depended on it," she admitted languorously, balancing herself by holding on to his shoulders while she drew her leg up slightly at the knee so that her shoe drifted more comfortably into his grip.

Unconsciously she had created such an artistic beauty of line and form that he had to stare some more, hoping to capture forever in his mind the lights and shadows of her loveliness.

"What are you doing now?"

"Taking off your shoes." The little buckle of her sandal felt cold against his fiery-hot fingers. He didn't hurry about it. She shifted restlessly, with her foot on his leg, while he insisted on undoing each buckle so that he could slide his finger along the back of each heel to soothe any pressure there, then under the foot, down under the arch. Finally after each shoe was cast aside, he cupped first one heel, then the other, in his hands.

Love is like a picture postcard, he thought in a new venture of lovestruck poetry while he flexed her pink toes in his fingertips, before bending low to kiss each slender arch. *A gift from faraway places you never think you can reach.*

"Rob—Rob darling!" The need in her voice was so urgent that he quit trying to control his desire.

But sometimes you do reach them. Sometimes you reach heaven.

She glided gracefully down beside him. He adjusted her position until she was lying on her side before him, facing the fire.

"I want to see you," he rasped, reaching for the hemline of the coat. He ran his fingers up the inside edge, letting the fur roll away until he had exposed a diagonal slash of her body all the way from her toes to her armpits. The broad curve of one pale hip and thigh rose high and pear-shaped above its pillow of fur.

"You have a perfect body for welcoming a man," he praised, running his hand along her wide pelvis, over the muscled belly, pausing over her curl-bedecked mystery of womanhood. She seemed breathless with waiting.

"I can't get used to your touching me with your left hand," she gasped when he began to fondle her.

"I'm ambidextrous at the important things," he bragged huskily, showing her. Her sighs turned to throaty moans and she slowly turned flat on the rug, exposing more of her body to his care. One breast was still partially covered, but he let that go for the moment while he stroked from her ankle to the amazing narrowness of her waist. Her other breast was bathed in passion's sweat and gleamed in the firelight. He circled it with one finger, then lay down beside her and watched its tightening as he teasingly doodled imaginary designs all over it.

He must have pushed her a bit too far, for she grabbed his hand and forced it to her mouth so she could suck at his fingertips.

Excited, he jerked his hand away, spread the coat open and began on both breasts, throwing his leg over hers when she tried to writhe away from him.

"Rob, don't tease me like this." She pulled at his hair, trying to force his mouth full over her breasts.

He held back, determined to pleasure her as she had never been pleasured before. Her struggles required some manipulating on his part to accomplish his purpose, and he was lying fully across her when her breasts were eventually molded and kissed into the two hard globes he wanted to see.

"Take off this coat." He was beginning to feel frustrated himself.

"Not yet! Let me undress you." She wriggled beneath him, kissed pleadingly at his face, pushed at his shoulders.

"Soon!" She fought him until he began to suck strongly at her breasts and rub his thigh against her legs. Then she fell still instantly. Eventually he crouched on his knees and slid his hands under her back. She rose easily within his lifting arms, arching highest at the wet, pinkened tips of her breasts, her head hanging back limply in ecstasy, her hair streaming to the floor. He held her there and leaned over to lick delicately each throbbing nipple, feeling through his tongue the rhythmic beat of her excitement. Then he eased her out of the sleeves of the coat.

"Ah, Meghan Dowell, you are so beautiful."

"Rob, take your clothes off!" She struggled to sit and became filled with urgent energy, angry with the stubborn buttons of his shirt.

"Meg..."

She had never undressed him before. It was surprising how good she could be at it when she made up her mind. In only seconds she had removed his shirt, shoved his now-cooperating bulk to the rug and was crouched above him, magnificently vibrant to watch. Slowly she began to tease him as he had teased her. Then, just when he thought he could take no more, she backed off and went to work on his slacks. Eventually she had everything off but his socks and was spreading hot kisses over his chest.

"We'd better take care of this coat." He rolled to his side and pulled the fur out from under him, thinking that she would not want her present damaged.

"I want that!" Undiplomatically she jerked it out of his hand and spread it back on the floor, fur side up to make a bed for them.

Amused, he still hesitated until she stretched out on it before him. "We won't be as hard on it as the animals have been," she pointed out huskily.

"Are you trying to tell me I'm acting like an animal?" He eased down beside her.

"Yes! Don't stop."

He lay upon her and framed her face in his hands. "Don't say I didn't give you a chance to be practical," he warned wryly, threading his fingers through her hair and slowly bringing his lips toward hers. She held him inches away with a hand along his jaw.

"Never doubt I want you more than I could ever want a fur coat," Meg admitted huskily, her face wreathed in smiles before she brought his mouth to hers.

Her joy became a catalyst to his own. He began to laugh. Sliding to her side to spare her his weight, he said, "Now here is my first animal kiss."

She didn't like the teasing lightness of it and rolled over on top of him. "Butterflies aren't animals," she objected, deepening the kiss. "You've forgotten your encyclopedia B's—Rob!"

He squeezed her delicately on the rump to stop her ramblings. Then they laughed, cried and hugged each other, rolling around and around in their nest of fur like two playful puppies.

Eventually their play slowed, became gentler yet more urgent; her arms tightened around him and he knew it was time. Looking into her eyes, entrusting his whole soul to her safekeeping, he lifted himself above her. When she tilted her welcoming hips and eased him into her enveloping warmth, it was as if that symbolism accepted everything else he had to offer her, too. He felt himself swelling to that need nearest to death until she began to move beneath him, babying him, encouraging him with her hoarse cries of wonder.

"Home is where..." It seemed important to tell her. But his words were garbled in his ecstasy. "Home is...darling!"

"IT WASN'T THE WEDDING PRESENT..."

Meg said the words against the hollow of his throat, where somehow she had burrowed.

"Hm?" His lazy query was perfunctory, she knew. He was still dozing and could not have cared less what she was saying, as long as she didn't move away from him. Every time she had shifted even slightly, he had pulled her closer against him.

But the words were important to her. She had to be certain he understood. "It wasn't the wedding present. Not the fur coat."

He seemed to be struggling to raise from the lethargic oblivion to which they had surrendered themselves for some hours. The errant fall-winter storm had settled into crisp quiet; the night had shrouded the windows, and only the soft whooshing sounds of the gas logs and the wavering colors of its warmth kept them company in their luxuriously soft love nest.

"Do you want to go to bed?" He tested her warmth with his hand. She was toasty fine.

"I want to be wherever you are." She didn't mind that the unliberated response sounded almost smug.

"Bed it is, then." He unwound his lanky form, then raised her to her feet beside him. She stood with her hand in his, unashamed of her nakedness.

When he straightened up, he groaned a little and smiled ruefully. The hours of sleeping on the floor seemed to have taken its toll on his joints. "What was it you said about me being forever young? Liar!"

While they walked to the shower hand in hand she laughed at the picture he made limping exaggeratedly, naked except for the dark socks that came almost to his knees.

"This is the first time I ever got so overcome by lovemaking that I left my socks on." He caught the edge of the sink to balance himself while he elevated one foot.

"You look cute," she quipped, escaping his punishing arms to step in the shower. He followed her as soon as he could fling the dark socks into the corner.

"I was telling you about the coat," she began again when they were standing together under the soothing warmth of the liquid spray. She began soaping his chest as if she had performed this service every night for him since their marriage. It was remarkable fun and she wondered why, indeed, she had not.

"I'm inhibited," she interjected for her own information.

"The hell you are. And what does that have to do with the coat?"

"Oh. Oh! Rob, you mustn't believe I...I did this because of your giving me the coat."

"Did what?" Grinning audaciously, he turned so she could cleanse his back.

"Why do you have to make this explanation so difficult?" She began sloshing rinsing water over him with the large washcloth. "I'm trying to tell you something important."

"So..." He turned and stood at one edge of the shower stall, watching while she washed herself. "I'm behaving myself now. Why did you do... it?"

"Because I couldn't think of any other way to tell you I love you!"

He burst into delighted laughter.

He was still laughing after the water had rinsed away her own passion residue and he had toweled them both dry. Shivering, they ran together to the warmth of their bed.

"It isn't as if I ride around in cars naked every day," she kept trying to explain while they pulled downy blankets up around their chins and cuddled spoon fashion against each other until their mutual body heat created a relaxing haven.

"Thank God you don't," he said, chuckling. "I almost had one of Charlie's heart attacks on the way home from the post office. Next time, would you consider a mild treatment for my prostate instead?"

"Rob, I'm trying to tell you I love you. It may not be important to you, but it's very important to me."

"Your happiness is the most important thing in the world to me," he admitted gruffly.

He grew still against her back, and she turned to frame his face with her hands.

"I love you," she repeated tenderly, kissing him lightly on the mouth.

"Why was that so hard to say?"

"It isn't the saying that's hard; it's living the meaning. A funny thing happened to me today."

"You mean in New York?"

"No, at the store. When I saw you with Susan's baby."

He watched the changing expressions flit across her face.

"I realized I could trust you. It was that simple."

"That was what's been between us all the time?"

"Don't be hurt. It had nothing to do with you. Surely you understand that."

He lay back, staring at the ceiling. She started massaging his shoulder, reaching down healingly across his chest. Suddenly he began to chuckle.

"Rob, are you taking me seriously?" Now she was the one who was hurt.

His laughter increased. "I was just wondering how you're possibly going to top this act and stay out of jail." His voice steadied. "Because you'll need to tell me you love me over and over again. I can never hear it too often."

THEY SPENT A LAZY DAY waiting for Mike to get home. And after he had arrived and all the flurry of hearing his news, filling him up with his mother's cooking, and seeing him into bed was over, they were again in each other's arms before the fireplace.

"This velvet love seat is better for my bones than the floor—" Rob smiled against Meg's cheek "—but not nearly as much fun."

She sighed her contentment and cuddled closer to his side, taking one of his hands in hers. "I feel as if

I've started a new life today. Belonging to you—really belonging to you and knowing you belong to me—has given me the most incredible feeling of freedom."

He straightened her hand in his and traced the smooth surface of the wedding band on her slender finger.

"Rob, I've been thinking about Dane and Mike."

The tracing stopped momentarily, then resumed again.

"You have to understand that he tried to quit drinking two or three times when we were first married, and the most it ever lasted was three months. Much as I want to encourage him, I can't seem to forget those other attempts."

"He seems to be doing very well," Rob said carefully.

"He does," she agreed. "And I want Mike to know he has two fathers who love him. But I've realized I can't handle a meeting here. I'd be so apprehensive that I'd ruin any chance they had for establishing a good rapport."

"Is there any way I can help?"

"It's not the ideal solution, but could you take Mike to see them?"

"I'd be honored to. You know that."

She did know. She knew it irrevocably now.

"If you're concerned about making this first meeting casual for Mike," he continued thoughtfully, "we could work it in with a Saturday trip I need to make to New Orleans. Mike would probably enjoy bumming around my office while I'm tied up, and if Dane and Karen could drive over from Baton Rouge to join us for lunch, it might not seem such an overwhelmingly momentous occasion for him."

Meg thought the idea was perfect. And when they called Dane and Karen, the plans were quickly made.

"You'll only be gone for the day?" she asked Rob anxiously when they were again side by side on the love seat, holding hands and staring at the fire.

"If this is going to be too traumatic for you, we can wait—"

"I have no doubts about your taking Mike to see Dane," Meg interrupted huskily, turning to stroke his face. "I was wondering how I could possibly get along without you for longer than a day."

Chapter Twelve

"You know what we've done wrong?" Rob asked Meg one morning when they were poking over breakfast after the confusion of getting Mike off to school. "Set up this lunch with Dane on the day before Charlie and Penny's wedding. If they plan any rehearsal festivities that night, our flight home would get in too late."

"I'll talk with Charlie," Meg said. "He's planning the wedding this time, so maybe we can arrange for Mike to practice the ring-bearing early."

"I'd hate to change things at this point. I think Dane needs this vote of confidence from you."

"You really want him to succeed, don't you?" Meg watched his caring face.

"Absolutely. For Mike, of course. But mostly for your sake; you invested a good part of your life in that man."

"I love you."

For a moment her spontaneous words seemed to fall on uninterested ears. He didn't look up, didn't throw her a kiss. Nothing. Then he suddenly put down his morning newspaper and cocked an eyebrow.

"Is that all you're going to do?"

"All I'm going to do?"

"Yes, is that it? You're just going to lean back and eat your breakfast and calmly say you love me? I thought you needed some dramatic medium for such a hard confession. Surely you could at least set up my own personal one-wife massage parlor? Or burst topless out of a home-made chocolate cake? Or how about—"

"You rat!" She was laughing and swinging at his ducking head with a rolled-up newspaper when he caught her around the waist and dragged her into his lap.

"Say it again!" He pinned her arms behind her.

"No."

"All right for you." His teasing voice was threatening as he transferred her hands to one of his, and with the other calmly started opening the buttons of her prim shirtwaist dress.

"Rob!" She began to wriggle, but it did no good. "I love you. Stop that!"

He kissed her breast through the bra and slip. She gasped, and he teased her more, before long forgetting what had started all this and loving her breasts as if he'd never touched them before.

"Stop that," she moaned.

"Are you certain you want me to?" he asked against her clinging lips. "Mike will be at school all day."

"You'll be late to the office."

"And you'll be late to the store. Will anyone worry?"

"They probably wouldn't start checking until— Rob!"

She had always thought it fiction that a man could lift a tall woman like herself and carry her comfortably into a bedroom. She found that she was wrong.

"YOU'RE AS NERVOUS AS A CAT. You'd think you were the one getting married tomorrow." Penny watched Meg sift through the requests for alterations twice without scheduling a single one on the seamstresses' books.

"I'm just wondering how Mike and Rob are getting along in New Orleans."

"What can go wrong in New Orleans, for heaven's sake? Besides, aren't they due home tonight?"

"Right. I suppose I'm being silly." She penciled some instructions on the alteration schedule and put it in the basket for the seamstress to pick up. They were having a relatively slow day, and it amazed her that Penny insisted on staying despite having a big church wedding the next afternoon. Charlie had invited several hundred people and was throwing a reception afterward at the country club. And Penny, who normally adored such social events, was behaving as if it were all a terrible bore that had nothing to do with her. Meg could only guess that it was because this third wedding meant more to her than she could bring herself to admit.

"We really appreciate your having had the rehearsal early this week so Mike would know what he's doing."

"I don't know why Charlie needed a rehearsal anyway," Penny grumbled. "You know that I blame this damn church wedding on you. Charlie liked all that family-and-friend togetherness you two put on."

"Penny, everything's going to be beautiful."

"I wanted a church wedding the first two times we were married and he absolutely refused," she continued, undaunted. "Said he didn't want to shop for a new suit. Now that he's retired, I swear he has too much time on his hands. He's been wearing my feet off with his damn shopping trips. Flowers. Caterers. Musicians. All I want to do is get this legality over with."

"You haven't told me yet what you're going to wear."

"And that's another thing," Penny raged. "Charlie keeps wanting me to wear white. Can you imagine that idiot? A woman my age marrying the same man for the third time and showing up in white?"

"Are you going to?"

"Never! I told him so. I'm wearing that champagne satin cocktail suit I bought from Palini. Charlie can take his white dress and shove it."

"Penny, you have a very bad attitude." Meg couldn't stop her laughter.

Between Penny's grumpiness and Meg's preoccupation with Mike and Dane, it was a wonder Penelope's survived that day under their management. By late afternoon even the most loyal and discreet employees were urging Penny and Meg to stay in the office out of everyone's way.

"I think we have goddamned insubordinate workers," Penny huffed, hitching back her flowing sleeve and lighting a rare cigarette. "That Susan, that part-time Susan, had the nerve to tell me that if I didn't quit giving her conflicting instructions she was going to take the rest of the afternoon off."

Meg watched her nervously blow smoke rings in the

air. It looked like fun and she reached for the cigarette pack, awkwardly lighted one and managed to avoid coughing while she tried to form rings herself. Blobs of smoke spread in a cloud over the room. Shrugging her shoulders, she gave up on the project.

"Betty, in alterations, told me there was no way she could adjust the collar and cuffs of a swimsuit," Meg eventually admitted, again watching Penny creating perfect fragile circles of smoke. "She suggested that I go home for a nap and let her write the instructions on the alteration schedule."

Suddenly they both began laughing.

"Maybe I should go home," Penny admitted. "I'm sure as hell not doing much good here."

"You'd be worse off at home. I can tell when you start all this swearing that you're worried about something. The wedding's going to go off fine."

"I'm not worried about the wedding. I'm worried about the marriage."

"Penny, you and Charlie could never break up. You're as committed to each other when you're divorced as when you're legally man and wife. Why did you decide to marry him again if you're worried about getting along living in the same house?"

Penny stubbed out the cigarette.

"Maybe because it's the first time I really wanted to make him happy. I admit I'm selfish. It's a congenital trait. My mother was the most selfish woman in the world. Anyway, I've always expected Charlie to make me happy, and if he didn't, I called everything off."

Meg listened silently. Penny reached for another cigarette, then stuffed it back into the pack.

"You know what he said to me when he asked me to marry him again? He brought over this insurance statistics chart about how much longer women live than men. And he said, 'Penny, I'm ten years older than you, and by statistics you should be on your own already. Now, we can spend whatever years I have left together, or we can spend them apart. But at some point here you aren't going to have that choice any longer.'"

"Charlie's going to live to be a hundred," Meg said reassuringly, smelling one of that rascally old man's charming subterfuges.

"Maybe he won't. It scares me. He's crude and stubborn and wants his own way and works much too hard, and he won't change. Except for music, he hates all the things I like, but I think I'll die when he's not around anymore. I'd never thought seriously about that before."

Meg stared at her. She had never visualized Penny so terribly vulnerable. "Rob lives a philosophy I'm trying to learn. He just takes one day at a time. It works better that way."

They were both sitting thoughtfully at their desks when Susan tapped on the door.

"Meg?"

"Come on in. We guarantee to bark before we bite." She laughed.

"You have a long-distance call from Baton Rouge. It's on line two."

She grabbed for the phone. Penny watched in concern as she answered.

"It's who?" Meg asked, the woman's voice not

registering because she was expecting news of disaster.

The woman said her name again and the familiarity of it finally made sense. "Oh, Karen! Is everything all right?"

"Everything's fine. We just got home from New Orleans. It's been like opening sunshine into our lives to be with Mike today, and we just had to call you. We can't thank you enough for sharing him with us."

Meg slumped forward in relief. For a moment she was smiling mistily. When Penny realized that the call was not a cause for alarm, she stepped out with Susan and closed the door behind her.

"How's Dane?" Meg had recovered her senses.

"I'm here on the other line, Meg. Rob was right. Mike is a fine boy. He told us about his baseball team and about his friend Corey."

"And about how long the school day is," Karen inserted eagerly. "He reminded me so much of my littlest brother. He hated school until he discovered physics in college. Now he's about to graduate."

"I thought Mike would be a little shy with you."

"At first he was, but no more than we were with him." Dane laughed. "He kept telling me I looked like him. I think that was as big a surprise to him as it was to me. I know you'd told me that, and I'd seen the pictures, but I wasn't prepared for it."

"Me, either." Karen laughed. "He even twists his right thumb around his knuckles when he's nervous, like Dane."

"Was he very nervous?"

"Not after the first few minutes. Rob smoothed

everything over for him. I'm glad you found that man, Meg."

"I am too, Dane." She gripped the phone tightly.

"It's really special to see them together," Karen added. "Rob seems naturally to be giving Mike the support families of alcoholics need. Every time Mike seemed to feel overwhelmed, Rob grinned at him, and he was all right again."

Meg flushed with warmth, so very grateful she hadn't, in her own ineptness, destroyed the relationship of the man and the boy she loved so much.

"We're keeping you from your work," Karen apologized. "We just had such a good time seeing Mike, and were so proud of him, that we wanted to thank you for making it possible."

"Meg, I'll drop Mike a line soon, if you don't mind."

"I'd like that, Dane. I think it's done Mike good to know his father cares about him."

"I can see I won't ever have the place in his heart that your husband does," Dane said with some sadness. "But I hope someday I'll earn my own place."

"I think you will, Dane...and I wish you and Karen all the success in the world."

She couldn't wait for them to get home. Rob had left his car at the airport to save her the trouble of coming after them, but now she was impatient that she had to wait just that much longer to see them. It seemed an eternity since they had driven away early that morning.

She was putting a load of clothes in the dryer when they pulled into the driveway, so she didn't hear the car. All of a sudden there was a thundering across the floor and arms were being flung about her and there were laughter and explanations and questions all at the same time.

"Mom, this man who's my father looks just like me!" Mike explained, dumping his toy bag on the floor. "But his wife doesn't look like me. And Dad's office people all say hello. And I ate a raw oyster. But don't try it, because they taste yucky."

"Where are you going?"

Mike turned from the back door.

"Oh. It's not too dark and I thought Corey might be playing outside with his sister. Is that all right?"

"Of course it's all right," Meg said huskily, wiping at her eyes. After he was gone, she looked lovingly at Rob.

"And that's it? This meeting I've been dreading?"

He grinned at her. "That's it. Your son handled it like a trooper. I wouldn't say they immediately hit it off as best of friends. You know how it usually takes Mike a while to warm up to people. But he didn't seem too curious at that point about why he hasn't seen his father before. Dane had taken me aside and asked if we thought he should explain anything, and I felt you'd want him to wait until Mike asked."

"I think I'm going to cry."

"Tears of joy are okay," Rob said huskily, taking her into his arms.

CHARLIE DID HIMSELF PROUD at his third marriage to Penelope Sands. The church was overflowing with flowers and glowing candles. Orchids of every color had been flown in from Hawaii to cover the altar. Along each pew lining the center aisle was fastened a nosegay of yellow, white and pink rosebuds. A string quartet played classical music for the overflow crowd before dramatically launching into the traditional wedding march.

Meg and Rob had a good view because Charlie and Penny had insisted they sit at the front as family of the bride and groom. An elderly couple who had been witnesses at both of the Peabodys' other weddings were happily performing the function again, and they came down the aisle first. Then Mike followed them.

His grin as he passed them, carefully balancing a lacy puff of a pillow holding diamond-encrusted rings, went proudly from ear to ear, making his freckles pop out more and flashing that new space he had after losing a tooth only that morning.

Next there was the rolling down of the white bridal carpet.

Meg wondered at first if Penny had changed her mind and decided to wear a long white wedding gown. But when everyone stood up to watch the bride walk down the aisle on the arm of her twice-already husband, Meg saw at once that she was wearing Palini's champagne satin.

"That's the first time I've ever seen a virgin groom," Rob whispered in her ear.

Suddenly the carpet made sense.

Charlie, dear crazy Charlie, faced with an uncooperative bride, had dressed appropriately himself. He was positively radiant. He had inventively worn white tie and tails, white cummerbund, and had a white rose in the lapel. His white hair was slicked back and he looked like an aging white knight.

Meg wanted to run out and kiss him.

Penny seemed to have gotten over her bridal nerves of the day before, and while perhaps looking a little overloaded carrying her funeral-parlor-sized spray of white orchids, was certainly a lovely bride. As they came even with the pew where Meg and Rob were standing, Penny cast a resigned look at Meg, lifted a hand slightly off her flowers, and discreetly gestured toward the floor. Meg's eyes obediently followed the direction in which she was pointing.

Charlie was wearing white cowboy boots.

Choice of shoes, however, was his only lapse in decorum throughout the entire ceremony. He said his vows clearly and with conviction. Meg even teared a little at the loving way he lifted the veil of Penny's hat and framed her face for a brief kiss.

It was absurd. But everyone burst into applause when Penny Peabody and Charlie Peabody started back up the aisle, again a married couple.

"Mom, Charlie's giving us his lake house," Mike hissed out of the corner of his mouth after the applause died down and he followed the happy couple up the aisle.

"What did he say?" Meg whispered to Rob.

"I think you heard him right," Rob whispered back.

"YOU CAN'T GIVE SOMEONE your house, Charlie," Meg protested over a glass of champagne at the country club.

"Why not? It's my house."

"I'll help take care of it, Mom." Mike was cheerfully on his second Coke and didn't understand what the argument was about.

"Take the dreadful place, Meg," Penny begged. "I never want anyone to know I've been out there."

"I'm getting my old fishing shack back," Charlie explained. "I never liked that fancy lake house."

"Then you can sell it to us," Rob said firmly. "You know I've been putting out feelers to you for months to buy it."

"I don't want to sell it. Penny and I are both selling our other houses. I don't need any more capital gains."

"Then where are you two going to live? And don't tell me that fishing shack, because I won't believe you."

"We're building his-and-hers homes on that acreage along the river near the LSU Shreveport campus." Penny said a little sheepishly. "They're Charlie's version of mother-in-law houses. One wing will be his shack, and the other wing will be my decent house. We'll have a breezeway between them."

"You have to be kidding," Meg said, not believing them for a moment.

"I think they're serious," Rob warned.

"Damn right we're serious," Charlie insisted. "She doesn't like the way I squeeze toothpaste, and I don't like all her frilly stuff cluttering up every place you want to sit. This way we'll both have a retreat when we get mad, and the family room and kitchen in the main house will be neutral ground."

"Actually it sounds like a rather good idea, under the circumstances," Meg said diplomatically.

"So take that lake house off my hands. The boy will love it out there, and besides, you'll have some more little ones running around soon and you'll need the space."

Meg was thoroughly rattled by then. But Rob kept his aplomb. "We won't let you give it to us, Charlie, but we'll haggle about price after you and Penny get back from your trip to Europe. Never let it be said that I passed up a good business deal."

"Did you mean that? About buying Charlie's lake place?" Meg turned into Rob's arms in the quiet after-midnight hours, when the wedding party was long over and their household was settling for sleep.

"We do need a bigger house. What do you think?"

"It would be marvelous to live out there all year round," she admitted dreamily. "I could drop Mike off at his magnet school, and he could still walk to my parents' house and stay until I could pick him up after work."

"The pool is already fenced, and I know I could fence the dock area attractively enough if we put in some plantings. It could be safe for children."

"Rob..." She ran her hand up his chest to touch his jaw. He turned his head just enough to kiss her fingertips. "Rob, what did you think about the other?"

"Other what?"

"Charlie's other idea. That we'd have more kids running around to make room for?"

"What do you think about it?" He lay very still.

"I'd like to have your child. You ought to have a family of your own."

Breathing a great sigh, he took her hand in his. "I already have a wife and son of my own. If we're lucky enough to have others join us, I'd welcome them, but I could never be any happier than I am now."

HE WAS WRONG, of course. Love has a way of increasing happiness beyond any possible expectations.

When Sara Ann Dowell was born on her parents' first wedding anniversary, Rob was awed at the prospect of their family having a new little human creature to love. He and Mike immediately went to the hospital gift shop and bought her a pink teddy bear dressed in a red T-shirt that said "Mascot of Shreveport."

For weeks thereafter Rob passed out free cigars with pink-and-blue bands that said: "Courtesy of Robert Clark Dowell, father of Michael John Bronson and Sara Ann Dowell."

"Why am I on there?" Mike asked when they had first opened the shipment.

"Because I didn't get to brag about you when you were born," Rob said proudly, helping himself to one of the cigars and sliding the band onto Mike's sturdy finger.

Sara Ann had her mother's blond coloring and blue-gray eyes. But by the time she could hold a rattle in her tiny fingers it was obvious that she would be left-handed like her father and brother. The two men in her life doted on her, but her mother never worried about her becoming spoiled. For Meghan Dowell knew from experience that wise loving never hurt anyone.

HARLEQUIN *Love Affair*

Now on sale

RAINBOWS AND UNICORNS   *Rebecca Flanders*

Faith Hilliard had only fallen from a stepladder in the Little Creek church when Ken Chapman caught her . . . yet he behaved as though she had fallen from the clouds like a gift from heaven.

But that was typical of Ken, a man who believed in miracles. And when she was with him, Faith almost believed in them herself. Every word Ken spoke resounded with love, hope and an unshakable belief in humanity, and he radiated a goodness so pure it melted her heart.

Faith could not help being drawn to him, but she knew she had to be careful not to get too close, lest the gentle light die in his eyes. . . .

TOUCHED BY LOVE   *Elda Minger*

The band Tough Cookie would go straight to the top. Talent manager Michael Stone knew that the first time he heard them play in a Los Angeles club. But it was the lead singer who particularly caught his attention. Dressed entirely in black, Cheri Bradley was magnetic . . . electrifying . . . phenomenal.

Cheri wasn't looking for fame, but that wasn't the reason she was reluctant to sign with Michael. While she could give body and soul to a performance, she could never give that to a man . . . and she knew that Michael would settle for nothing less.

SECRET LONGINGS   *Sharon McCaffree*

She had forgotten how to date.

Was it the blossoming of spring in Shreveport or the chance phone call that caused Meg Bronson to take a fresh look at Robert Clark Dowell? Suddenly the man she had always considered a sedate bachelor was having an odd effect upon her. On their first date he was charming and gracious, while Meg was awkward, nervous as a schoolgirl. The evening was a fiasco, and Meg was certain he would never want to see her again.

But when Rob made plans for another date, Meg realized she had underestimated him. Unfortunately, she hadn't learnt from her mistake. . . .